Electronic Document Preparation and Management

for CSEC®

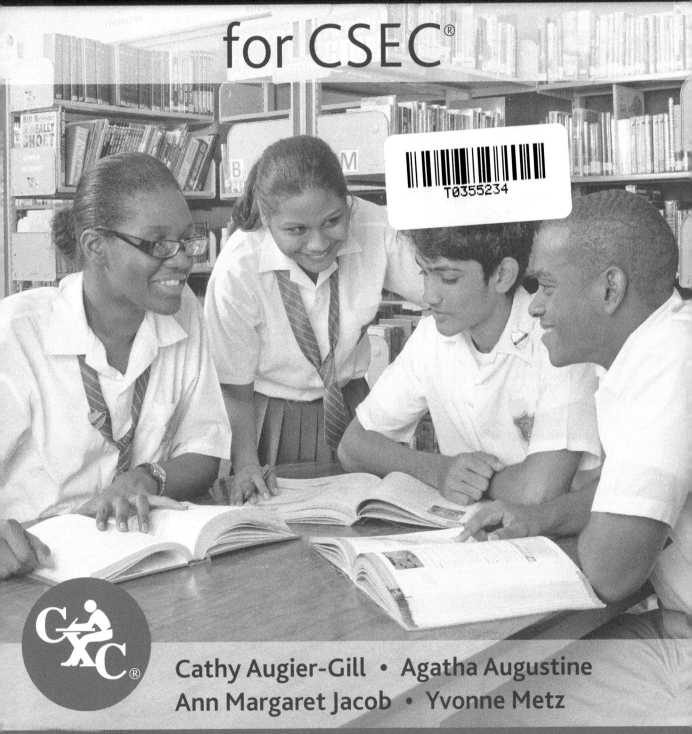

Cathy Augier-Gill • Agatha Augustine
Ann Margaret Jacob • Yvonne Metz

A Caribbean Examinations Council® *Study Guide*

Great Clarendon Street, Oxford, OX2 6DP, United Kingdom

Oxford University Press is a department of the University of Oxford.
It furthers the University's objective of excellence in research, scholarship,
and education by publishing worldwide. Oxford is a registered trade mark of
Oxford University Press in the UK and in certain other countries

British Library Cataloguing in Publication Data
Data available

978-1-4085-2251-6

10

Printed in Great Britain by CPI Group (UK) Ltd., Croydon CR0 4YY

Acknowledgements

Cover photography: Mark Lyndersay, Lyndersay Digital,
Trinidad, www.lyndersaydigital.com
Illustrations: Newgen Publishing and Data Services, Pantek
Media, David Russell Illustration, Tony Forbes of Sylvie Poggio
Artist Agency and Harry Venning
Page make-up: Pantek Media, Maidstone

Thanks are due to Cathy Augier-Gill and Yvonne Metz for their
contribution in the development of this book.

Microsoft product screenshots reprinted with permission from
Microsoft Corporation.

Microsoft and its products are registered trademarks or
trademarks of Microsoft Corporation in the United States and/
or other countries.

The author and the publisher would also like to thank the
following for permission to reproduce material:

Text: p88, Professor Howard Stevenson quote sourced
from Eisenmann, T.R. 2013. Entrepreneurship: A
Working Definition. Retrieved from http://blogs.hbr.org/
hbsfaculty/2013/01/what-is-entrepreneurship.html; p136,
Henry Wadsworth Longfellow, *The Arrow and the Song*; p138,
William Shakespeare, *Macbeth*; p139, Floyd Dell, *The Angel
Intrudes* (Charleston, BiblioLife, 2009); p158, United Nations
article sourced from the United Nations News Centre, 'Deputy
UN Chief Calls for Urgent Action to Tackle Global Sanitation
Crisis', 21 March 2013, http://www.un.org/apps/news/story.asp?
NewsID=44452&Cr=sanitaion&Cr1=#.UiSgcH9K01z.

Images: pp4–9, all iStockphoto; p12, Norton Antivirus
screenshot; p59 and 122, iStockphoto; p138, Hill Street
Studios/Blend Images/Corbis; p151, 154, 160 and 169;
iStockphoto; p152 cropped screenshots of Mozilla Firefox
browser.

Although we have made every effort to trace and contact all
copyright holders before publication this has not been
possible in all cases. If notified, the publisher will rectify any
errors or omissions at the earliest opportunity.

Links to third party websites are provided by Oxford in
good faith and for information only. Oxford disclaims any
responsibility for the materials contained in any third party
website referenced in this work.

Contents

Introduction   1

Introduction to Electronic Document
Preparation and Management   2

Section 1   Fundamentals of computing

1.1 The computer   4

1.2 Input devices   6

1.3 Output devices   8

1.4 Storage media   10

1.5 Software   12

1.6 Computer care and safety   14

Section 2   Keyboard mastery

2.1 Introduction to keyboarding   16

2.2 Working with punctuation   18

2.3 Manuscript correction signs   20

2.4 Headings and paragraphing   22

2.5 Abbreviations, figures and ellipsis   24

Section 3   Introduction to application software

3.1 Introduction to word processing   26

3.2 Introduction to spreadsheets   28

3.3 Introduction to database
management systems   30

3.4 Introduction to presentation software   34

Section 4   Use of application software

4.1 Formatting features: characters   36

4.2 Formatting features: paragraphs   38

4.3 Formatting features: page   42

4.4 Editing   44

4.5 Simple tabulation   46

4.6 Advanced tabulation   48

4.7 Applying tabulation   50

4.8 Creating presentations 1   52

4.9 Creating presentations 2   54

Section 5   Business document preparation

5.1 Identification and selection
of stationery   56

5.2 The business letter   58

5.3 Letterheads   62

5.4 The blocked letter format   64

5.5 The semi-blocked letter format   66

5.6 The indented letter format   68

5.7 Short and long letters   70

5.8 Circular letters   72

5.9 Mail merge   74

5.10 Letters with insets   76

5.11 Letters with enumeration   78

5.12 Letters with tables   80

5.13 Envelopes and labels   82

5.14 Composition of business
communication   86

5.15 Memoranda   90

5.16 Notices and agendas   92

5.17 Minutes of meetings   96

5.18 Working with graphics   98

Section 6   Specialised document preparation

6.1 Columnar work   100

6.2 Creative displays 1   102

6.3 Creative displays 2   104

6.4 Flow charts   106

6.5 Organisation charts   108

6.6 Charts and graphs   110

6.7 Newsletters   112

6.8 Reports and proposals   114

6.9 Press releases   116

6.10 Legal documents   118

6.11 Wills   120

6.12 Leases   122

Contents

6.13 Conveyance documents   124

6.14 Agreements   126

6.15 Contracts   128

6.16 Specifications   130

6.17 Bills of quantity   132

6.18 Scope of works   134

6.19 Literary work   136

6.20 Trial balances and balance sheets   140

6.21 Income and expenditure statements   142

6.22 Bank statements and receipts   144

6.23 Forms   146

6.24 Wizards and templates   148

Section 7 Electronic communication

7.1 Types of electronic communication   150

7.2 The Internet   152

7.3 Facsimile and multifunctional devices 154

7.4 Email   156

7.5 Communication media   158

Section 8 Document management

8.1 Filing systems   160

8.2 Electronic filing systems   162

8.3 File integrity and security   164

8.4 File retention and traceability   166

Section 9 Ethics

9.1 Intellectual property   168

9.2 Copyright and plagiarism   170

9.3 Standards of work   172

9.4 Desirable habits and attitudes   174

Practice exam questions   176

Glossary   180

Index   186

This Study Guide has been developed exclusively with the Caribbean Examinations Council (CXC®) to be used as an additional resource by candidates, both in and out of school, following the Caribbean Secondary Education Certificate (CSEC®) programme.

It has been prepared by a team with expertise in the CSEC® syllabus, teaching and examination. The contents are designed to support learning by providing tools to help you achieve your best in Electronic Document Preparation and Management and the features included make it easier for you to master the key concepts and requirements of the syllabus. *Do remember to refer to your syllabus for full guidance on the course requirements and examination format!*

Inside this Study Guide is an interactive CD which includes electronic activities to assist you in developing good examination techniques:

- **On Your Marks** activities provide sample examination-style short answer questions, with example candidate answers and feedback from an examiner to show where answers could be improved. These activities will build your understanding, skill level and confidence in answering examination questions.

- **Answers** are included for each of the Practice exam questions in the book so that you can check your work.

- **Additional practice exam questions** similar to those at the end of the Study Guide have been included to help you practise for the Paper 2 examination.

This unique combination of focused syllabus content and interactive examination practice will provide you with invaluable support to help you reach your full potential in CSEC® Electronic Document Preparation and Management.

Introduction to Electronic Document Preparation and Management

Structure of the examination

The examination consists of three papers:

Paper 1	Paper 1 is a one-hour written examination that consists of 10 compulsory questions. This examination assesses the first two profile dimensions. This paper is compulsory for all candidates.
Paper 2	Paper 2 is a two-hour practical examination that assesses your ability to copy-type, prepare letters, manuscripts, tables, reports, business forms and creative displays. This is a compulsory paper. All three profile dimensions are assessed.
Paper 3	Candidates at a school are required to produce three school-based assessments (SBAs) and a portfolio. These are compulsory for in-school candidates. Private candidates do not produce SBAs. Instead, they are required to do the alternative examination called Paper 3/2. The alternative to the SBA will test the same skills as those tested for in-school candidates by means of the SBA. Private candidates are therefore advised to pay careful attention to the structure and content of the SBA.

Electronic Document Preparation and Management (EDPM) is designed to help you develop essential skills in the use of computers in the business environment. More specifically, this course focuses on the creation, storage, transmission and management of electronic documents.

In this Study Guide we have provided information to help you use certain features of word processors, spreadsheets, database management systems and presentation programs. We have tried to cater for as wide a variety of software as possible by providing both guidelines for software in general, and specific instructions for Microsoft Word, Excel, PowerPoint and Access 2003 and 2007. Significant changes occurred in the transition from Office 2003 to 2007, with the introduction of ribbons instead of the menus that characterised previous versions, which is why we focus upon these two versions. You should note that in Office 2007, there is a Home button rather than a File option as in 2003 and 2010. Where possible we have also provided notes for Office 2010 when it differs from 2007. We hope that in doing this the Study Guide will be useful for all students.

Please note that Figure 2.1.1 on p16 illustrates the American keyboard layout. This places the @ on the 2 key and the " on the ' key. You are advised to check the layout of the keyboard that you will use.

Aims of the course

The main aims of this course are to:

1 develop an understanding of the importance of Information and Communication Technology (ICT) in a modern office environment

2 equip students with the requisite skills to perform clerical and administrative roles

3 lay the foundation for career development and advancement in a business environment

4 develop knowledge and skills useful for specialised training for secondary and post-secondary studies and future careers

5 foster disciplined and ethical behaviours within the work environment

6 develop effective document management capabilities

7 enhance the quality of life and promote personal growth and development.

By the end of this course, you should have developed the knowledge, skills, values and attitudes needed to be creative and productive Caribbean citizens. This includes having self-confidence and self-esteem, respect for human life, appreciation of diversity, a positive work ethic and technological competence.

School-Based Assessment

The School-Based Assessment (SBA) consists of four items.

Assessment 1

This assignment is a timed, teacher-supervised activity in which you are expected to correct text from the author's original work with amendments and printers' correction signs. You are expected to interpret these signs, make the necessary changes, and present documents in a style consistent with universally accepted standards.

Assignment 2

You are expected to conduct research on an assigned topic and present the findings electronically using your developed skills. The research paper must be disseminated via email and must include an appropriate bibliography. You are assessed in areas such as the use of Internet and electronic mail.

Assignment 3

This assessment is based on real or imagined scenarios that will allow you to use various applications to design documents, such as, flyers, menus, invitations and newsletters. You are expected to demonstrate your creative abilities and effectively use application software such as PowerPoint or Lotus Presentation.

The portfolio

You are required to produce a portfolio that consists of 10 error-free samples of your work. Each portfolio must contain the following:

Item	Sample
Letters	Two-page indented OR blocked style letter A circular letter OR form with a tear-off slip
Manuscript	A report OR specification OR play (with actor's part)
Tabular work	An example of ruled tabulation with main heading and multiple columnar headings applying oblique or vertical heading and sorting
Committee documents	A notice of a meeting with an agenda for a meeting A chairman's agenda OR minutes of a meeting
Display	An invitation with a menu OR programme (a creative design should be used) A flow chart OR organisational chart (with or without use of template)
Legal work	A lease OR hire purchase agreement OR will with an endorsement. A contract of employment

Assignment 1

You are assessed in areas such as:	
✓	Spelling, grammar and word usage
✓	Keeping eyes on the copy
✓	Hand and arm position and posture
✓	Accurate keyboarding
✓	Arrangement of work space
✓	Speed
✓	Document formatting
✓	Use of graphics

Assignment 2

You are assessed on your use of the Internet and electronic mail to:	
✓	Open a web browser
✓	Open a webpage of known address
✓	Print a webpage
✓	Use a search engine
✓	Compose, edit and spell check
✓	Add attachments and weblinks
✓	Create and use an address book
✓	Save email
✓	Send email, including multiple recipients
✓	Print email
✓	Forward email
✓	Use copy features
✓	Organise and store email

Assignment 3

You are assessed on your ability to:	
✓	Create, open, modify and save presentations
✓	Add slides or cards
✓	Insert text, format text or add a text box
✓	Insert and modify graphics
✓	Insert or change slide or card design
✓	Navigate using scrollbar, slide sorter, menu, key commands
✓	Apply backgrounds and objects appropriately
✓	Use tools
✓	Save presentation
✓	Print slides

1 Fundamentals of computing

1.1   The computer

LEARNING OUTCOMES

At the end of this topic you should be able to:

* define the computer
* identify types of computer
* discuss the advantages and disadvantages of computer usage.

RESEARCH IT

Find out at least six ways in which computers have affected the business world. Make brief notes to summarise your findings.

DID YOU KNOW?

Cellphones now offer many of the features of a PDA plus email, Internet, audio recording, photographs and video.

A **computer** is an electronic machine or device that accepts and processes data to produce information. Table 1.1.1 shows the definitions of the basic terms used in this topic.

Table 1.1.1 Computer terminology

Hardware	The physical components of a computer system, that is, all the parts that you can see and touch, including the computer itself, as well as input, output and storage devices.
Software	A collection of programs, procedures and routines that direct the operations of a computer.
Central processing unit (CPU)	Considered the brain of the computer. It is the piece of hardware that carries out all the instructions from the software.
Peripheral	Any hardware device connected to and controlled by the central processing unit.

Types of computers

There are three basic types of computer: **mainframes**, **minicomputers** and **microcomputers**.

* **Mainframe**: a large-scale computer with a variety of peripheral devices, large storage capacity and a fast central processing unit. Mainframe computers can handle thousands of users simultaneously.
* **Minicomputer**: a computer whose size, speed and capabilities lie between those of a mainframe and a microcomputer. Minicomputers were designed to simultaneously support hundreds of users while occupying less space than a mainframe.
* **Microcomputer**: a computer based on a single microprocessor. A microcomputer is designed to be used by one person. It is also called a personal computer (PC). There are many different sizes of microcomputers (Table 1.1.2).

Table 1.1.2 Types of microcomputers

	A **desktop** is a PC that is designed to be set up in a permanent location. This type of computer is most commonly found in homes, schools and offices. They are usually cheaper to buy and easier to maintain and repair than portable devices such as laptops or palmtops.
	A **laptop** or **notebook** combines all the parts of a typical computer in a lightweight battery-powered case often no larger than an average textbook. They are useful for people who need to take work home, travel for work or have limited workspace.

	A **tablet** is a thin, flat panel with a touch-sensitive screen. This recently developed computer is becoming very popular with business people, professionals and students who want a small light-weight easy-to-use device.
	**Palmtop** computers or personal digital assistants (PDAs) are hand-sized devices used for managing schedules and storing contact information.

Advantages and disadvantages of computer usage

The main reasons for the widespread use of computers are their speed, accuracy, reliability, storage capability, versatility and accessibility.

- **Speed**: a computer can improve the speed and efficiency of business operations as it can carry out calculations in a fraction of the time it would take the average person. For example, the use of computerised accounting systems.
- **Accuracy**: a computer is able to perform very complex calculations without making errors.
- **Reliability**: a computer will do exactly the task it was instructed to do for as many times as it was instructed without becoming tired or bored. For example, 24-hour banking machines.
- **Storage capability**: a computer can store vast amounts of information in a very small space. For example, all the volumes of a set of encyclopaedia can fit on a single CD, together with audio and video clips.
- **Versatility**: a computer can be programmed to do a wide variety of tasks, including document preparation, data management and communication.
- **Accessibility**: computers make it possible for people and organisations to quickly access information and communicate with people throughout the world.

However, the use of computers has created new challenges:

- **Poor health**: excessive or improper computer use can result in illness or injury.
- **Dependency**: people can become overly dependent on computers, reducing the amount and quality of their interactions with family, friends and colleagues.
- **Unauthorised access**: data can be accessed by unauthorised people (hackers) or damaged by malicious programs (viruses).
- **Unreliability**: some businesses cannot operate if the computer system breaks down or there is a power outage.
- **Change in human input**: some employees may lose their jobs where computers can complete tasks in less time and for less cost. Additional resources for training may also be required where new technology has been introduced into the workplace.

SUMMARY QUESTIONS

1 Define the following terms:
   a computer
   b hardware
   c software
   d central processing unit
   e peripheral device.

2 Describe each of the following types of computer:
   a microcomputers
   b minicomputers
   c mainframe computers.

3 In the past VasTec Manufacturing Company has only used computers in the office. However, they are now investing in computerised systems for all their operations.
   a Discuss at least three ways in which the business will benefit from this change.
   b Identify at least three challenges that the company might experience as a result of having fully computerised operations.

Input devices

Figure 1.2.1 | A light pen

An **input device** is any piece of hardware that is used to enter data or to control signals to the computer. Input devices include the keyboard, mouse, light pen, microphone, document scanner, character readers and bar-code readers.

Keyboard

A **keyboard** is an input device used to enter information and instructions into a computer by pressing various keys. Standard keyboards have 101 keys. Multimedia keyboards have additional keys that control functions such as sound, visual display and Internet connections. Keyboards are used for a wide range of business purposes, including the typing of documents such as letters, memoranda and reports.

Mouse

A **mouse** is a handheld input device that controls the movement of the cursor, or the pointer, that is seen on a computer screen. The cursor moves in response to the movement of the mouse on a flat surface. There are several variations to the mouse, including the trackpoint, touchpad, trackball and joystick. These are collectively referred to as **pointing devices**. A mouse is used to open programs, select options and move items.

Light pen

A **light pen** is a light-sensitive input device which detects the presence or absence of light when it touches the screen. It is used to select an entry or indicate a position on a display screen (Figure 1.2.1). The user points the light pen at the screen to move the pointer and choose objects. The user is then able to select the object, write or draw. The light pen is very useful for designers and artists because they can create freehand drawings directly on the screen.

Touch screen

A **touch screen** is sensitive to human touch, so users can select and move objects with their fingers or a **stylus** (a pointed device, similar to a pen, designed to be detected by the touch screen) instead of using a mouse. Touch screens are now quite affordable, so some businesses and home users choose to buy them instead of the standard monitors.

Microphone

A **microphone** allows the user to send sound into the computer system. In the business world computers equipped with microphones are used for communication, to record audio files, or to dictate notes to software that convert voice to text.

Document scanner

A **document scanner** is a device that converts existing images or documents to a digital image on the computer (Figure 1.2.2). A scanner bounces a beam of light off the document and records the reflected light as a computer code. A document scanner enables a business to store copies of paper documents on the computer.

| Figure 1.2.2 | A document scanner |

Character readers

A **character** is a letter, digit, punctuation mark or other symbol that is represented on a computer. Each character is represented on the computer by a unique code. Table 1.2.1 explains how different types of character readers work.

Table 1.2.1 Types of character readers

Optical character recognition (OCR)	OCR is the scanning and conversion of paper documents into text that can be edited or changed. OCR involves three basic steps: **1** The device scans the document into the computer, character by character. **2** A computer program analyses each scanned character to determine which stored text character it most closely matches. **3** The computer program converts the set of scanned characters to a text document that can then be opened and used.
Optical mark reader (OMR)	An OMR is used to recognise dark pencil marks that are made in specific positions on forms such as multiple-choice answer sheets or questionnaires. Data can be input quickly and easily without the need for manual typing, but marks must be placed precisely where indicated and must be dark enough to be read by the scanner.
Bar-code reader	A **bar code** consists of a set of vertical lines of various widths that are printed on almost all products that are sold. Each bar represents a number. The bar code is read by an optical scanner called a bar-code reader. Businesses use bar codes to accurately record their stock and reduce the time customers spend at their checkout counters. When stock is received, the code is scanned using the bar-code reader and the information relating to the product is typed into the computer system. This information includes the product name, price and quantity in stock. When the cashier scans the code, the product name and price are displayed on the computer screen. After the payment is registered, the amount sold is deducted from the quantity in stock.

Digital cameras

A digital camera uses an electronic sensor to take videos or still photographs that you can view immediately on the camera's display screen. The images are stored in a code that can be read by a computer, inserted into documents or published on the Internet.

RESEARCH IT

Find out about other input devices such as webcams, digitising tablets, magnetic character readers and magnetic strips. Summarise your findings.

SUMMARY QUESTIONS

1 Define the term **input device**.

2 Explain how each of the following input devices would be used:
   a   keyboard
   b   touch screen
   c   light pen
   d   document scanner
   e   bar-code reader.

3 Explain the difference between an optical character reader and optical mark reader.

Output devices

Output devices are used to send messages out of the computer in the form of text, images, sounds or coded signals, either directly to the user or to another computer. Output devices include monitors, printers, speakers and multimedia projectors.

Monitors

A **monitor** is a television-like device used to display data. It is sometimes called a visual display unit or VDU. The screen is the display area of the monitor. At the front of the monitor, below the screen, you will most likely find buttons to control the size, brightness and contrast of the on-screen display.

Printers

A printer is a device that takes the information on your computer (soft copy) and produces a hard copy, that is, it transfers the information to paper. There are two basic classes of printer – impact and non-impact. In the examples discussed below, you can see that their characteristics make them more suitable for certain areas of business.

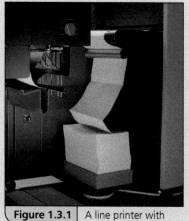

Figure 1.3.1 | A line printer with continuous paper

Impact printers

Impact printers create a printout by using metal pins to press an inked ribbon onto a sheet of paper. In the past, impact printers such as daisy wheel and line printers were commonly used. However, non-impact printers such as inkjets and laser printers are now more popular, because they are quieter, faster and capable of printing in colour.

Non-impact printers

Non-impact printers are much quieter than impact printers as their printing heads do not strike the paper. The advantages of non-impact printers are:

• They are quieter and faster than impact printers, because there is no contact between the print head and the paper.
• They can print in black and white and colour, on most types of paper and transparencies.
• The print quality is better than that of impact printers.

However, they are generally more expensive and less durable than impact printers.

Table 1.3.1 describes some examples of impact and non-impact printers.

Table 1.3.1 Examples of different types of printers

Impact printers	
Dot-matrix printer	• Uses a series of dots to create an image (Figure 1.3.2) • Durable, fast and the ink ribbon is far cheaper than an inkjet cartridge or laser toner • Print quality is poor and they are very noisy • No longer popular but still used to produce bills and invoices in places such as hospitals and utility companies
Line printer	• High-speed, similar to a dot-matrix printer in that it uses pins to strike the paper • While the dot-matrix creates one character (letter, number or symbol) at a time, the line printer creates an entire line • Relatively fast, printing more than 1,000 lines per minute • Still used by some businesses because of their speed, durability, low cost and their ability to print on a wide variety of media including cards and box labels
Non-impact printers	
Inkjet printer	• Uses a series of fine jets to squirt ink at the paper • Output is similar to a dot-matrix because the image consists of a series of dots • The dots are tiny, so the print quality is suitable for most educational, home and business purposes
Laser printer	• Uses a laser beam to attach dry powdered ink to a sheet of paper • Originally only printed in black and white, but colour laser printers are now available • More expensive than inkjets or impact printers • Produces a superior quality printout at high speeds – used by organisations that want to produce glossy, photo-quality documents such as brochures and newsletters

Figure 1.3.2 A dot matrix printout

DID YOU KNOW?

3D printers are now available for home use, although they are still fairly expensive. These printers add successive layers of material to transform drawings into three-dimensional objects you can use.

RESEARCH IT

Find out about other devices such as interactive whiteboards/ smartboards, e-book readers and 3D printers. Summarise your findings.

Speakers

A speaker produces output in the form of sound. Some computers have built-in speakers. However, external speakers are also commonly used.

Multimedia projector

A **multimedia projector** takes the image from a computer screen and projects it onto a larger screen or wall so that it can be seen by a large audience.

SUMMARY QUESTIONS

1 Describe three output devices other than printers.

2 Jaskin is trying to decide which printer he should purchase for his newly-established graphics design business. He is seeking your advice.

   a Differentiate between impact and non-impact printers.

   b State the advantages and disadvantages of each of the following types of printer:
      i   Dot-matrix
      ii   Line
      iii Inkjet

   c What properties of laser printers make them the best choice for Jaskin's business?

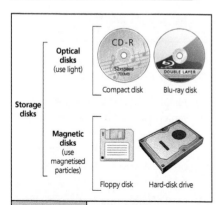

Figure 1.4.1 Types of disk

When a computer is switched off, everything in the main memory of the central processing unit is erased. Programs, data and information that are needed must be saved onto a storage medium such as a hard disk, compact disk, flash drive or memory card.

Storage is the process by which data is retained on a computer for future use.

Types of storage

The term **backing storage** refers to memory external to the central processing unit used for storage of large quantities of data or large programs. Backing storage is also known as a secondary store, auxiliary store or external store. Examples of backing storage include hard disks, compact disks and flash drives.

Immediate access storage is the memory within the central processor. It is also referred to as main memory or main storage.

The terms **storage device** and **storage medium** do not mean the same thing. The storage device is the equipment that is used for recording data, for example a CD drive or a floppy-disk drive. The storage medium is the material on which the data is recorded, such as a CD or a diskette.

Magnetic and optical disks

Disks (also spelled discs) are either magnetic or optical (Figure 1.4.1).

A **magnetic disk** is a circular plate on which electronic data can be stored magnetically. Magnetic disks include floppy disks and hard disks.

An **optical disk** stores data as microscopic light-and-dark spots on the disk surface. The optical disk drive uses a laser light to read this data. Optical disks include compact disks (CDs) and digital video disks (DVDs).

Floppy disk

A **floppy disk** or **diskette** is a flexible magnetic coated disk, housed in rigid plastic casing. It has a sliding shutter which automatically closes when the disk is received from the disk drive. They were once a popular means of transporting information, but they have generally been replaced by higher capacity alternatives.

Hard disk

A **hard-disk drive** is a metallic case that contains a set of inflexible disks that are stacked one above the other on a spindle. There is a read-write head for each disk. This is a device that senses (reads) and records (writes) data on the disk. Although hard drives are usually stored inside the computer case, external hard drives are also available. Hard disks are the most commonly used storage media. This is because:

- hard disks can store large amounts of data
- the information on a hard disk can be easily viewed, modified and deleted
- data stored on a hard disk can be accessed very quickly
- they are relatively cheap.

Compact disk

A **compact disk (CD)** is made of aluminium-coated plastic. CDs can store large amounts of information. Most CDs store about 700 MB of data. However, depending on the on the disk quality and technology used, a CD can often store up to 870 MB. A compact disk may be CD-ROM, CD-R or CD-RW. Table 1.4.1 lists the details of the three types of CD.

Table 1.4.1 Types of CD

Type of CD	Stands for	Features
CD-ROM	Compact disk read-only memory	Your computer can only read the data on a CD-ROM. You cannot write any additional data to it.
CD-RW	Compact disk – read/write	Your computer can erase and write over existing data on a CD-RW.
CD-R	Read-only CD	You can only write data to a CD-R once.

Digital video disk

A **digital video disk (DVD)** can store over 4 GB of data, allowing you to record large files, such as movies, on a single disk. DVD-RW disks may be reused several times. Blu-ray disks can store up to 128 GB of data, and larger capacity disks are being developed.

Flash drives

A **flash drive** is a small, relatively inexpensive, portable storage device that connects to the computer via a USB port. It is also known as a memory stick, thumb drive, USB drive, key drive, finger stick, pen drive, jump drive, disk-on-key and memory key. Some flash drives have up to 1 TB of storage, and the capacity continues to increase.

Memory cards

A **memory card** is a small plastic-coated rectangle that can be used to store data, on computers, digital cameras, music players, cellphones and game consoles. A memory card is actually a flat version of a flash drive. Memory cards are popular because of their small size, large capacity and versatility.

RESEARCH IT

Use the Internet to find information on the capacity and use of different types of optical disks.

EXAM TIP

Ensure that you can discuss the characteristics, advantages and disadvantages of each storage device.

RESEARCH IT

Many individuals and organisations are now choosing to store their data and information online. Research 'cloud computing' and summarise its advantages and limitations.

SUMMARY QUESTIONS

1 Explain the difference between each pair of terms:
  a Optical disk and magnetic disk
  b Immediate access storage and backing storage
  c Storage device and storage medium

2 Define each of the following types of storage and state two reasons why each is used:
  a Hard disk
  b Memory card
  c Flash drive

LEARNING OUTCOMES

At the end of this topic you should be able to:

- distinguish between operating system software and application software
- identify various types of application software.

DID YOU KNOW?

In the past, DOS (Disk Operating System) was the most popular and widely used operating system. Microsoft software such as Windows XP, Windows Vista and Windows 7 and the Mac OS for Apple computers are now the most commonly used.

EXAM TIP

Ensure that you can select the appropriate application software for specific purposes.

As you have already learned, a computer is able to perform tasks automatically. A program is a set of instructions written in a logical sequence, which directs the computer. Computer programs are known as software. As a computer is a programmable machine, it needs software before it can do any useful work. There are two main types of software: operating system software and application software.

Operating system software

Operating system software is a set of programs that coordinate the activities among computer devices. They contain instructions that allow the user to run application software. The computer cannot function without an operating system. For example, it tells the computer how to:

- recognise keystrokes and mouse clicks that the user makes, such as when you double-click to open a program
- load the program that you want to use into the main memory
- keep a record of all the files that are stored on the hard disk
- organise the contents of disks into folders or directories
- delete unwanted files from the hard disk
- manage the input and output devices that make up the hardware components of a computer
- send what appears on the screen to the printer when a user gives a command.

Antivirus software

A **virus** is a harmful program that destroys files or damages the operation of a computer. They are transmitted from one computer to another on removable storage devices such as flash drives or via the Internet. **Antivirus** programs are often classed as utility programs and are designed to prevent, search for and remove viruses (Figure 1.5.1).

Application software

The term **application software** refers to programs that perform specific tasks for users, including, word-processing software, spreadsheet software, database management software and presentation software. Table 1.5.1 shows some different types of software applications and their uses.

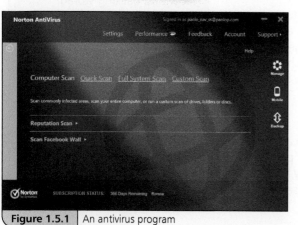

Figure 1.5.1 | An antivirus program

Table 1.5.1 Types of application software

Type of application	Uses	Examples
Word-processing software	• This software allows you to create, edit, format and print documents that are mainly made up of text, such as letters, papers and reports. • It also allows you to change what is written without having to retype the entire document or use correction fluid. You can insert new characters and delete existing ones, and move blocks of text from one part of a document to another. • After ensuring that the document is perfect, you can print as many copies as you want.	Microsoft Word, Microsoft Works, Apple iWork, Lotus Word Pro, TextMaker and Word Perfect
Spreadsheet software	• This software allows you to enter, display and manipulate data that is arranged in rows and columns. • It is mainly used for mathematical calculations, comparison of information, statistical analysis, and the creation of a wide variety of charts and graphs.	Microsoft Excel, Lotus 1-2-3, OpenOffice Calc, Corel Calculate
Database management software	• This is an organised collection of data files that may be used by a number of applications. The storage and access to the data is controlled by a set of programs known as a **database management system (DBMS)**. • A database management system is a combination of programs and database files that allow timely and easy controlled access to data by a number of users. • Databases are used to manage mailing lists, catalogues, inventories and personnel files. They also enable you to generate statistics, print reports and produce mailing labels.	Microsoft Access, Oracle, MySQL, IBM DB2
Presentation software	• This software allows you to create presentation documents called slides. A presentation consists of a series of slides, arranged in a logical order, which is usually used by a speech-maker or lecturer. A multimedia projector can be connected to the computer to project the slides onto a screen or wall, so that they can be viewed by the audience. • The slides can also be printed and used as handouts.	Microsoft PowerPoint, Lotus Presentation and OpenOffice Impress

SUMMARY QUESTIONS

1 Explain the difference between operating system software and application software.

2 State the purpose of each of the following types of software:
   a Antivirus
   b Word processing
   c Database management
   d Spreadsheet
   e Presentation

RESEARCH IT

Investigate and prepare a report on methods by which computer viruses are transmitted and strategies for preventing their transmission.

1.6 Computer care and safety

LEARNING OUTCOMES

At the end of this topic you should be able to:

- describe ways of caring for computer peripherals in the working environment
- discuss health factors associated with computer use.

RESEARCH IT

Carpal tunnel syndrome is a painful condition that develops in the wrists of people who often type on computer keyboards for long periods of time. Find out about at least four other repetitive strain injuries that can affect computer users.

DID YOU KNOW?

Injuries to the arms, shoulders and neck are among the most common work-related disorders in the world.

EXAM TIP

You should be able to discuss these health and safety concepts, not simply list them.

General care of the computer

Some guidelines for the general care of the computer include:

- Follow all the manufacturer's instructions.
- Keep the computer, peripherals and work area dust free. Use a soft brush or feather duster to dust the monitor, keyboard, mouse, systems unit, scanner and other devices. Wipe the screen and scanner glass with a soft lint-free cloth that is slightly moistened with a screen-cleaning liquid.
- Cover the computer and its peripherals with dust covers when the equipment will not be used for a long period.
- Never eat or drink near the computer.

Safety

Safety standards are designed to minimise the risk of harm or injury. Three areas of particular concern to computer users are as follows.

- **Overloading electric sockets**: never overload electrical outlets as this can damage your computer and create a fire hazard. Instead you should use a surge-protector with multiple outlets to safeguard the equipment from sudden changes in electrical voltage.
- **Position of work stations**: ensure that your computer is placed on a stable, level surface. Protect the computer from excessive heat, moisture and extended exposure to direct sunlight.
- **Location of extension cords**: route all cords so that they do not cross passageways. Ideally, the computer desk should be positioned 8–10 cm (3–4 inches) from the wall, adjacent to an electrical outlet, so that all cables will be safely out of the way.

Ergonomics

Ergonomics is the science of designing the job, equipment and workplace to suit the worker, to reduce fatigue, discomfort and injury. It includes:

- workspace design such as office layout and size, seating, lighting and ventilation
- furniture and equipment
- work habits.

Effects of extended use

Repetitive strain injuries occur when the muscles, tendons, nerves or other tissue experience stress or strain because a task is performed repeatedly, such as extended use of the computer. **Static forces** are pressures exerted on parts of the body that are caused by maintaining the same position for a prolonged period of time. To help reduce the effects of extended use you should:

- take short breaks (10 to 60 seconds) throughout the work day. Look away from your work, blink several times and flex and stretch your muscles
- get out of your chair every 20 to 40 minutes
- alternate tasks if possible in order to avoid having overly long periods of the same activity.

Table 1.6.1 provides checklists to ensure you have the correct lighting, furniture and posture in your work environment.

Table 1.6.1 Guidelines for correct lighting, furniture and posture

Lighting: inadequate lighting can cause headaches and eye strain.	**Furniture:** inappropriate furniture can cause discomfort and pain in the back, neck, shoulders, arms and wrists.	**Posture:** bad posture can cause muscular aches and pains. Figure 1.6.1 shows some key requirements for maintaining correct posture.
✓ The lights should be bright enough for you to see properly, without causing glare or discomfort. ✓ The computer should be positioned so that light does not shine directly into your eyes or reflect off the screen. ✓ If it is not possible to reduce the amount of light, then an anti-glare filter should be placed over the screen.	✓ You chair should be comfortable with adjustable height, lower-back support and adjustable armrests. ✓ Your desk should be wide enough so that you can position your monitor 60–75 cm (24–30 inches) away from your eyes or approximately an arm's length away from your body. ✓ The height of the desk should allow your shoulders to be relaxed and to hang naturally. You should use a desk with a keyboard tray for typing. ✓ The surface should be non-reflective to minimise glare.	✓ Sit with your back erect and your shoulders down and back. ✓ Do not be stiff or tense; relax, but do not slump. ✓ Adjust the chair height so that your knees bend at a 90° angle. Your thighs should be horizontal and your feet should rest firmly on the floor. ✓ Your keyboard should be positioned so that your upper arms will hang naturally at your sides. Your forearms should be parallel with the keyboard. Your wrists should be straight. ✓ Avoid postures that require extended stretching, twisting or unnatural curvature of the spine.

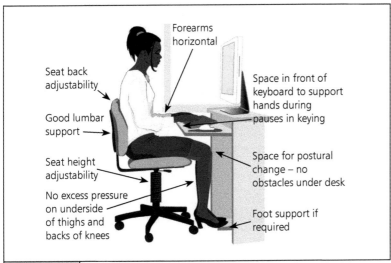

Figure 1.6.1 | Correct posture helps to promote efficiency and good health

SUMMARY QUESTIONS

1 Describe at least four ways of caring for computer peripherals in the work environment.

2 Discuss the standards that should be followed to minimise the impact on the health and safety of computer users. Use the following headings:
   a Positioning of work stations
   b Selection of furniture
   c Lighting
   d Extended use
   e Posture

2 Keyboard mastery

2.1

Introduction to keyboarding

At the end of this topic you should be able to:

- demonstrate correct posture for typing at the computer
- demonstrate competence in keyboarding techniques
- demonstrate competence in the use of special keys.

The term **touch keyboarding** refers to the process of typing data into a computer without looking at the keyboard. When you are first learning to use the computer you should practise the correct techniques for typing and using the keyboard. This will help you to type documents rapidly and accurately.

Posture

Review ergonomics in 1.6 to ensure your posture is correct. Note that the keyboard should be flat and at or below the level of your elbow.

Keyboarding techniques

Use all of your fingers when typing. Lightly rest the fingers of your left hand on **ASDF** and the fingers of your right hand on **;LKJ**. These are the **home keys**. The **A** key on the left and semicolon key (**;**) on the right are called the **guide keys**. When the little fingers are over the guide keys, it is easy for the other fingers to find their respective home keys naturally. Strike the space bar once with the right thumb to create a space after you have typed a group of letters or a word.

Aim to type accurately without looking at the keyboard. Keep your eyes on the **copy**, that is, the text from which you are keyboarding. You must practise consistently to attain the keyboarding speed of 35 words per minute that is required for this course. There is a speed test included as the first practice exam question at the end of this Study Guide, to help you practise.

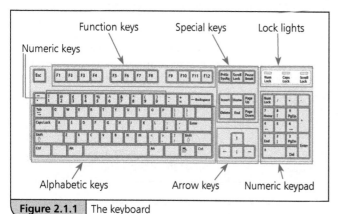

Function keys   Special keys   Lock lights

Numeric keys

Alphabetic keys   Arrow keys   Numeric keypad

Figure 2.1.1 The keyboard

The keys on the keyboard

Before you can demonstrate competence in keyboarding, you must learn the positions and functions of the various keys (Figure 2.1.1). Locate the following keys on your own keyboard.

The Escape key

The **Escape** (Esc) key allows you to quit some of the tasks you are doing.

The function keys

The **function keys** are labelled F1 to F12. The program being used determines their purpose. For example, in Microsoft Word F1 opens the Help feature, F4 repeats the last action and F12 activates the Save option.

Character keys

The **character keys** are displayed in the rows below the function keys. They consist of letters, numbers, punctuation marks and other symbols. The **space bar** is the longest key on the keyboard.

Modifier keys

The **Caps Lock** and **Shift** keys are called **modifier keys** because they modify or change the function of the character keys. They enable you to enter text in upper case (capital letters), for example ABC. If you want a single capital letter, hold Shift and press the letter key, then release both keys. The Shift key also enables you to type the symbols that are displayed at the top of the number and punctuation mark keys.

Use Caps Lock only if you want to type a large block of text in capital letters. When you have finished typing the block of text, press Caps Lock again to return to lower case. A light at the top right side of the keyboard or on the Caps Lock key indicates when Caps Lock is on.

Command keys

The **Ctrl** and **Alt** keys are special **command keys** or **system keys** that you use in combination with other keys to perform specific tasks. For example, simultaneously pressing the Ctrl, Alt and Delete keys will allow you to log off, lock, or change the password for the computer. For more information on these key combinations and their functions, see 3.1 and 4.2.

Other important keys

Table 2.1.1 shows other important keys that you should learn how to use.

Table 2.1.1 Important keys and their uses

Enter (↵)	Moves cursor to a new line
Backspace	Removes the character to the left of the cursor
Delete	Removes the character to the right of the cursor
Insert	Changes the computer to overwrite mode, so that existing text is replaced as new text is typed
Tab	Moves the cursor to the right of the page in large jumps, or from one section of a table to another
Arrow keys (←→↑↓)	Control the cursor so you can move it around a document without clicking the mouse. There are four arrow keys together in a group
Home	Moves the cursor to the beginning of the line. Holding the Ctrl key and pressing Home will move the cursor to the beginning of the document
End	Moves the cursor to the end of the line. Holding the Ctrl key and pressing End will move the cursor to the end of the document
Page up (Pg Up)	Scrolls up so you can view upper sections of a document
Page down (Pg Dn)	Scrolls down so you can view lower sections of a document

Working with punctuation

There are specific rules governing the amount of character spaces that you should leave before and after each punctuation mark.

• As a general rule, leave two spaces at the end of a sentence, whether it ends with a full stop, exclamation mark or question mark.
• Leave one space after the comma, semicolon and colon.
• Do not leave a space before any of these punctuation marks.

Full stop

Use a full stop (also called a period) to mark the end of a statement. **Do not put a space before a full stop.** Use two spaces after the full stop when it is used at the end of a sentence.

You can also use a full stop to show abbreviations or with initials in a name. In this case, use only one space after the full stop.

Comma

Use a comma to show a brief pause in a long sentence or for separating items in a list. **Do not put a space before the comma.** Use one space after a comma.

Colon

Use a colon before an explanation, an example or a list. **Do not place any space before the colon.** Use one space after the colon.

Semicolon

Use a semicolon to join two complete and very closely-related sentences. **Do not use any space before the semicolon.** Use one space after the semicolon.

Question mark

Use a question mark at the end of a sentence that is a question. **Do not use a space before the question mark.** Use two spaces after the question mark.

Exclamation mark

Use an exclamation mark at the end of a short sentence to express strong emotions such as pleasure, surprise or horror. **Do not use a space before the exclamation mark**. Use two spaces after it.

Apostrophe

Use an apostrophe before a letter s ('s) to show possession such as in 'Peter's bag'. **Do not leave any space before or after an**

apostrophe when it is used before an s to show possession. Use one space after a word that ends with an apostrophe, such as in 'babies' rattles'.

Also use the apostrophe to show where letters are omitted in contracted words such as don't and they're. **Do not leave any space before or after the apostrophe when typing contractions.**

Parenthesis

A parenthesis is one of a pair of signs, also called brackets, which enclose an explanation or afterthought. Use one space before the opening parenthesis, but do not include a space after it. **Do not put a space before the closing parenthesis, but include one space after it.**

Quotation mark

Quotation marks show the exact words that a person has spoken. You can use either single or double quotation marks. Use one space before the opening quotation mark, but no space after it. **Do not use any space before the closing quotation mark, but leave one space after it.**

ACTIVITY

Apply the punctuation rules you have learned as you type the following passages:

Passage 1 – Use of the comma, full stop, parenthesis and colon.

Productivity tools are a wide range of programs (also known as software) that are designed to increase efficiency in the workplace. These programs include: word-processing, spreadsheet, database, presentation and desktop publishing.

Passage 2 – Use of the exclamation mark, question mark, apostrophe and double quotation marks.

"Oh no!" Vashelle exclaimed, as she came to an abrupt stop.

"What is wrong?" asked her friend Hayleigh.

"I left my cellphone at home. You know that I can't survive without it."

Passage 3 – Use of the semicolon and single quotation marks.

Choose your words carefully. Pearl Strachan Hurd once said that 'words have more power than atom bombs'. Ensure that the dictionary you use is up to date because language changes constantly; new words are introduced, existing words may develop new meanings or may no longer be used.

SUMMARY QUESTIONS

1 Type the following sentences, ensuring you apply appropriate punctuation and spacing:

   a   Hard disk drives keyboard and monitors are examples of computer hardware

   b   Do you know where I can find Avery asked James

       Yes Cherise replied He went to the computer lab a few minutes ago

   c   Three ergonomic guidelines for computer users are Use blinds drapes or an anti-glare filter to reduce glare from the monitor screen Maintain proper posture while typing Avoid extended computer use get up and walk around or switch activities after thirty to forty minutes

Manuscript correction signs

A **manuscript** is the original handwritten or typewritten work of an author that is used to prepare an error-free document you can print and/or send. The manuscript may contain abbreviations that must be spelled out (see 2.5) and correction signs, symbols or marks that must be interpreted and applied.

You should learn how to correctly interpret each correction sign. Table 2.3.1 shows commonly used manuscript correction signs and their meanings.

Table 2.3.1 Commonly-used manuscript correction signs

Instruction	Marginal mark	Textual mark
Stet (leave unchanged)	Stet or ⊘	set of signs ~~and symbols~~ stet
Run on (continue work without a new paragraph)	Run on or ⤸	Ensure that your work is free from errors.⤸ ⤹Omissions, transpositions and insertions are some common typing errors.
Type in lower case	lc	Manuscript Correction Signs
Type in upper case	uc	san fernando is a city in Trinidad
New paragraph	NP or [or //	You can change the spacing between the lines or the spacing before or after each paragraph. [Letters are usually typed using single-line spacing.
Indent	→	→Letters are usually typed using single-line spacing.
Line up (align)	‖	Please bring the following items with you: Masking tape Sharp scissors ‖ Paper glue A pencil An eraser A ruler ‖
Move to the left	←	← Paragraphs are not indented when letters are being typed in full block layout.
Start lower on the page	↙	↙A margin of 1 inch or 2.54 cm is left at the top of the letter.
Move up	↗	One clear line space should be left between each paragraph. ↗ If you depress the Enter key too long, more than one line space will be created.

Instruction	Marginal mark	Textual mark
Insert	λ	Your word processor usually inserts λ text wherever the cursor is positioned. (new)
Delete	↻ or π	Omissions, transpositions and insertions are ~~some~~ common ↻ typing errors.
Transpose these words	1 ⌣ 2 The numbers indicate the new word order	3 2 1 The grammar and spelling checker contains several editing options.
Type in initial capitals (initial caps)	ic or ini caps (a double underline is used)	Annual general meeting
Closed capitals	cl. caps (a double underline is used)	Graduation Programme
Spaced capitals	Sp caps	Chairman's Agenda
Close up space	close up/	To horizontally centre a document you use equal ⊂ left and right margins.
Insert a space where shown	#	The letters OVR will appear on the statusbar #
Move the section in the balloon to the indicated position	⟳→	The street sweepers reported for duty at 5.30 a.m. just before sunrise

ACTIVITY

Apply the manuscript signs you have learned as you type the following passage:

Do you know the
West Indian Cherry?   lc
It is a small berry that
grows on a ~~short~~ bushy   ↻
shrub. It is known by
several other names,
including the Barbados
cherry and the
acerola. The humble
West Indian cherry
is world-renowned
because it is the fruit
with the highest
con ⊂ centration of   close up/
vitamin C.   uc

SUMMARY QUESTIONS

1 Write out the meanings of the following correction signs:

  a λ
  b ⌣
  c ⊘
  d ↻
  e [

2 Write the correction signs that mean each of the following:

  a move to the indicated position
  b spaced caps
  c transpose
  d indent
  e line up.

Headings and paragraphing

EXAM TIP

You should leave a clear line space after each paragraph.

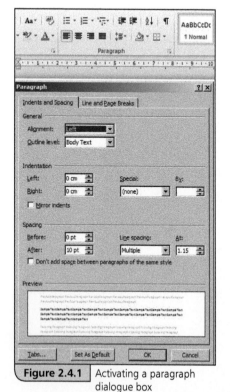

Figure 2.4.1 Activating a paragraph dialogue box

Headings

A **heading** is text that indicates the topic of a document or section within a document. There are several types of headings, with specific formatting rules governing each type. The headings most commonly used in business documents are:

- **main heading** – used to indicate the general subject matter of the entire document
- **subheading** – used to indicate the specific subject matter of the document
- **shoulder heading** – used to indicate the main idea of a section of a document
- **paragraph heading** – used to indicate the specific idea of a paragraph
- **marginal heading (side heading)** – used in displayed work such as programmes and plays.

You may sometimes be given specific instructions for the formatting of the headings. Where no instructions are given, use the formatting information in Table 2.4.1 as a guideline.

Paragraphing

There are four main types of paragraphs in manuscripts and business documents. They are:

- blocked
- indented
- hanging
- inset.

You can usually select which type of paragraph style you want to use throughout your word-processing document (Figure 2.4.1). For example, in Microsoft Word you can set indents using the **Paragraph** dialogue box. To activate this feature in Word 2003, click on **Format** and then **Paragraph**. In Word 2007, click on the small arrow in the bottom right-hand corner of the **Paragraph** section of the **Home** ribbon.

A **blocked paragraph** is the most commonly used paragraph style. Each line of the paragraph begins at the left margin.

In an **indented paragraph**, the first line starts at a distance (usually 1.27 cm or 0.5 inches) from the left margin. All other lines begin at the left margin.

With a **hanging indent** only the first line begins at the left margin. All other lines begin away from the margin (usually 1.27 cm or 0.5 inches). You can use hanging indents when typing entries in bibliographies and reference lists. Numbered and bulleted lists also use hanging indents, in that the first line is typed at the left margin, but all other lines begin away from the margin.

In Word 2007 you can access the numbered list options by clicking the numbering drop-down arrow in the **Paragraph** section of the **Home** ribbon.

An **inset** is used to clearly identify a particular section of a document such as a lengthy quotation. Each line of the inset paragraph begins and ends at a distance from the left and the right margins, as is shown below.

> The job interview is one situation that illustrates the truth of the axiom, 'If you fail to prepare, then prepare to fail'. Being well prepared will maximise the chance that you will be offered a job. Being well prepared will help you feel more relaxed and appear more confident.

Table 2.4.1 Guidelines for formatting headings

Heading	Formatting
Main heading	• Placed at the top of the first page of the document, either aligned left or centred. • Typed in the largest font in the document in **either** bold closed capitals with one or two spaces between words or spaced (expanded) capitals with three spaces between words • May be underlined
Subheading	• Placed immediately below the main heading with a clear line space between • Typed in slightly smaller font than the main heading • Either aligned left or centred • Typed in **either** bold closed capitals with one or two spaces between words or **initial capitals (title case)** with underlining
Shoulder heading	• Two clear line spaces between the preceding paragraph and the shoulder heading. Placed above next paragraph with a clear line space between heading and paragraph, left-aligned • **Either** closed capitals with or without underlining or initial capitals with underlining or bold • May be enumerated using either letters or numbers
Paragraph heading	• Placed in the first line of the paragraph • Left-aligned or indented according to the style of the paragraph • **Either** closed capitals with or without underlining or initial capitals with underlining or bold • **Either** followed by a colon or full stop with three spaces after the punctuation mark or with two spaces after the last word of the heading or with one space after if it is part of the opening sentence
Marginal heading (side heading)	• Placed in the left margin, left-aligned or indented • Typed in closed capitals or initial capitals in the same font and size as the paragraph • May or may not be underlined or bold

DID YOU KNOW?

In word-processing programs you can also set indents from the ruler that is displayed above the document. Use the Help feature of the software to find out how.

ACTIVITY

Type any passage from this Study Guide and then apply a different type of indent to each paragraph.

SUMMARY QUESTIONS

1 Outline the layout and use of each of the following:
   a main heading
   b subheading
   c shoulder heading
   d paragraph heading.

2 State at least one use of each of the following indents:
   a hanging
   b inset.

Abbreviations, figures and ellipsis

At the end of this topic you should be able to:

- prepare typescript from manuscript or typed notes using accepted rules for abbreviations, figures and ellipsis
- apply appropriate language skills to produce a professionally finished document.

Abbreviations

When writing a draft, the author may use abbreviations or contracted words to save time. Some of these abbreviations are commonly used and may be familiar to you. However, many abbreviations may have been created by the writer. You must therefore read carefully and interpret the meaning of these abbreviations in the context of the document you are typing.

It is acceptable to use the abbreviations shown in Table 2.5.1 when composing business documents. These are typed as seen so you do not expand these abbreviations.

Most other manuscript abbreviations must be expanded. Table 2.5.2 contains some examples and their expanded form.

Table 2.5.1 Abbreviations that are commonly used and can remain contracted

Open punctuation	Closed punctuation
eg	e.g.
etc	etc.
ie	i.e.
Messrs	Messrs.
Mr	Mr.
Mrs	Mrs.
Ms	Ms (full stop not necessary)
am	a.m.
pm	p.m.

Table 2.5.2 Abbreviations that should be expanded

Abbreviation	Expand to
accom	accommodation
advert	advertisement
a/c	account
approx	approximately
appt	appointment
bn	been
co	company
dr	dear
dept	department
ffly	faithfully
fr	from
hv	have
necy	necessary
ref	reference
sh	shall
shd	should
sin/sinc	sincerely
th	that
w	with
wl	will
yr	year/your
yrs	yours

DID YOU KNOW?

The closed punctuation style uses punctuation marks with abbreviations. Some letters are typed using open punctuation, a style that helps to increase typing speed by omitting all unnecessary punctuation. Full stops or commas are not used in the addresses, salutation or complimentary close of the letter. Full stops are also omitted from some abbreviations (see Table 2.5.1).

Figures

Numbers as figures or words

Type all numbers as numerals in statistical tables, reports, house numbers, postcodes, insurance policies and certificates.

Spell out the word when the numeral one (1) stands alone or when a number begins a sentence.

Date

The American style for typing dates is as follows: month, date, year (for example June 3, 2014). In the Caribbean the UK style is more commonly used: date, month, year (for example 3 June 2014). Avoid using slashes to abbreviate dates, such as in 03/05/2014. Days of the week should be typed out in full. See the different date styles to apply to different letter formats in 5.4 to 5.6.

Time

If you are expressing time using the 12-hour clock, separate the hour from the minutes with a full stop or colon and add a.m. or p.m. at the end, for example 9.47 a.m. or 5:20 p.m.

If you are expressing time with the 24-hour clock you may use four unspaced digits, such as 1720 hours. Alternatively you can use a period to separate the hours from the minutes: 17.20 hours.

Numbers with symbols

Use numerals with percentage and currency symbols, for example 33% of $45.60.

You should also use figures to express measurement and quantity, such as 388 km, 25 °C, and '10 boxes of paper clips'.

Money expressed within text

Type currency symbols first. Use a decimal point to separate the dollars from the cents or the pounds from the pence. Two figures must follow the decimal point, for example $952.99 or £23.05.

Fractions

Some word-processing programs automatically display the following fractions in the format shown: ½ ¼ ¾. Type the numerator followed by the solidus (oblique) and the denominator then strike the space bar. The desired fraction will appear in the document. Other fractions usually display as typed, for example 2/3 or 1/10.

If you are typing a number that consists of a whole number followed by a fraction, leave a space before starting the fraction, for example 1 ½ or 42 3/5.

Ellipsis

An **ellipsis** is a set of three spaced full stops used to show that words have been omitted from a quotation. The omission may occur anywhere in the passage. If the omission is at the end of a sentence, a fourth spaced full stop is added to mark the end of the sentence.

SUMMARY QUESTIONS

1 Write out the following abbreviated sentences in full:

   a By now you wl realise that employment in the word-processing dept of a co requires good lang skills.

   b Among the workshop expenses were $1,500 for ads and $2,200 for food and accom. These amts shd be drawn from the school a/c.

   c I will be back from vac in approx ten days' time. Ensure that you do not make any appts before then.

   d It is necy to get refs from at least two trustworthy people, eg a former teacher, your religious minister, etc.

2 Outline the guidelines that should be observed when typing each of the following:

   a dates

   b fractions

   c currency

   d time.

3 Introduction to application software

Introduction to word processing

Purpose of a word processor

A word processor is a program that allows the user to type, edit and format text-based documents. There are several advantages to using a word processor, including:

• You can see your work on the screen, read it and make adjustments before it is printed.
• You can use a wide variety of formatting options, including font type, colour, line spacing and borders.
• You can quickly address the same letter to many recipients.
• You can save and reuse your work as needed.
• Many word-processing programs contain **templates** that make producing documents easier. A template determines the basic structure for a document and contains document settings such as AutoText entries, fonts, page layout, special formatting and styles.

You would use a word processor to prepare documents that consist mainly of text, for example business letters and wills, or where text manipulation is required to make certain areas of text stand out, such as in flyers or notices.

Features of a word processor

The features of a word processor allow you to type, edit and format text and save and print your work. Many word processors have shortcut buttons for these functions which allow you to complete tasks more quickly. Table 3.1.1 shows the meanings of some of the most common shortcut buttons. You should learn the purpose of each button shown in the table, as well as the others on your screen. You will also be expected to know the keyboard combinations shown in Table 3.1.2.

Table 3.1.1 Common shortcut buttons in a word-processing program

Button	Command	Button	Command
	Create a new blank document		Open a saved document
	Save the document		Print this document
	Show a print preview of the document		Activate the spelling and grammar check
	Open a research task pane to use the thesaurus and translator		Cut (used to remove selected text and graphics from their location and place them on the clipboard)
	Copy the selected text and graphics onto the clipboard		Paste the contents of the clipboard
B	Make text **bold**	*I*	Put text in *italics*
U	Underline text		Activate a help feature

Table 3.1.2 Microsoft Word keyboard combinations

Command	Key combination
Make letters bold	Ctrl + B
Make letters italic	Ctrl + I
Underline letters	Ctrl + U
Decrease font size	Ctrl + Shift + <
Increase font size	Ctrl + Shift + >
Remove paragraph or character formatting from selected text	Ctrl + Space bar
Copy the selected text or object	Ctrl + C
Cut the selected text or object	Ctrl + X
Paste text or an object	Ctrl + V
Undo the last action	Ctrl + Z
Redo the last action	Ctrl + Y
Open a document	Ctrl + O
Create a new document	Ctrl + N
Print a document	Ctrl + P
Save a document	Ctrl + S
Single-space lines	Ctrl + 1
Double-space lines	Ctrl + 2
Set 1.5-line spacing	Ctrl + 5
Add or remove one line space preceding a paragraph	Ctrl + 0 (zero on the alpha part of the keyboard)
Close the program window	Alt + F4

Introduction to spreadsheets

Purpose of a spreadsheet

A **spreadsheet** is a program in which data is displayed in table format. It is designed for the manipulation of numerical data, such as the calculation and comparison of costs, and to represent data using charts and graphs. Businesses therefore use spreadsheets to:

• produce financial documents such as estimates, invoices and statements of income and expenditure

• produce statistical reports, for example, to compare quantities of goods that are sold over a period of time

• represent data in graphical format.

You would choose a spreadsheet if you are working mainly with numbers that require calculations.

Features of a spreadsheet

Think of the spreadsheet as a workbook with an unlimited number of pages. Each page is called a **worksheet**. A new workbook contains three blank worksheets, but you can insert or delete sheets if you wish.

If you open a spreadsheet program you will find that some of the features and shortcut buttons resemble those in a word processor. The worksheet, however, looks quite different from a word-processing document because it is covered with a set of blocks, called a grid.

• The grid in a worksheet consists of vertical lines that create columns and horizontal lines that create rows.

• Columns are labelled by letters, whereas rows are labelled by numbers. These labels look different from the rest of the worksheet because they are usually grey or blue, whereas the worksheet is white.

• The block that is created by the intersection of a column and a row is called a **cell**. Cells can contain text, numbers or mathematical formulae.

• Each cell is identified by the column letter followed by the row number. This combination of letter and number is called the **cell address** (see Figure 3.2.1 where there is a bold black border around cell address A1).

• A group of adjacent cells is called a **range**.

The toolbar

While many of the shortcut buttons in spreadsheet programs are the same as those in word processors, additional options are designed to make it easier to manipulate data quickly. The shortcut buttons in Table 3.2.1 provide you with some examples, demonstrating how spreadsheets are useful for working with data. More information on using these functions is given in 4.6 and 4.7.

Figure 3.2.1 | A worksheet

Table 3.2.1 Common shortcut buttons in a spreadsheet program

Button	Command	Button	Command
Σ	Autosum – adds up the contents of a group of adjacent cells	%	Applies per cent format to the number in a cell
A Z ↓	Sorts text data in ascending order from A to Z and numerical data from the smallest to the largest	,	Adds commas to the number in a cell, e.g. 1,275,399
Z A ↓	Sorts text data in descending order from Z to A and numerical data from the largest to the smallest	←.0 .00	Increases the number of digits after the decimal point
📊	Activates a chart wizard to insert a chart using selected data	.00 →.0	Decreases the number of digits after the decimal point
$	Applies currency format to the number in a cell		

Manipulating worksheets

Table 3.2.2 summarises the instructions for some common tasks in Excel.

Table 3.2.2 Instructions for common Microsoft Excel tasks

Task	Action
Enter data	Click on a cell to select it. A border will appear around the selected cell. Type the data.
Modify existing data	Double-click on the cell.
Merge cells	Select adjacent cells by clicking and dragging. In Excel 2003, select **Format**, then **Cells**. Click on the **Alignment** tab in the **Format Cells** dialogue box that appears. Click **Merge Cells**. Click **OK**. In Excel 2007, select the cells and then select **Merge Cells** from the **Merge & Center** drop down list on the Home ribbon.
Add a row	Right-click on the row label and then click **Insert** on the pop-up menu.
Add a column	Right-click on the column label and then click **Insert** on the pop-up menu.
Delete a row or column	Right-click on its label and then click **Delete** on the pop-up menu.
Resize rows and columns	Drag the line that separates the row or column labels. You may also right-click on the row/column label and the option to change the height or width will appear in the menu.
Select an entire row or column	Click in its label.

SUMMARY QUESTIONS

1 State at least four purposes of a spreadsheet.

2 Write out the functions of the following shortcut buttons:

a $

b Σ

c ←.0 .00

3 Outline the steps you will follow to do each of the following tasks. Use the Help function of your software if needed.

a Insert a worksheet

b Rename a worksheet

c Insert a row

d Change the width of a column

e Merge a group of cells

Introduction to database management systems

Purpose of a database

A **database** is a collection of structured data that is arranged to allow its contents to be easily retrieved, managed and updated. For example, a school may keep a database with information on all its students and staff. A teacher's record might include name, address, date of entry to the profession, subjects taught and classes assigned. This information can then be used when planning the school timetable.

You can manipulate and use the data stored in a database in a variety of ways, including:

- creating tables
- sorting data into order, such as alphabetically or chronologically
- searching for and retrieving specific information
- preparing reports.

Features of a database management system

Fields

A **field** refers to a single attribute of a record. That is, it stores data on only one part of a record. Table 3.3.1 shows some examples of field types.

Table 3.3.1 Database field types

Field type	Used for
Text	Words or combinations of words and numbers such as names, addresses and vehicle numbers Numbers that do not require calculation, such as telephone numbers, postal codes or the serial numbers on devices
Currency	Amounts of money
Number	Numerical data to be used in mathematical calculations
AutoNumber	Allowing the computer to automatically number the records when they are inserted
Date/Time	Dates and time
Picture or OLE object	Items that were created in other programs such as pictures, sounds, Word documents or spreadsheets
Yes/No	Data for which there are only two options, such as Yes/No, True/False, On/Off, Male/Female
Memo	Long text such as descriptions or notes
Hyperlink	Words or graphics that can be clicked to go to another location such as a page on the Internet
Look-up wizard	Creating a list of values that can be selected. For example, a list of subjects offered in your school

To create a field:

1 Type in the field name.

2 Select the data type based on the what you want stored in that field.

3 Declare the field size.

4 Set the format.

5 Insert the number of decimal places.

Note that steps 3–5 may not be necessary depending on the field or data type.

Records

A group of related fields is called a **record**. For example, in the school's database, all of the information about a specific teacher makes up that individual's record.

Tables

Related records are stored in a **table**. The columns in a database table contain fields, whereas each row contains a record. You should use a separate database table for each group of records. For example, in a library database there will be separate tables for members, staff, books and equipment.

Database

A database is a collection of data organised in tables. See Figure 3.3.1, which shows the hierarchical structure of a database.

Figure 3.3.2a Getting started in a database

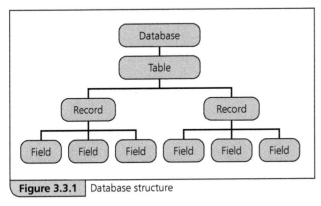

Figure 3.3.1 Database structure

Manipulating a database

This topic provides guidance on how to create and modify a database.

When you open the database program, a **Getting Started** task pane will usually open. It can look like one shown in Figures 3.3.2a and 3.3.2b, depending on the program that you are using.

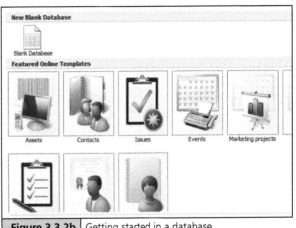

Figure 3.3.2b Getting started in a database

Working with a blank database

To obtain a database in which you must create and name the tables manually:

1 Select the option labelled **Blank Database**.

2 Type the name of the database in the appropriate space to the right of the task pane and click **Create**. A blank database table will be displayed.

3 Right-click on the column titles and select **Rename Column** to enter the field names.

4 Type the data in the respective cells. A new row (a record) is automatically added whenever you press the **Enter** key on the keyboard.

Working with a template

If you want to use a pre-designed database in which the tables are automatically created:

1 Select one of the options in the **Templates** section of the task pane. For example, use **Contacts** for storing names, addresses, and so on.

2 Type the file name in the appropriate space to the right of the task pane and click **Create**. The selected template will be displayed on the screen.

3 Right-click on the column name and select **Delete** to remove any field you do not want to use.

Queries

Databases can contain numerous records. Consider, for example, the amount of data about students that might be stored in your school's database. It is usually not practical to manually search through the database to locate records and data fields. A **query** is a database tool

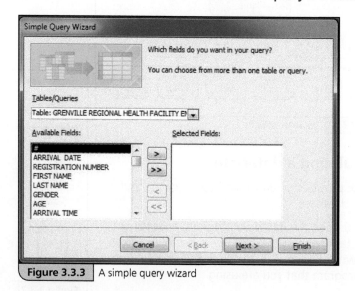

Figure 3.3.3 A simple query wizard

> **TRY IT!**
>
> Create a database called *Friends*. Create a contacts table and save the first names, surnames, dates of birth, gender, addresses and telephone numbers of at least six of your friends.

that is used to automatically find and select information from tables for specific purposes. For example, your school can use a query to display the names of all 13–15-year-old students who have scored more than 75 per cent in the most recent English examination.

To perform a simple query:

1 Open the database, and select **Query wizard** from the **Create** toolbar or ribbon.

2 Select **Simple query** from the dialogue box that will appear (similar to the one in Figure 3.3.3), and then click OK.

3 Select the table that contains the data that you want to use from the **Tables/Queries** drop-down list.

4 Click on the fields that should be displayed in the query and click the right-pointing arrow (>) to add them to the **Selected Fields** list. Click **Next**.

5 Type in a name for the query, and then click **Finish**. The results of the query will be displayed as a table in a new database window.

TRY IT!

Perform a query that will show only the first names and telephone numbers of the friends in your database. Print the results of your query.

SUMMARY QUESTIONS

1 The manager of KLTec Book Store has asked for your advice about establishing a database management system for his business.

  a Define the terms:
    i table
    ii record
    iii field
    iv database.
  b Explain at least three purposes for which the database can be used.

2 a Create a database called **XYCOM Ltd**.
  b Create a table called **Customers** with the following information:

First name	Last Name	Email Address	Phone	Company	Job Title
Sanderson	Grant	s.grant@wefty.com	1 609 555 4234	WEFTY Sales and Services Ltd	Manager
Broderick	Bailey	brodbailey34@frl.co	1 990 5552 322	Ferdinand Redistributors	Sales Supervisor
Florence	Ali	flo.ali@enter_prise.com	1 234 555 7890	A Ali EnterPrises	Operations Manager

  c Amend the table to include the following records:
    Vincent Trimm, the Chief Executive Officer of Jiganson Electronics, whose email address is v_trimm@jiganson.net.tt and his administrative assistant Heather Kinland, whose email address is hlkinland@jiganson.net.tt. Their company's phone number is 1 868 555 0909.

  d Do a query to display the full names and email addresses of all people in your database. Print the results of your query.

3.4 Introduction to presentation software

LEARNING OUTCOMES

At the end of this topic you should be able to:

- explain the purpose of presentation software
- determine the appropriate software to be used to perform specific tasks.

TRY IT!

Look at the formatting options and shortcut buttons in your presentation program. Like the buttons in Microsoft Excel that are designed to enable you to manipulate data efficiently, the functions in presentation software enable you to change the design and effects of your presentation quickly and easily.

ACTIVITY

You should practise summarising information, so that you can make your points brief but informative. Summarise the main idea in the following paragraph into a single statement using eight words or less.

The ability to keep information to yourself is an indication of your professionalism. Even when you are not specifically instructed to keep a matter confidential, you should refrain from discussing details about your employers or your job.

Purpose of presentation software

A **presentation program** is used to create slides containing a variety of elements such as text, pictures, sounds, graphs and video clips. You would use a slideshow when making a presentation to an audience, such as giving a report in a meeting, speaking at a conference or when teaching a lesson. In addition to providing information, a presentation could also be used to persuade or motivate people. Microsoft PowerPoint is an example of application software that is used to create presentations.

Features of presentation software

The 'pages' in a presentation program are called **slides**. The design elements, such as text and graphics, can be freely moved to any location on the slide. You can add animations to these objects so that they move when the presentation is viewed as a slideshow. More information on using presentation software is provided in 4.8 and 4.9.

Preparing a presentation

Some people mistakenly think that they should type out their whole speech on the slides. This is not correct. The slide should contain a point-form summary of the main ideas. It should not consist of large blocks of text.

- As a general rule you should use no more than eight words per line and no more than six lines per slide.
- Make your presentations interesting. Know your audience and design a presentation that will capture and keep their attention.
- Be informative. Ensure that your presentation teaches or reinforces valuable information.

It is a good idea to draft out your presentation on paper before creating it on the computer.

- First list the main ideas that you want to communicate to your audience. Each main idea should utilise at least one slide. The main idea should be used to compose the slide's title.
- After you have prepared the outline, list no more than six points that you will make on each slide. Keep in mind that if the slide contains pictures you must use less text.
- Do not use a picture simply to make your presentation look pretty. Graphics should illustrate an essential point. Identify the key points that you will want to illustrate with a photograph, drawing or graph.

Selecting the most appropriate software

The four applications that are most frequently used in business situations include word processors, spreadsheets, database management systems and presentation software.

You should be able to determine which type of software is most appropriate for performing specific tasks. As you began to use some of these applications, you might have observed that they have some features in common. Certain features in one program, however, might make it more appropriate for one particular task than another. For example, you can type text in each of the four applications described, but a word processor allows you to easily manipulate the text to present it as an effective business document. Table 3.4.1 summarises the four applications and the tasks for which they are designed.

Table 3.4.1 Purposes of applications

Word processor	Most appropriate for preparing and manipulating text-based documents such as letters, memos, wills, leases and hire-purchase agreements
Spreadsheet	Designed for the manipulation of numeric data such as the calculation of costs and preparation of graphs
Database management system	Best suited for storing, organising and retrieving collections of interrelated data
Presentation software	Used to produce sequences of slides with text and graphics that present information on a topic, usually for use with a multimedia projector

SUMMARY QUESTIONS

1 Outline at least six principles that should be observed when preparing a presentation.

2 State at least three uses of presentation software.

3 When Flame De Gannes approached the Small Business Development Agency for a loan to start up a clothes store, the loans officer asked for the following:

   a a detailed statement of the expenses that will be incurred in starting up the business

   b a letter outlining her business plan

   c a set of graphics and text that effectively summarise the main features of her proposed business.

State the most appropriate software for Flame to use when preparing each of the requested items.

ACTIVITY

Your school's football coach is planning a training camp for the team. What software should he use for each of the following purposes?

1 To prepare a budget.

2 To use when speaking to the team about the camp's rules and regulations.

3 To organise each player's personal information.

4 To type a note informing parents about the training camp.

5 To produce a schedule of each day's activities.

6 To create motivational posters for the dormitory walls.

4.1 Formatting features: characters

Font refers to the shape and design of the characters. Font may be plain or very decorative. You should select the type of font according to the nature of the document you are preparing. For most business letters you should use plain font type such as Times New Roman or Arial.

The specific process for formatting font will differ depending on the software you are using. Microsoft Word 2003 features a formatting toolbar, similar to the one shown in Figure 4.1.1. You will have to click on the **Format** menu to see other formatting options. Word 2007 features a **Home** ribbon with shortcut buttons for the most common formatting tasks. If you wish to use more advanced formatting options, you must click on the tiny arrows found at the bottom of the ribbon.

Figure 4.1.1 | A formatting toolbar

Table 4.1.1 Text formatting options

Button	Name
Calibri (Body)	Font face
11	Font size
A▴	Grow font
A▾	Shrink font
B	Bold
I	Italics
U ▾	Underline
abc	Strikethrough
x₂	Subscript
x²	Superscript
A ▾	Font colour

How to format characters

Follow these steps to format characters:

1 Select the text.

2 Click the desired formatting button (see Table 4.1.1 for examples). Some of the buttons feature an arrow that is used to access a longer list of options. This is called a **drop-down menu**.

3 If you want to choose the font type, click on one of the font names and you will see the changes made to the highlighted text.

4 Click anywhere on your on-screen page to deselect the text.

You can also use the keyboard to apply formatting, by clicking the combination of keys shown in Table 4.1.1.

Selecting font styles

Bold, *italics* and underlining are mainly used to draw attention to specific words. You should use these styles sparingly because they can make a document difficult to read. You should avoid using bold, italics and underlining for emphasis when you are typing a business letter. However, in other business documents, the guidelines in Table 4.1.2 are applicable.

Table 4.1.2 Font styles and their uses

Bold	Use bold to darken key words that relate to the topic of the document, thereby making them stand out from the rest of the text. Use sparingly when you are preparing a document.
Italics	Use italics to draw attention to key words or to introduce a new word that will be explained later on in the document. However, in business documents, including letters, italics are used to type words that are: • the titles of works such as poems, stories, newspaper articles, magazines or books • foreign language words • the names of ships or aircraft.
Underlining	People using typewriters used underlining for emphasis because bold and italics were not available. Unless you are specifically instructed, do not underline text when creating a word-processed document.

Selecting size

Most of the documents for this course must be typed in size 12 Times New Roman. Size 16 is used for main headings and size 14 for subheadings. You can use a wider variety of font sizes when producing creative work such as flyers, programmes and invitations.

RESEARCH IT

Find out the keyboard shortcut for each of the tasks in Table 4.1.1 where possible.

Selecting colour

You should type business documents in black. Avoid using coloured text within the body of the document. You may use colour when designing letterheads and logos.

Symbols

You already know how to type symbols such as the percentage sign (%) and ampersand (&) (see 2.1). However, there are many other symbols that are not on your keyboard. You can use the **Symbol** dialogue box to enter these symbols anywhere in your document. The Symbol dialogue box can be found by using the **Insert** menu or tab.

DID YOU KNOW?

Fonts such as Wingdings and Webdings consist entirely of symbols.

DID YOU KNOW?

The font that the program automatically uses is called the default. You can use the **Font** dialogue box to change the default font.

SUMMARY QUESTIONS

1 Outline the steps that should be followed to format text.

2 List at least six guidelines that should be followed when formatting text for business documents.

3 State the purpose of each of the following shortcut buttons:

a   b   c   d

EXAM TIP

Unless you are otherwise instructed, you should type business documents in Times New Roman size 12.

Formatting features: paragraphs

At the end of this topic you should be able to:

• apply appropriate paragraph formatting features to enhance specific documents.

The text in business documents is usually divided into paragraphs, that is, groups of sentences related to a main idea. It is sometimes necessary to apply special formatting to paragraphs. For example, a report is usually typed in double line spacing so that it is easier to read.

You can format paragraphs by selecting the text you want to change and clicking the desired formatting button, as you did for font in the previous topic. Table 4.2.1 shows some common formatting buttons. They can usually be found in the **Home** ribbon or **Formatting** toolbar.

Table 4.2.1 Paragraph formatting options

Shortcut button	Name	Keyboard combination	Purpose
	Bullets	(no keyboard combination given)	Start a bulleted list with a distinctive symbol at the start of each list item. Click ▼ to select the symbol.
	Numbering	(no keyboard combination given)	Start a numbered list. Click ▼ to select the numbering style such as roman numerals.
	Decrease indent	Ctrl+Shift+M	Reduce the distance from the margin at which the paragraph begins.
	Increase indent	Ctrl + M	Increase the distance from the margin at which the paragraph begins.
	Align text left	Ctrl + L	Ensure that the left margin is even. The lines end at different distances from the right margin.
	Centre	Ctrl + E	Ensure that each line of text is spaced an even distance from the left and right margins.
	Align text right	Ctrl + R	Ensure that the right margin is even. The lines begin at different distances from the left margin.
	Justify	Ctrl + J	Align text to both the left and right margins, adding extra spaces between words if necessary.
	Line spacing	See Table 3.1.2	Change the spacing between lines of text or paragraphs. Click ▼ to select the options.
	Shading	(no keyboard combination given)	Colour the background behind the selected text. Click ▼ to select the colour.
	Borders	(no keyboard combination given)	Create an outline around selected text. Click ▼ to select the options.

Line spacing

Line spacing is the amount of space from the bottom of one line of text to the bottom of the next line. Most word processors adjust the line spacing to accommodate the largest font or the tallest graphic in that line. You can change the spacing between the lines or the spacing before or after each paragraph.

You should usually type letters using single-line spacing with an extra line space between paragraphs. You should type manuscripts using double line spacing unless you are otherwise instructed.

Alignments

There are four options for paragraph alignment: left, right, centre and justified (see Figure 4.2.1).

Left-alignment causes the first letter of each line in
a paragraph to be in line with the left margin. This
paragraph is left-aligned.

Right-alignment causes the last letter of each
line to be in line with the right margin. This
paragraph is right-aligned.

Centre causes each line of text to be evenly spaced
between both the left and right margins. This
paragraph is centred.

Justify causes the text to be evenly distributed between both margins so
that the first and last letters of each line are in line with the respective
margins. Because the last line of text in a paragraph is often shorter than
the other lines, it may not appear to be justified. This paragraph is justified.

Figure 4.2.1 | Types of paragraph alignment

Tabs

A **tab stop** instructs the cursor to move to a specific position on a line. The default tab stop is 1.27 cm (0.5 inches). This means that each time you press the **Tab** key on the keyboard, the cursor will move to the right by 1.27 cm. You can use the **Tab** button on the **Paragraph** dialogue box to set different tab stops.

When you set a tab stop its character is displayed on the ruler at the top of your word-processing document. You can then change the position of the tab stop by dragging its character to a new place on the ruler. Dragging the character off the ruler removes the tab stop. Table 4.2.2 summarises the tab stop characters and their effects.

Table 4.2.2 Tab stop characters and their effects on text

Tab character	Name	Effect
 **L**	Left tab	Text is aligned to the left in relation to the tab stop position.
 ◢	Right tab	Text is aligned to the right in relation to the tab stop position.
 ⊥	Centre tab	Text is evenly positioned to the left and right of the tab stop position.
 ⊥	Decimal tab	Numbers are aligned so that the decimal points are lined up one under the other.
		Bar tab	A vertical line is drawn at the tab stop position. It can be used whenever you are typing data in a tabular layout.

Create the price list as shown in Figure 4.2.2 by following these instructions:

1 Open a new document.

2 Open the **Paragraph** dialogue box, click on the **Tabs**… button and set a centre tab at 5.1 cm (2 inches) and a right tab at 10.2 cm (4 inches). Type the header row in bold font. Remember to press the **Tab** key on the keyboard to create the desired spaces.

3 Go to the next line. Open the paragraph box and clear all tabs. Set a decimal tab at 5.1 cm (2 inches) and a right tab with leader dots at 10.2 cm (4 inches). Type the next three lines.

a Type the following list:

Mangoes

Oranges

Bananas

Pineapples

b Select the list and define a new bullet.

Leaders

A **leader** is a solid, dotted or dashed line that is used to fill the space created by a tab character. The price list shown in Figure 4.2.2 illustrates the use of several tabs and a leader.

Book Title	Unit Price	Condition
Happy Days	$17.95	...Gently Used
Andy and I	$9.50	...Used
To Catch a Thief	$38.00	...New
The Return	$1.99	...Back cover missing

Figure 4.2.2 | Use of tab stops and a leader

Bullets

A **bullet** is a symbol that is placed before text to indicate a list of items or key points. Word offers several different bulleting styles. You can access these through the **Bullets** dialogue box or drop-down menu. The dialogue box enables you to select a symbol, picture or font as the bullet (Figure 4.2.3). You may also use this box to set the alignment of the bulleted list.

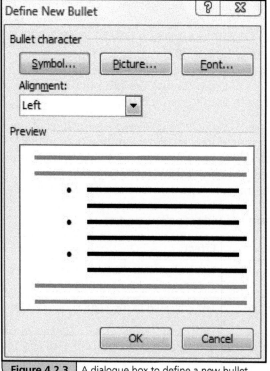

Figure 4.2.3 | A dialogue box to define a new bullet

Numbering

Numbering is used to show the sequence of items in a list. For example, numbering is used in this Study Guide to clearly identify each step of a process. There are several different numbering formats, as is shown in the drop-down menu on the numbering button in the Paragraph section of the Home ribbon in Word 2007.

A word-processing program can be set to automatically number a list. If this feature is active, the program automatically formats text as a numbered list if you start a paragraph with a number followed by a full stop and then a space. See 5.11 for more about enumeration.

Borders and shading

Borders are used to outline words, paragraphs, entire pages or cells in a table. Borders may be simple lines or decorative frames. You can apply page borders to one or more sides of the document.

Shading changes the background colour of the text. There are several shading patterns to choose from with an almost infinite range of colours.

Borders and shading are used in this Study Guide for features such as 'Did You Know?' and 'Summary Questions'.

SUMMARY QUESTIONS

1 State the key combination that can be used to perform each of the following tasks:
  a right-align a paragraph
  b increase a paragraph indent
  c centre the selected text.

2 Explain the purpose of each of the following formats:
  a leaders
  b bullets
  c decimal tabs
  d bar tabs.

3 State the purpose of each of the following shortcut buttons:
  a   b   c   d

4 List the steps that should be followed to:
  a set a tab
  b use a bullet that is not displayed in the drop-down menu.

EXAM TIP

Make sure that you learn how to quickly access the different paragraph formatting options.

4.3

Formatting features: page

At the end of this topic you should be able to:

• apply appropriate page formatting features to enhance specific documents.

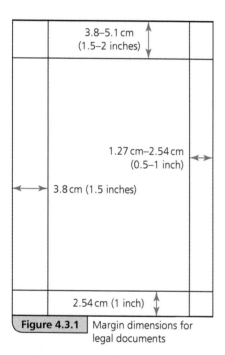

| **Figure 4.3.1** | Margin dimensions for legal documents |

The diagram shows: 3.8–5.1 cm (1.5–2 inches) at top; 1.27 cm–2.54 cm (0.5–1 inch) at right; 3.8 cm (1.5 inches) at left; 2.54 cm (1 inch) at bottom.

DID YOU KNOW?

The use of watermarks dates back to the 13th century. Papermakers in Europe first used watermarks to identify their products. Watermarks are now often used as a security feature on banknotes and postage stamps.

There are specific requirements for the page layout of professionally prepared documents. These are discussed below.

Margins

The **margins** are the blank areas that surround the content of a page. Business letters are typed with 2.54 cm (1 inch) margins at the top, bottom, left and right. Legal documents such as wills and leases are typed with the margins shown in Figure 4.3.1.

Backgrounds and watermarks

Backgrounds are colours, patterns or pictures that cover the page behind the text. You should not use backgrounds in business letters or legal documents unless you are specifically instructed to do so. However, they are acceptable for design work, such as invitations, menus or programmes for events. If you use a background:

• ensure that there is sufficient contrast between the background and the text, so that the document is readable

• avoid backgrounds that distract because of their brightness or content

• use colours that blend well together for the background, text and borders, to create a visually appealing effect.

Watermarks are text or pictures that are placed behind the text in a document. They are used to:

• add interest

• identify the status of the document, such as 'Draft', 'Confidential' or 'Urgent'

• show the producers of the document such as a company's name

• reduce the possibility that other people can simply photocopy and present the document as their own.

Watermarks should be carefully selected and positioned so that they do not obscure the text or distract from the contents of the document.

Headers and footers

Headers and **footers** are areas in the top and bottom margins of the page into which you can insert text or graphics. Examples of items that are often inserted into the headers and footers are:

- the document's title
- a company logo
- the chapter or section number
- the author's name
- the date
- page numbers.

Page numbering

The second and subsequent pages of business documents should always be numbered. This helps the reader to easily put them in order if they get mixed up or separated. Numbers may be placed in the header or footer, aligned to the left, right or centre.

Footnotes and endnotes

A **footnote** is a notation at the bottom of a page that is used to explain, comment on, or provide references. **Endnotes** are used at the end of a document to cite sources of the information that were used in your document.

How to format the page

Depending on the software you are using, most page formatting tools can be accessed through the page layout or page setup options available in the File menu or Home ribbon. For a table of instructions for using these formatting features in Microsoft Word, please see the accompanying CD.

SUMMARY QUESTIONS

1 Outline the guidelines that should be followed for the selection of backgrounds.

2 State the purposes of each of the following:
   a watermarks
   b footnote
   c endnote.

3 Explain the process for inserting:
   a a footer
   b a footnote
   c page numbers
   d backgrounds
   e watermarks.

Editing

EXAM TIP

Make sure you practise identifying and correcting errors in text, as this skill is frequently assessed.

DID YOU KNOW?

The word-processing program may flag correctly spelled words such as unfamiliar names or foreign words. You should therefore ensure that you know how to correctly spell all the words you use.

EXAM TIP

Take care if you use the **Replace All** option. The software will not be able to tell if the word you are replacing is part of another word. For example, if you use **Replace All** to change 'sand' to 'mud', 'sandwich' will be changed to 'mudwich'.

Editing

Editing involves making changes to a document. It includes the identification and correction of errors. However, editing also involves other essential processes such as:

• condensing to avoid unnecessary wordiness or repetition
• rearranging words to ensure a smoother flow of ideas
• ensuring that the language and contents are suitable for the intended reader
• clarifying ambiguous or confusing statements
• verifying that information is accurate and up to date
• ensuring that the tone of the document is appropriate for its purpose
• using the appropriate styles and layouts for documents.

Table 4.4.1 summarises some of the most commonly used editing features in Microsoft Word. Remember that you can use keyboard shortcuts for some of these tasks.

Proofreading

Editing is not synonymous with proofreading; however, they are closely related. **Proofreading** is the process of reading through a document word by word to identify and correct errors in spelling, grammar, sentence construction, word usage and punctuation. Proofreading requires an excellent command of the language and careful attention to detail.

Spelling and grammar checker and thesaurus

Most word-processing programs contain a utility for checking spelling and grammar as you type or after typing the entire document. Possible errors are flagged or identified by a wavy underline. Word uses the following underlines:

• green to identify grammatical errors, such as incorrect order of words, non-agreement between subject and verb, and incomplete sentences
• red to identify words that are not in its dictionary
• blue to identify possible errors in word usage, such as using *there* for *their* and *it's* for *its*.

You can right-click on the flagged word and decide whether to ignore, change or add it to the dictionary.

You can also use the right-click option to access a thesaurus, which is a list of synonyms.

AutoCorrect

Some word-processing programs automatically correct certain typographical errors. For example, if you type *can;t* plus a space, AutoCorrect replaces what you typed with *can't*.

Table 4.4.1 Steps for using editing features in Microsoft Word

Move text or graphics	1 Select the text or graphic to be moved. 2 Right-click and select **Cut** to remove the item from its current position. 3 Click to position the cursor where you want the item to be placed. 4 Right-click and select **Paste**.
Copy text or graphics	1 Select the text to be copied. 2 Right-click and select **Copy**. This leaves the original text in its current position and places a copy of it on the clipboard. 3 Click to position the cursor where you want the text to be placed. 4 Right-click and select **Paste.**
Search for a specific word	1 In Word 2003, click **Edit** then **Find....** In Word 2007, click the **Find** button on the **Home** ribbon. A dialogue box will appear. 2 In the **Find what:** box, enter the text for which you want to search. 3 Select any other options that you want, such as: **Match case, Find whole words only** or **Find all word forms**. 4 Click **Find Next**.
Automatically replace text	1 In Word 2003, click **Replace...** on the **Edit** menu. In Word 2007, select the **Find** button on the **Home** ribbon. 2 Enter the text that you want to search for in the **Find what:** box. 3 Enter the replacement text in the **Replace with:** box. 4 Select any other options that you want. 5 Click **Find Next**, **Replace** or **Replace All**.
Turn on the automatic spelling and grammar checker	1 In Word 2003, click **Tools,** then **Options...**, and then click the **Spelling & Grammar** tab. 2 Select the **Check spelling as you type** and **Check grammar as you type** check boxes. In Word 2007 this can be done by selecting the **Spelling & Grammar** button under the **Review** tab, and then clicking **Options...**.
Use the automatic spelling and grammar checker	1 Type the text. Right-click a word with wavy red or green underlining and then select the spelling or grammar alternative that you want. To check the spelling and grammar all at once: 1 In Word 2003, click **Tools,** then **Spelling and Grammar....** In Word 2007, click on the **Review** tab and then click the **Spelling & Grammar** button. 2 Type or select the desired change and click the **Change** button. 3 Make all of the desired corrections until the checking process is complete. Click **Close**.

Type Over and Insert modes

In **Insert mode**, your word processor inserts new text wherever the cursor is positioned. Existing text is shifted to accommodate the new text. Your computer will usually be in Insert mode.

Alternatively, in **Type Over** or **Overwrite mode**, existing text is erased as you type. If your computer is set up for this feature, then you can access it by pressing the **Insert** key on the keyboard.

SUMMARY QUESTIONS

1 Identify at least six ways in which a document might be edited.

2 What is proofreading?

3 Discuss three uses of the spelling and grammar checkers.

4 Outline the steps that you will follow to:
   a   search for a specific word in a document
   b   move text or graphics
   c   activate the spelling and grammar checker.

Column and row headings

The first cell of a column or a row is called the heading. This is different from the greyish-coloured headers that Microsoft Excel uses to display the column letters and row numbers. A **column heading** or **row heading** is used to describe the category of data that it contains. Look, for example, at Table 4.5.1. The column headings are: Students, English, Maths, Science, Art and Music. The row headings are the names Anthony Henry, Monifa Lekan, Shariff Khan and Mei Li Chen.

Table 4.5.1 Column and row headings

Students	English	Maths	Science	Art	Music
Henry, Anthony	75	78	82	74	87
Lekan, Monifa	79	92	85	67	62
Khan, Shariff	65	87	90	93	71
Chen, Mei Li	88	62	51	66	64

Formatting headings

Column headings are usually typed in bold and you may use slightly larger font. The first word of each column and row heading must be capitalised. Unless you are otherwise instructed, all headings should be left-aligned. For example, you will observe that one of the headings in Table 4.5.2 is centred.

Multiple-columnar headings

A multiple-columnar heading spans several columns, as is shown in Table 4.5.2. There should be a row that contains individual column headings above or beneath the multiple-columnar heading.

Table 4.5.2 Multiple-columnar headings

Students	Subjects				
	English	Maths	Science	Art	Music

Oblique and vertical headings

You may use oblique and vertical headings to label narrow columns. In **oblique headings** the text is slanted relative to the rest of the table, for example, at 45°. In **vertical headings** the text is perpendicular (90°) to the rest of the table.

Apply borders

A table that is prepared in Excel is **unruled**. The grey gridlines that you see are simply to identify the limits of the cells and are not usually printed. However you might be instructed to show all borders when typing a table.

How to format spreadsheet tables

Table 4.5.3 shows you how to apply table formatting in Excel.

Table 4.5.3 How to apply table formatting in Microsoft Excel

Task	Method
Change text direction	**1** Select the cells for which you want to change text direction. **2** Right-click then select **Format Cells…**. **3** Click on the **Alignment** tab in the **Format Cells** dialogue box that appears. **4** Type in or select the number of degrees at which you want the text displayed. Click **OK**.
Prepare a ruled table (show borders)	**1** Select the cells to be bordered. **2** Right-click then select **Format Cells…**. **3** Click on the **Borders** tab. **4** Select the border style and colour. The selected border style may be applied by clicking on the presets buttons, preview diagram or the specific border buttons. Click **OK**.
Centre the table on the page	**1** In Excel 2003, select **File** then **Page Setup…**. This option is also available in the **Print Preview** menu. In Excel 2007, click the **Page Layout** tab and then the **Margins** button. Select **Custom margins…**. **2** Click on the **Margins** tab of the **Page Setup** dialogue box. **3** Click **Center on page** and click **Horizontally** and **Vertically**, so that check marks appear next to these options. Click **OK**.
Sort data by a single row or column	**1** Select the cells that will be sorted. **2** Click the **Sort Ascending (A–Z)** button or **Sort Descending (Z–A)** button on the standard toolbar (Excel 2003) or **Data** ribbon (Excel 2007).
Sort data by multiple columns	**1** Select the cells, rows or columns that will be sorted. **2** In Excel 2003, select **Data** then **Sort** from the menu bar. In Excel 2007, click on the **Data** tab and then the **Sort** button. The **Sort** dialogue box will appear. **3** Select the first column for sorting from the **Sort by** drop-down menu and choose either ascending or descending. **4** Select the second column and, if necessary, the third sort column from the **Then by** drop-down menus. **5** If the cells you highlighted included the text headings in the first row, mark **My data range has** and **Header row** and the first row will remain at the top of the worksheet.

SUMMARY QUESTION

a Prepare the following table. Show all borders.

Representatives	Gross sales figures						
	January	February	March	April	May	June	Total
Victor, Anderson	$14,993	$9,000	$11,789	$10,075	$11,755	$9,328	$66,940
Bertram, Barry	$9,886	$15,550	$9,772	$12,322	$11,987	$11,907	$71,424
Young Lai, Chrissy	$12,007	$10,630	$10,390	$14,598	$13,231	$12,654	$73,510
Narine, Savitri	$11,832	$11,422	$8,472	$10,762	$14,554	$11,900	$68,942
Total	$48,718	$46,602	$40,423	$47,757	$51,527	$45,798	$280,816

b Print the table centred on the page.

Advanced tabulation

Using formulae and functions

Formulae are used to instruct spreadsheets to perform calculations. You can create formulae by following certain conventions when you type into a cell. For example, the formula **=A2+B2+C2** tells the computer to add the total of these three cells. Similarly, the formula **=F2*A7** means that the computer should multiply the numbers contained in those two cells.

A **function** is a preset instruction that is built into the spreadsheet program. For example, the function **=Average(B3:G3)** will find the average of the numbers in cells B3 to G3. Likewise the function **=Min(B3:G3)** will find the minimum (smallest) value in the range of cells, whereas **=Max(B3:G3)** will find the maximum value.

Using Autosum

If you want to add up the contents of many cells, then it is best to use the **Autosum** function. To use Autosum:

1 Select the cells for which you want to calculate the total, ensuring that the adjacent cell in which the total will be displayed is empty.

2 Click the **Autosum** button Σ on the standard toolbar.

3 The total will appear in the empty cell.

Data formats

You should use the cell formatting options to specify number formats such as currency, percentage, fraction, date and time (see Table 3.2.1). This eliminates the need to repeatedly type symbols such as the dollar sign. It also enables calculations to be performed on numbers expressed with special formatting, such as time expressed as hour:minute:second (for example 03:45:15).

Charts and graphs

Charts allow you to present data entered into the worksheet by using a variety of graph types. You must first enter data into a worksheet before you can make a chart. Table 4.6.1 provides instructions for converting the data into a chart.

EXAM TIP

You are expected to apply formulae and functions in the practical examinations.

Table 4.6.1 How to create a chart in Microsoft Excel

To create a chart in Excel 2003	To create a chart in Excel 2007
1 Select all the cells that will be included in the chart including headers. 2 Click the **Chart Wizard** button on the standard toolbar to view the first **Chart Wizard** dialogue box. 3 Choose the **Chart type:** and the **Chart sub-type:**. Click **Next**. 4 Select the data range (if different from the area highlighted in step 1) and click **Next**. 5 Enter the name of the chart and titles for the X and Y axes and click **Next**. 6 Click **As new sheet** if the chart should be placed on a new, blank worksheet or select **As object in:** if the chart should be embedded in an existing sheet, and select the worksheet from the drop-down menu. 7 Click **Finish** to create the chart.	1 Select all the cells that will be included in the chart including headers. 2 Click the **Insert** ribbon. 3 Choose the chart type from the options available. The chart will be automatically created as an embedded object on your Excel worksheet. To create a chart on a new sheet: 1 Click on the chart to select it. 2 Click on the **Design** tab that becomes available, then on the **Move Chart** button. 3 Choose where you want the chart to be placed, then click **OK**.

SUMMARY QUESTIONS

1 Marcel receives a weekly allowance which he uses as follows:

Transportation:$80   Entertainment: $50
Lunch and snacks:$65   Savings: $35
Stationery: $20

Enter the information in a spreadsheet and

a   calculate his total allowance

b   create a pie chart to represent this data.

2 You have been asked to prepare a statistical report on the fundraising ventures of your sports club for January to March of this year. The following is the raw data:

January: sponsorship $3,800; members' contributions $1,400; raffle $2,900; cake sale $875.

February: members' contributions $986; raffle $1,655; ice-cream sale $670. There was no sponsorship.

March: pie sale $735; sponsorship $1,000; raffle $1730; members' contributions $1,100.

a   Enter the raw data using the following column headings: Month, Sponsorship, Sales, Raffle, Contributions.

b   Apply currency format to all figures.

c   Calculate the totals for each row and column.

d   Use functions to identify the highest, lowest and average earnings.

e   Use a column graph to represent the earnings for January.

Applying tabulation

At the end of this topic you should be able to:

• prepare invoices, debit notes and credit notes.

Many spreadsheet and word-processing programs contain pre-designed invoices that can be used for educational purposes. However you must check the product licence to find out whether the templates can be used in a business.

The abbreviation **E&OE** means errors and omissions excepted. This is printed on an invoice to allow a company to legally correct legitimate mistakes that might be made on an invoice. These corrections are usually made by issuing debit notes or credit notes.

Invoices

An **invoice** is a bill that a business sends to a customer. It lists the items, quantities and agreed prices of the goods or services that the customer obtained. It is considered a legal document, as it indicates that the purchaser has an obligation to pay the amount shown.

ACTIVITY

Apply your knowledge of spreadsheet formulas, functions and formatting to create the following invoice and calculate all totals:

INVOICE No. 145321   **Date:** Use current date

CUSTOMER:
Z M Longdon and Associates
32 Kipling Lane, Bridgetown
Phone 555 8991

Typist: Insert appropriate logo here

SERVICE ADDRESS:
The Crystal Room
Golden Flamingo Conference Centre
Union Hall

Clarise's Catering Company
Glitchfield Street, Arlington
Phone 555 5555
Email clarisecatering@mymail.com

Qty	Item	Unit Price	Cost
100	Caribbean puffs	$0.15	
50	Grilled chicken with three bean pilaf	30.00	
35	Seafood platter with coconut rice	35.99	
15	Spicy tofu, vegetables and noodles	28.95	
100	Tossed salads	17.50	
		*TOTAL	

PAYMENT METHOD
☐ Cash
☐ Certified cheque
☐ Credit card
☐ Debit card

* *All prices include sales tax and service charges*
E&OE

Debit notes

A business will send out a debit note to a customer in the following circumstances:

• when the invoice was wrongly calculated so that the amount shown was too low

- when charges, such as transport costs, have been paid by the seller when really they should have been paid by the purchaser.

Clarise's Catering Company discovered that they had omitted the cost of desserts and charged $0.15 for Caribbean puffs instead of $1.50, a difference of $1.35. Prepare and print the following debit note to correct these errors:

Clarise's Catering Company Glitchfield Street, Arlington Phone 555 5555			*Typist: Please calculate totals*	
DEBIT NOTICE				
Z M Longdon and Associates 32 Kipling Lane, Bridgetown Phone 555 8991			Date: *Use current date*	
			INVOICE NO.:	
QUANTITY	DESCRIPTION		UNIT PRICE	COST
100	Desserts – Omitted from invoice		$14.95	
100	Caribbean puffs – undercharged		$1.35	
	TOTAL			
E&OE				

Credit notes

A business will send out a credit note when:

- goods are returned (for example, if they are the wrong goods or they are defective)
- the buyer is given an allowance (such as for repair of damaged goods)
- there is an overcharge on the invoice.

The format of the credit note is identical to the debit note, except for the following:

- the words **CREDIT NOTE** are printed after the business's contact information
- the credit note is usually printed in red to distinguish it from a debit note.

Clarise's Catering Company realised that they had charged the customer for tossed salads, when the contract stated that salads are free with all meals. Prepare a suitable credit note.

AAO Entertainment Services Limited of 90 Francis Lane, Rousillac billed Charlesworth Douglass Primary School of 12 Devlin Street, Corinth for the following services at the price shown:

Supply of two bouncy castles at $800 each

Face painting of 250 children at $5 per child

10 novelty events at $60 each

4 hours of DJ music at $240 per hour

1 Prepare an invoice using today's date.

2 One of the bouncy castles was not useable because it did not inflate. Prepare the required document.

3 Prepare a document to correct the fact that 15 novelty items were supplied, not 10 as shown in the invoice.

4.8

Creating presentations 1

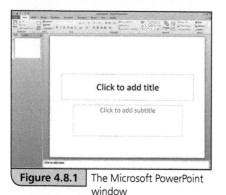

Figure 4.8.1 | The Microsoft PowerPoint window

Presentation programs enable you to easily insert and manipulate design elements such as text boxes, word art, pictures, photographs and charts. They are also used to create graphical documents such as certificates, banners, posters and flyers.

Slides

A presentation slide is a page onto which you may place text and graphics. When you open a new presentation program window you will see a blank title slide, similar to the one shown in Figure 4.8.1. The rectangles enclosed by the dotted lines are **placeholders**. A placeholder is a section of a document into which you may put text.

To the left of the window is a small representation of the slide called a **thumbnail**. As you add new slides, their thumbnails will automatically be displayed in this section.

Title slide

A presentation should begin with a title slide. The title of the presentation is usually typed in the upper placeholder whereas a subtitle, such as the name of the presenter or organisation, is typed in the lower placeholder.

Layouts

Layout refers to the relative positions of design elements on the slide.

• Use the same position for headings, subheadings and body text throughout.
• Ensure your layout is simple and uncluttered.
• Ensure that your text and images are well balanced, so that they are not concentrated in only one section of the slide.
• Make text and graphics as large as possible to ensure readability. However, you should not place them too close to the edge of the slide.

PowerPoint offers several pre-designed layouts. In PowerPoint 2003 you can access these layouts by clicking on ▾ near the top right of the toolbar; in PowerPoint 2007 this is found next to the **New Slide** button on the **Home** ribbon.

You will observe that in some slide themes, in addition to text, placeholders may be used for content such as tables, charts, pictures and movies. Once a new slide is opened, simply click on the type of content you wish to insert, and PowerPoint will display the appropriate dialogue box.

Slide templates

A slide template is a design that controls the appearance of the slides, such as background, placement of text and graphics, bullet styles and font. PowerPoint offers a variety of design templates.

Slide masters

A **slide master** stores information about the slide template. You can use the slide master to make changes that will affect all the slides in the presentation. For example, if you want to use a company logo throughout the presentation, then it should be inserted on the slide master.

Appropriate font

Table 4.8.1 shows the guidelines you should follow when formatting text for presentations.

Table 4.8.1 Guidelines for formatting font in presentations

Type	You should not use more than two different font types within a single slide. Ensure that you choose plain, clear fonts that are easy to read.
Style	**Bold text** is more readable than normal text in a presentation. Avoid typing in *italics* because they are very difficult to read.
Size	Ensure that the font size is large enough to be comfortably read when standing 4–5 metres from the monitor.
Colour	Avoid a wide variety of colours on one slide. Make sure that there is sufficient contrast between the text colour and the slide background. Avoid red or purple font as they do not display well with some projectors.

Graphics

Visual images and graphics are used to help the presenter to express information that would be difficult to describe in words. A well-chosen chart, graph or picture is usually more effective than many lines of text. Select graphics that enhance your presentation. Try to use no more than one or two graphics per slide and ensure that they are large enough to be seen. Make sure that the graphics do not become blurred or distorted when you enlarge them. If a graphic is included on a slide there should only be 1–2 text statements included.

SUMMARY QUESTIONS

1 Define the following terms as they relate to presentations:
   a slide
   b placeholder
   c template
   d slide master
   e graphic
   f thumbnail.

2 List at least three guidelines for each of the following features of a presentation:
   a layout
   b graphics
   c font.

LEARNING OUTCOMES

At the end of this topic you should be able to:

• create simple presentations using presentation software including the use of animations, transitions, timing and effective communication.

Motion effects such as animations and transitions can add impact to a slideshow. However, their overuse can be very distracting, as the audience will become more interested in the special effects than in the information presented. You should therefore limit your use of these features.

Remember that you can use the **Help** feature of your software for assistance in using these tools.

Animations

Animations are motions that can be added to slide elements such as text and graphics. These items can be made to fly, spin, bounce, flash on, fade, and much more. Use only one animation effect consistently throughout a slideshow. It should only be used to emphasise a very important point.

Transitions

Slide transitions are motion effects that are created as you move from one slide to another. Most presentation programs offer a wide variety of transitions including fade, wipe, dissolve in, chequerboard and blinds, to name a few (see Figure 4.9.1). You can also select whether the transition should be fast, medium or slow. Avoid distracting transitions. As with animations, use one transition consistently throughout your slideshow.

DID YOU KNOW?

You will not see your transitions and animations while the presentation is in **Normal** view. You must select **Slide Show** from the **View** menu to see the effects that you have applied.

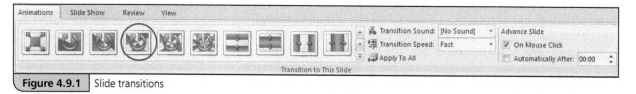

Figure 4.9.1 Slide transitions

Timing

Slideshows can be set up so that slides change automatically or each time the mouse is clicked. These options are displayed adjacent to the slide transitions.

To rehearse the timing for your slide show:

1 In Microsoft PowerPoint 2003 click **Slide Show**; in PowerPoint 2007 click on the **Slide Show** tab.

2 Click **Rehearse Timings**. A full-screen slide show will be launched.

DID YOU KNOW?

Outline view, available in Microsoft PowerPoint 2007 and 2010, shows only the text that is used in a presentation, not the graphics.

3 The computer will begin to record how long you stay on each slide. Click on the **Next** arrow of the **Rehearsal** box to move through the show (similar to that shown in Figure 4.9.2).

4 Press the **Esc** key on your keyboard to leave the rehearsal. A box will appear that offers you the option to save the slide timing.

Figure 4.9.2 | A rehearsal box

Effective communication

The following guidelines will help you to effectively communicate information in your presentations:

- Plan your presentation carefully (see 3.4).
- Include only necessary information.
- Communicate your information in short, simple sentences rather than long paragraphs.
- Avoid abbreviations and acronyms.
- Use layout, colours and styles consistently on all the slides.
- Do not type in block capital letters.
- Use graphics only when they directly relate to the main idea of the slide.
- Use animations sparingly.
- Use light words against a dark background if you will be using a projector. However, use dark words against a light background if a monitor is to be used or if slides must be printed.
- Rehearse your presentation several times, until you can deliver it effectively.

DID YOU KNOW?

You may rehearse a slideshow as many times as you want, until you are satisfied with the timing. You can use this as you practise the presentation to decide how long is needed on each slide.

TRY IT!

You have observed that many of your classmates are having difficulty with creating effective presentations.

1 Prepare an eight-slide presentation with relevant notes to assist them.

2 Explore the different **Print** options that are available. Print out the following:

a a colour handout of your presentation with four slides per page

b a greyscale handout of your presentation with eight slides per page

c the notes pages

d an outline view.

SUMMARY QUESTIONS

1 Outline the guidelines that should be followed to ensure that a presentation:

a is easy to read

b holds the audience's attention

c is relevant to the topic.

2 You want to start up a business and want to convince friends and relatives to invest in your enterprise. Prepare a slideshow that can be used with your presentation.

5 Business document preparation

5.1 Identification and selection of stationery

The term **stationery** refers to a wide range of writing materials and office supplies. However, in the context of this course, stationery means the paper and envelopes used for business documents.

Paper sizes

It is vital that you know which size of paper is the most appropriate for each assignment. Unless you are otherwise instructed, you should use A5 paper for short letters, short memoranda and notices, and A4 paper for longer items, including letters, memoranda, agendas and legal documents. You are required to learn the full range of international paper sizes and the purposes for which each size is used (Table 5.1.1).

Table 5.1.1 International Organization for Standardization (ISO) sizes of paper

ISO name	Measurement in mm	Measurement in inches (approx.)	Uses
A0	841 × 1,189	33.1 × 46.8	Posters, wall maps
A1	594 × 841	23.4 × 33.1	Posters, wall maps
A2	420 × 594	16.5 × 23.4	Posters, folded maps, plans, timetables, travel schedules, wall calendars, advertisements
A3	297 × 420	11.7 × 16.5	Legal documents, balance sheets, financial statements, travel schedules, shares, maps, advertisements
A4	210 × 297	8.3 × 11.7	Business letters, reports, circular letters, minutes, agenda, chairman's agenda, specifications, long memoranda, manuscripts, tabular work, forms, programmes, display work, specifications, itineraries, legal documents, invoices, literary work, advertisements
A5	148 × 210	5.8 × 8.3	Short letters, short memoranda, notices, agendas, invitations, debit notes, credit notes, invoices, circulation slips, forms, vouchers, advertisements
A6	105 × 148	4.1 × 5.8	Postcards, index cards, petty-cash vouchers, credit notes, debit notes, invitations, telephone message pads, compliment slips, receipts, agendas
A7	74 × 105	2.9 × 4.1	Address labels, index cards, compliment slips
A8	52 × 74	2.1 × 2.9	Business cards, address labels
A9	37 × 52	1.4 × 2.1	Folder and document labels

In addition to the ISO paper sizes, you also need to know about letter-sized and legal-sized paper. **Letter-sized paper** measures 216 mm × 279 mm (8.5 inches × 11 inches) and **legal-sized paper** measures 216 mm × 356 mm (8.5 inches × 14 inches).

Paper layout

Page **orientation** is the direction in which a rectangular page is displayed or printed (Figure 5.1.1). A sheet of paper is in **portrait** orientation if it is in vertical format, that is, if it is taller than it is wide. For example, the pages of this Study Guide are printed in portrait orientation. In contrast, **landscape** orientation is in horizontal format, that is, it is wider than it is tall.

You can change the orientation of your word-processing document by accessing the page layout or page setup options (see 4.3).

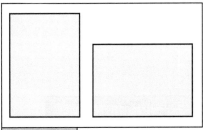

Figure 5.1.1 | Portrait and landscape orientation

Envelope sizes

The size of envelopes should be appropriate for the paper size of your document. As a general rule, the paper should fit into the envelope without requiring more than two folds. See the specific sizes of envelopes in 5.13 so that you will be able to make the best selection.

Types of stationery

Business organisations sometimes use specific types of stationery such as letterheads, memos, copy paper, forms, labels, index cards and document covers.

A **letterhead** is a piece of stationery that is imprinted with the organisation's name, logo and contact information.

A **memorandum** or **memo** is a short written message sent from one person to another in the same organisation. Memoranda are usually written according to a specific format, so the business might use templates.

Copy paper is the good-quality, lightweight paper that is used in printers and photocopiers. The two most commonly used sizes of copy paper are letter-sized and legal-sized paper.

A **form** is a preprinted document with blank spaces into which information is entered.

A **label** is usually a self-adhesive piece of paper onto which information is written or printed. For example, labels with mailing addresses might be affixed to envelopes.

An **index card** is heavy paper cut to a standard size, which is used to record small amounts of information. It can be ruled or plain.

Document cover is relatively thick, durable paper which is used for making covers for publications such as pamphlets and brochures.

Computers are now used to prepare most business documents. Many businesses use computers to create and save document designs instead of ordering preprinted stationery. See 6.24 for more about these templates.

SUMMARY QUESTIONS

1 Define the following terms:
   a stationery
   b portrait
   c landscape
   d template.

2 State the dimensions and three uses of each of the following stationery:
   a A3
   b A4
   c A5
   d A6.

3 Identify two appropriate sizes of envelopes for each paper size listed in Question 2 above. Refer to Table 5.13.1 if needed.

4 Briefly describe at least three types of preprinted stationery that might be used in a business.

LEARNING OUTCOMES

At the end of this topic you should be able to:

• identify some common types of business letter and their purpose

• produce business letters.

RESEARCH IT

Under what circumstances does the law or protocol of your country require that a business letter be written?

Electronic mail and telephones provide businesses with instantaneous methods of conveying information and are among the most frequently used means of communicating. Nevertheless letters continue to play an important part in business communication. This is because they:

• may be required by law or protocol

• provide a permanent record of communication

• are useful when communicating complex or detailed information

• are effective when communicating with someone you do not personally know.

Business letters are written for professional or official purposes such as to:

• make an enquiry

• advertise or sell a product or service

• request information

• place an order

• apply for employment

• lodge a complaint

• express appreciation or commendation.

Table 5.2.1 shows some common types of business letters and their purposes.

Table 5.2.1 Types of business letter

Type	Description
Enquiry	Written to obtain information, usually about a product or service.
Response to enquiry	Used to supply information as requested or to express regret at the inability to provide requested information.
Sales	Designed to capture the recipient's attention, stimulate interest, build a desire to obtain the product or service, and prompt the reader to purchase it.
Complaint	Used to express dissatisfaction about a product or service, convince the reader that you have valid grounds for your dissatisfaction, and prompt a desired action in recompense.
Response to complaint	Used for one of the following purposes: • to acknowledge that the complaint is valid and notify that the requested solution is being granted • to acknowledge that the complaint is valid and to propose an alternative solution • to indicate the reasons why the complaint is not valid and therefore express refusal to grant the proposed solution. **Note:** Regardless of the response, always use a courteous, concerned tone. Ensure that the letter indicates that the customer is valuable and shows that the business is fair and reasonable.

Writing effective business letters

Business letters are official communication and are therefore written in formal language and must be prepared using specific layouts and formats. They create a lasting impression and influence the reader's perception of the sender (Figure 5.2.1).

The following guidelines will help you to compose letters that make a positive impact.

- Always maintain a courteous tone.
- Ensure that you communicate clearly so that your message cannot be misunderstood.
- Be as brief as possible, but ensure that you include all necessary information.
- Make sure that your letter is free of errors in spelling, grammar, punctuation or word use.
- Conclude by clearly indicating the action you want the reader to take.
- Print on clean, neat, good-quality paper.

Font format

Business letters are usually typed in Times New Roman, size 12, black. Some businesses might choose to use other plain, easily read fonts such as Arial, Calibri or Garamond.

Paragraph format

Set paragraphs to single-line spacing and set spacing before and after paragraphs to zero.

Page format

Set the paper size to A4 for long letters or A5 for very short letters. Use portrait orientation. Set top, bottom, left and right margins to 2.54 cm (1 inch).

Structure of the business letter

Read the sample letter on p61 (Figure 5.2.2) and note the sequence of its different parts.

1 Sender's address
If you are not using a letterhead, type the sender's full mailing address. Do not abbreviate the names of streets or cities.

2 Date

Leave a clear line space before typing the date. Do not abbreviate the month.

3 Reference line

Some businesses use a code for tracking and filing their correspondence. If this is used, leave a clear line space before typing the reference line. When a business is responding to a letter that included a reference line, then the reference notation might be as follows:

Our ref:

Your ref:

Leave a clear line space between the date and reference line.

4 Inside address (also known as recipient's address)

Leave a clear line space before typing the recipient's name, position in the organisation and address.

Figure 5.2.1 | Ensure that your letters create a positive impact

EXAM TIP

The date format varies slightly according to whether the letter is blocked or indented (see 5.4 and 5.6). Ensure you know the appropriate date format for different layouts.

Attention line

If the name of a specific person was not included in the recipient's address, you may choose to include an attention line. Leave a clear line space between the address and the attention line.

5 Salutation

For formal letters, and if you do not know the recipient's name, use Dear Sir, Dear Madam, or Dear Sir/Madam.

6 Subject heading

This succinctly states the subject of the letter.

7 Body

This consists of one or more paragraphs. First state the purpose of the letter, then provide additional details. Conclude by clearly indicating the action you want the recipient to take. Leave a clear line space between each paragraph.

8 Complimentary close

If the recipient was addressed by name in the salutation you should close with 'Yours sincerely'. If the salutation was 'Dear Sir', 'Dear Madam', etc., then use 'Yours respectfully' or 'Yours faithfully'. Leave a clear line space before the complimentary close.

9 Signature block

Leave four clear line spaces for the signature. Then type the sender's name. Do not type a line for the sender's signature. An electronic or handwritten signature will be inserted here.

10 Designation

The sender's **designation** indicates his or her job title or position in the organisation.

11 Additional notations

An **enclosure line** indicates that there are additional documents in the envelope. One of the following abbreviations is used: enc, encl, Encl, ENC, encs or ENCS.

A **copy notation** indicates that copies of the letter have been sent to other recipients.

CC or cc (meaning Carbon Copy), followed by the names of the additional recipients, is typed on all copies of the letter. If the sender does not want the main recipient to know that copies are being sent, the abbreviation bcc (blind carbon copy) is typed on the additional copies only.

Business letters can be formal or informal. Informal business letters are usually written in a 'lighter', more conversational tone. A **postscript** is a brief note that is attached at the bottom of a letter. Postscripts should not be used in formal letters. However, they may be included in informal letters to send a personal message or to give information that is not directly related to the subject of the letter.

Villington Business Solutions Limited ①
379 Caribbean Avenue
Main Port
Sunnyside

25 August 2014 ②

Ref: SD/231 ③

The Human Resource Department ④
Haynes Tours Limited
Akella Street
Hopetown

Attention Mr Obasi Haynes

Dear Mr Haynes ⑤

Our Product Listing ⑥

In keeping with the request you made in our telephone ⑦
conversation on 21 August, I am pleased to send you a
complete listing of the product and services we offer.

As you will notice in the enclosed brochure, our products are
of the highest possible quality at unbeatable prices. We will
also be pleased to source any difficult-to-find items that you
might require.

Please call Aduke at 987-6543 or Krishna at 234-5678 to
place your orders or make enquiries.

Yours sincerely ⑧

Mai Chin Kee ⑨
Marketing Manager ⑩

Enc ⑪

| **Figure 5.2.2** | A sample business letter |

TRY IT!

You have opened a print company at your home address. It is a business that provides typing and photocopying services at competitive rates. Prepare an appropriate letter with an enclosed brochure to be sent to the manager of Gomes Building Contractors, located at 23 Industry Avenue, Notown.

DID YOU KNOW?

If your letter occupies only a small portion of the page, you may use two clear line spaces between the different parts of the letter. However, only one clear line space should be used between paragraphs in the body.

SUMMARY QUESTIONS

1 'Despite the ever-increasing availability of electronic communication, the letter continues to be the most essential means of conveying business information.' Explain why you agree or disagree.

2 You are employed in the offices of a prestigious manufacturing company and you have been asked to train Karissa, a new employee, to prepare effective business letters. Outline at least 10 instructions that you will give to Karissa.

3 Identify at least three common types of business letters and discuss the purpose of each.

5.3 Letterheads

A letterhead adds a professional look to any business communication. It should be clear, easy to read and attractive. Many of the sample letters in this book include letterheads.

Guidelines for letterhead text

The letterhead usually contains the following lines of text:

- *The organisation's name* printed in larger, distinctive but easy-to-read font, usually size 16.
- *The organisation's address* printed in smaller font such as size 12 or 10, in blue or black. Use plain font such as Times New Roman, Arial or Calibri.
- *Contact information* such as a telephone number, fax number and email address.

The letterhead is created in the **Header** section of your word-processor document. Revise using the header in 4.3 so you know how to access this.

The letterhead should be displayed on the first page only. It is always wise to set this up before you create the letterhead by checking the **Different First Page** box on the header and footer toolbar or tools ribbon (Figure 5.3.1). Once you have selected this box the letterhead will only appear on the first page of the document; headers on subsequent pages can then be edited differently.

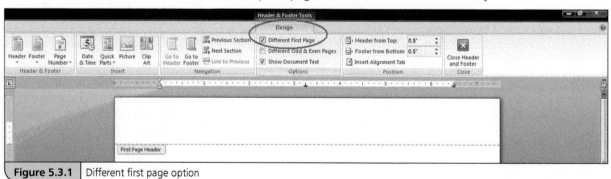

Figure 5.3.1 | Different first page option

LEARNING OUTCOMES

At the end of this topic you should be able to:

- prepare letterheads.

RESEARCH IT

Use the Internet to find letterhead designs. Study them to identify the effects created by their choice of colour, graphics and layout.

Why do some businesses avoid using pink, red and orange in their letterhead text?

Table 5.3.1 How to insert clip art in Microsoft Word

1	Place your cursor where you want the graphic. In Word 2003, click **Insert**, then **Picture**, and select **Clip Art**; in Word 2007 click on the **Clip Art** button in the **Insert** ribbon. A **Clip Art** task pane will open.
2	Type a word or phrase that describes the clip you want in the **Search for:** box.
3	Click **Go**.
4	All clips that match the keywords will be displayed in the results section of the task pane.
5	Click on the clip you want to use.

Inserting a logo

Most letterheads contain a **logo**, that is, a picture that represents the organisation.

Inserting clip art

Table 5.3.1 shows you how to find a suitable clip art in Microsoft Word. You may use clip art in your school assignments but note that unless you have permission, clip art should not be used in real business letters or for commercial purposes due to copyright.

Inserting pictures from a file

To insert a picture that is stored on your hard disk, flash drive or other storage location you can use the **Insert** button or ribbon in Word, as you did when using clip art, to add different picture types as you wish.

Changing the location and size of your graphic

You can use **text wrapping** to properly position your graphic.

The total height of your graphic should not exceed the lines of text in your letterhead. Table 5.3.2 includes instructions for positioning and resizing your logo.

EXAM TIP

Letters should never be typed in the header section of a document. Ensure you exit the header before typing the letter.

Table 5.3.2 How to position and resize graphics in Microsoft Word

Task	Word 2003	Word 2007
Select text wrapping	1 Right-click on the graphic, select **Format Picture** and click on the **Layout** tab. 2 Click on the preferred layout such as **Square** or **Tight** and click **OK**. You may then click and drag the graphic to the desired position.	1 Right-click and select **Text Wrapping** (in Word 2010 this is labelled **Wrap Text**). 2 Click on the preferred layout such as **Square** or **Tight**. You may then click and drag the graphic to the desired position.
Resize your logo	1 Place your mouse pointer over one corner of the graphic until you see a two-headed diagonal resize arrow. 2 Click and drag the corner of the image inwards to make it smaller or outwards to make it larger.	
Set an exact size for the logo	1 Right-click on the image. 2 Select **Format Picture**. 3 Click on the **Size** tab. 4 Type in the desired height and width and click **OK**.	1 Right-click on the image. 2 Select **Size** (in Word 2010 this is **Size and Position...**). 3 Type in the desired height and width.

Using the footer

The footer may be used to display the company's motto, a brief mission statement, or a memorable phrase with which you want your company to be identified. The footer button is usually displayed next to the header button on the toolbar or ribbon (in Word 2003 it opens automatically when you open the header).

TRY IT!

Create a name and contact information for each of the following types of business and design an appropriate letterhead:

Computer supplies and services

Law firm

Preschool

SUMMARY QUESTIONS

1 Discuss the main principles that should guide the design of a letterhead.

2 Outline how to do each of the following tasks:

 a add text to a header

 b ensure that a letterhead is displayed on the first page only

 c insert a logo that you have scanned and saved on a flash drive.

DID YOU KNOW?

The entire letterhead should be 2.54–3.81 cm (1–1.5 inches) high. It is usually centred at the top of the page, but some businesses use other alignments.

The blocked letter format

The layout of a letter is determined by the alignment of the 11 basic elements (5.2) to the left, centre or right of the page. There are three basic layouts for typing a business letter: blocked, semi-blocked and indented. This topic will focus on the blocked format.

Layout

The blocked layout is a modern, efficient style that seeks to reduce typing time by omitting all unnecessary keystrokes. Consequently:

• all the letter elements begin at the left margin (Figure 5.4.1)
• paragraphs are not indented
• punctuation marks are only used in the body of the letter
• the date is typed as day, then month then year, as shown in Figure 5.4.2.

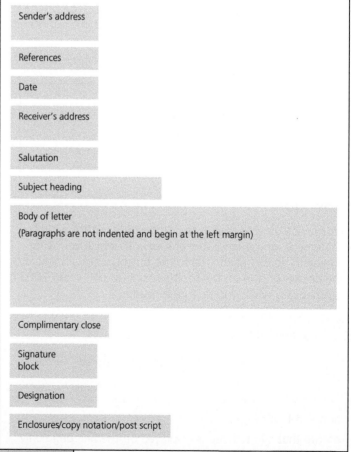

Figure 5.4.1 | The blocked format

Figure 5.4.2 is a product enquiry letter displayed in blocked format.

Letterheads in blocked format

When a letterhead is used, a clear line space is left before typing the date. The sender's address is not typed because it is already part of the letterhead. All other letter elements are left-aligned. This is illustrated in the following sample letter of response (Figure 5.4.3).

TRY IT!

Type the sample product enquiry letter (Figure 5.4.2) in blocked format.

Apartment 9B
Building 103
Hillside Drive
ROSEAU

2 June 2014

The Sales Department
Safe & Sure Roofing Systems Limited
23 Scott Industrial Complex
ROSEAU

Dear Sir or Madam

REQUEST FOR INFORMATION ABOUT IRONCLAD PRODUCTS

I am seeking details on the quality, cost and colour options for your newly released Triple Ripple Home Roofing System.

The project under consideration is the construction of a 6000 square foot seafront residence. This will necessitate a roofing system able to withstand the strong, moisture-laden winds and sea-spray that are characteristic of coastal areas.

Kindly provide a product costing, along with recommendations about the most suitable roofing option for this location.

Yours faithfully

Kareena Wills

Figure 5.4.2 | Example of a letter in blocked format

Safe & Sure Roofing Systems Limited
23 Scott Industrial Complex, ROSEAU
Phone/Fax 1-777-555-0000 email: info@ssrsl.com

Safe & Sure

12 June 2014

Ref 3R/Inq

Kareena Wills
Apartment 9B
Building 103
Hillside Drive
ROSEAU

Dear Ms Wills

SUBJECT Triple Ripple Home Roofing Product Information

We are pleased to provide the information you requested about our Triple Ripple Home Roofing System. As is shown in the enclosed brochure, this newly launched product offers unsurpassed beauty and protection for new and renovated buildings.

In addition to the standard colour range, Triple Ripple Roofing Sheets can be supplied in custom colours that exactly match your home design needs. We are so confident about the durability of this product that we offer an unprecedented 20-Year Warranty.

You are invited to visit our offices or call Michael at 555-4444 to obtain further information, view our extensive product range or to place your order.

Yours sincerely

Ambrose Caines
Marketing Manager

ENC June 2014 Product Brochure

Figure 5.4.3 | The blocked format with a letterhead

SUMMARY QUESTIONS

1 Describe three distinctive features of the blocked letter format.

2 You are seeking information on the post-secondary training programs that are offered by A1 Secretarial Institute of 54 College Street, Castries, St Lucia. Prepare an appropriate letter of enquiry in blocked format.

TRY IT!

Design a suitable letterhead and type the sample response letter (Figure 5.4.3) in blocked format. You may choose different fonts, colour and graphics.

The semi-blocked letter format

At the end of this topic you should be able to:

• produce letters using the semi-blocked format.

The semi-blocked format is considered to be less formal than the blocked format. There are several variations to this style. For example, some organisations right-align the date whereas others begin the date at the centre of the page. Unless you are otherwise instructed, you may use the following guidelines.

Layout

The following elements are aligned against the **left** margin:

• references
• recipient's address
• salutation
• subject heading (may also be centred)

• body of the letter
• additional notations such as enclosures, copy notation and postscript.

The following elements begin at the **centre of the page**:

• sender's address (if a letterhead is not used)
• date

• complimentary close
• signature block
• designation.

The date is typed on the same line as the reference (Figure 5.5.1). Where there are two references, the date is typed on the same line as Our Ref., aligned with the sender's address. Open punctuation is used.

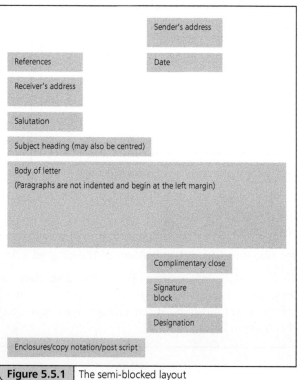

Figure 5.5.1 The semi-blocked layout

Figure 5.5.2 is a sample of a letter of complaint in semi-blocked format.

Letterheads in semi-blocked format

Figure 5.5.3 is a sample response to a complaint, prepared in semi-blocked format on a letterhead with a footer.

Ni-Nu Electronics Ltd
12 Antoine Street, BRIDGETOWN
Phone 1-246-555-4433

Ref: SC01/XM   18 January 2014

Ms Ashaki Kain
57 Potters Lane
CHRIST CHURCH

Dear Ms Kain

Re Your Request for a Full Refund
I sincerely apologise for the inconvenience caused by the failure of our Customer Service staff to resolve your complaint about your recently purchased X-Mobile Touch Screen Cellular Phone, Serial Number XM-246-864-SE.

We generally seek to address such complaints in keeping with our service warranty, however evidently on this occasion we have not met your expectations. In light of this, we have decided to grant you a full refund of your purchase price. Please return the phone, with all accessories and your original service receipt, contract and warranty to our Bridgetown branch. A cheque for the sum of $499.99 has already been prepared.

Please call our department's direct line at 1-246-555-6519 to indicate when you will be coming in.

Yours sincerely
for Ni-Nu Electronics Limited

THEODORE HENRY
CUSTOMER SERVICE MANAGER

At Ni-Nu Electronics customer satisfaction is our first priority.

Figure 5.5.3 The semi-blocked format with a letterhead

---

57 Potters Lane
CHRIST CHURCH

10 January 2014

The Manager
Ni-Nu Electronics Ltd
12 Antoine Street
BRIDGETOWN

Dear Sir

REQUEST FOR REFUND

On the 20th of December 2012 I purchased an X-Mobile Touch Screen Cellular Phone, Serial Number XM-246-864-SE, at your Christ Church branch. Unfortunately, the cellphone has not performed well because the battery consistently loses charge after approximately thirty minutes of use.

When I returned the phone for a replacement on 30th December, the Customer Service Representative denied my request, asserting that I had failed to properly condition the battery before use, as instructed in the User Manual. On the contrary, I had charged the battery for the recommended four hours. As I urgently needed access to a phone, I eventually purchased another unit from a different firm.

To resolve the problem, I would appreciate a full refund of my purchase price and a cancellation of my service contract. Enclosed are photocopies of the relevant documents.

Thank you for your anticipated assistance in settling this issue. Please contact me at 1-222-555-3000 and/or askain@livemail.com if you have any questions.

Yours respectfully

Ashaki Kain

Enclosures: Payment invoice, service receipt, warranty and contract

Figure 5.5.2 Example of a letter in semi-blocked format

TRY IT!

Type the letter in Figure 5.5.2 in semi-blocked format.

DID YOU KNOW?

The word **Re**, as used in the subject line of a letter, means *concerning* or *in reference to*.

TRY IT!

Type the letter in Figure 5.5.3 in semi-blocked format on a letterhead. You may vary the letterhead design.

SUMMARY QUESTIONS

1 Outline the major differences between the blocked and semi-blocked letter styles.

2 Imagine that when Ms Kain took the phone in to the service department at the Christ Church branch on 30 December, it was discovered that the battery was not the one originally supplied with the phone. Compose an appropriate response letter in semi-blocked format without a letterhead.

The indented letter format

Traditionally, letters were typed in the indented format. Although this style has become less popular, it is still used by many businesses.

A major difference between the indented format and the blocked and semi-blocked styles is that the first line of each paragraph is indented by 1.27 cm (0.5 inches). Another difference is that the indented layout uses full punctuation. Commas are used after the lines of the addresses and a full stop is used at the end of the final address line. Full stops are typed between the letters of abbreviations.

Layout

In the indented format the subject line is **centred**.

The following letter elements are **left-aligned**:

- references
- recipient's address
- salutation
- enclosures/copy notation/postscript.

The following items are set to the **right of the page**:

- sender's address (if a letterhead is not used)
- date, typed with a comma to separate the month from the year and ending with a full stop as shown in Figure 5.6.2

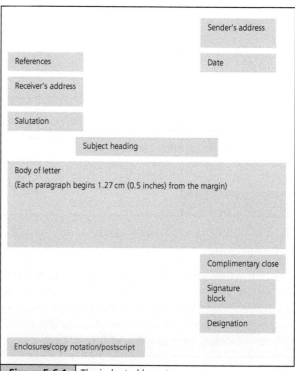

Figure 5.6.1 The indented layout

- complimentary close
- signature block and designation.

Figure 5.6.2 is a sample request letter in indented format.

Figure 5.6.3 is a sample response letter, prepared in indented format on a centred letterhead. There are no strict rules for the placement of the letterhead.

Dew Drop Apartment Hotel
Bliss Parade, BELMOPAN.
Telephone/Fax: 501-555-1323
Email: info@dewdrop.com

7th February, 2014.

ATTENTION: Gerald DuBois.

Hillview High School,
135 Half Moon Avenue,
BELMOPAN.

Dear Mr DuBois,

PERMISSION TO DO RESEARCH STUDY

We are pleased to grant you permission to do research for your School-Based Assessment in Office Administration at our premises on the 15th and 22nd of March, 2014 between the hours of 9:30 a.m. and 12:30 p.m.

To ensure that you derive the maximum benefit from your visit, we ask that you provide us with a more detailed outline of your study, including the questions you intend to ask in your interview.

Please call 501-555-5320 three days before the proposed date to confirm your visit.

Yours sincerely,

Kennedy James,
MANAGER.

Figure 5.6.3 The indented format with a letterhead

Hillview High School,
135 Half Moon Avenue,
BELMOPAN.

7th February, 2014.

The Manager,
Dew Drop Apartment Hotel,
Bliss Parade,
BELMOPAN.

Dear Madam,

REQUEST FOR PERMISSION TO DO RESEARCH STUDY

I am seeking permission to study your organisation to gather information for my School-Based Assessment in Office Administration.

I selected your hotel because it is a leader in the tourism industry. My study will investigate the role, function and duties of the Reception and Hospitality Department and the methods of communication that are used in the performance of these duties. It will be necessary for me to interview at least two workers, observe their activities, and view samples of the forms that they utilise.

I will greatly appreciate your permission to visit your premises on the 15th and 22nd of March, 2014 between the hours of 9:30 a.m. and 12:30 p.m. If these dates and times are not suitable, I will be happy to adjust my visits to your convenience. I will follow up with a telephone call next week and would be happy to answer any questions or concerns that you may have. You may call me at 501-501-5001 or email g.dubois@hhs.edu.

Thank you for your time and consideration in this matter.

Yours respectfully,

Gerald DuBois.

Figure 5.6.2 | Example of a letter in the indented format

TRY IT!

Type the letter in Figure 5.6.2 in indented format.

TRY IT!

Type the letter in Figure 5.6.3 in indented format.

Special notations

You will observe that the sample response letter contained a line with ATTENTION followed by the name of the intended recipient. In all layouts, this and other descriptors such as URGENT, PERSONAL or CONFIDENTIAL should be typed in closed capitals after the date, with a clear line space before and after.

SUMMARY QUESTIONS

1 Outline the major differences between the indented format and
   a blocked format
   b semi-blocked format.

2 Imagine that an emergency at the hotel has resulted in their inability to accommodate Mr DuBois on the scheduled dates. Compose an appropriate letter requesting that he reschedule. The letter should be in the indented style on an appropriate letterhead.

Short and long letters

At the end of this topic you should be able to:

- prepare short and long letters on appropriate stationery
- prepare continuation sheets for two-page letters.

Short and long letters

A5 paper should be used for short letters. Longer letters should be printed on A4 paper. Short and long letters must be printed in portrait orientation.

Wherever possible a business letter should be prepared on a single sheet of paper. However, do not try to force a long letter onto one page if it will be better presented on two pages.

Preparing continuation sheets

A **continuation sheet** is used if a letter is longer than one page. This sheet should be prepared in keeping with specific standards. Observe the following guidelines when preparing the continuation sheet.

Stationery

- Use headed paper (letterhead) for the first sheet only.
- For the second and subsequent pages use the same size, colour and quality paper as the first page. Print on one side of each sheet of paper.

Layout

- Use the same style and layout of the first page on the continuation sheet. This includes margin size, font, line spacing and punctuation.
- It is best to start the new page with the beginning of a new paragraph.
- Do not leave only the first line of a new paragraph at the end of a page.
- Do not carry over only the last line of a paragraph to the continuation page.
- Make sure that the continuation sheet contains at least two lines of text in addition to the complimentary close and signature block.
- Do not number the first sheet; all subsequent pages must be numbered.

Heading

The heading of the continuation sheet should include the following:

- the page number
- the date of the letter
- the addressee's name; the name of the organisation may be typed below the addressee, but this is optional.

There should be a clear space between each part of the continuation heading. Leave at least one line of space between the continuation heading and the text of the letter.

DID YOU KNOW?

In Microsoft Word you can hold the Control (Ctrl) key and press **Enter** to begin a new page wherever you want. This is called inserting a **page break**.

EXAM TIP

A continuation heading must be typed for every letter that runs on to a second page, even when you are not specifically instructed to prepare one.

Continuation page formats

The format of the continuation page will differ according to the letter format used. See the samples below for how they should be presented in each style.

Blocked layout

Lexington Court Hotel
1987 Coral Street
CASTRIES

9 July 2015

The Chief Executive Officer
St Lucia Marketing Board
Baptiste Street
CASTRIES

Figure 5.7.1a First page

Page 2

9 July 2015

The Chief Executive Officer

Figure 5.7.1b Continuation page

Semi-blocked layout

Lexington Court Hotel
1987 Coral Street
CASTRIES

9 July 2015

The Chief Executive Officer
St Lucia Marketing Board
Baptiste Street
CASTRIES

Figure 5.7.2a First page

Page 2

9 July 2015

The Chief Executive Officer

Figure 5.7.2b Continuation page

Indented layout

Lexington Court Hotel,
1987 Coral Street,
CASTRIES.

9th July, 2015.

The Chief Executive Officer,
St Lucia Marketing Board,
Baptiste Street,
CASTRIES.

Figure 5.7.3a First page

Page 2.

9th July, 2015.

The Chief Executive Officer.

Figure 5.7.3b Continuation page

SUMMARY QUESTIONS

1 Sashelle Francis, the Marketing Manager of Oneko Trading Company Limited of 23 High Street, San Fernando, has instructed you to type a two-page letter to Jeremy Sieupersad, the Procurements Manager of Jinen Manufacturing Company of LABIDCO Industrial Estate, La Brea. Using the current date, prepare the heading for the first and second pages in each of the following layouts:

   a blocked

   b semi-blocked

   c indented.

2 You have been asked to guide Henderson, a trainee word-processing clerk, in the proper preparation of two-page letters. List five guidelines that he should follow.

Purpose of circular letters

A circular letter is a standard letter that is sent to a number of recipients. The letter is prepared once and then multiple copies are printed for distribution. A circular letter can be used for a variety of purposes, for example:

- to give information such as a change in the business address, the appointment of new management, the introduction of new products or services, or the opening of a new branch
- for sales promotions
- to issue official guidelines or instructions to employees.

Preparing circular letters

Use an indented, blocked or semi-blocked layout, ensuring that the variations below for date, recipient, body and close are followed (Table 5.8.1).

Table 5.8.1 Guidelines for circular letters

Date	Unless otherwise instructed type either the words **Date as postmark** or the month and year only. The day of dispatch may then be inserted individually.
Recipient	Leave 10 single-line spaces for the insertion of personalised recipient information. If a general salutation is not used, then type **Dear** followed by space for a name to be inserted or leave the required number of line spaces.
Body	Directly address the reader in the body of the letter. For example, say 'We are pleased to inform you...' instead of 'We are pleased to inform our customers...'.
Close	The sender's name is usually typed, and may be followed by the sender's job title or the organisation's name.

The salutation might use a general name, such as *Dear Householder, Dear Wholesalers, Dear Customer* or *Dear Parent or Guardian*. However, it is best to personalise the letter by adding the names and addresses of the intended recipients. This can be done very easily by using the mail merge feature of the word-processing program (see 5.9).

Letters with a cut-off slip

Some circular letters contain a **cut-off slip**, also called a **response form**, that the recipient is expected to complete and return to the sender. Follow these guidelines for the preparation of the cut-off slip:

- Leave at least two line spaces after the letter before beginning the cut-off slip.

- Use a continuous line of unspaced full stops or hyphens from one margin to the other to separate the cut-off slip from the rest of the document.
- You can insert the symbol of a pair of scissors to the left or centre of the separation line.
- Leave two line spaces after the separation line.
- Use continuous unspaced full stops or underscore the blank spaces to create the lines on which the reader should write the information they are returning (writing lines).
- Leave at least one space after a word before beginning a writing line.
- Leave double-line spacing between writing lines and triple-line spacing for the signature.
- Apply your formatting skills effectively to give your cut-off slip a pleasing, uniform layout.

Figure 5.8.1 is a sample circular letter.

TRY IT!

Type the sample circular letter (Figure 5.8.1) with a tear-off slip on A4 paper.

EXAM TIP

You are required to prepare a circular letter with a tear-off slip for the reference manual of your School-Based Assessment. Ensure you know how to do this.

Right Start Early Childhood Centre

Paul's Avenue, KINGSTOWN
Telephone: 784-555-0990

7 October 2015

Dear Parent or Guardian

We are pleased to inform you that we have arranged for Ms Daphne Carrington, a highly qualified instructor, to provide gymnastics lessons for our students on Thursdays from 1:00 to 2:00 p.m.

Ms Carrington has agreed to accept a significantly reduced monthly fee of $50 per child. Please complete the attached form to register your child for this fantastic learning opportunity.

You are warmly invited to our Parent Teacher Meeting next Wednesday, when we will be happy to answer any questions you might have.

We look forward to your full support and participation.

Bridgette Abraham
Principal

✂..

Right Start Early Childhood Centre

Paul's Avenue, KINGSTOWN

I .... hereby register for my child .... to receive gymnastics classes at the school on Thursdays from 1:00 to 2:00 p.m. I enclose the required monthly fee of $50.

....
Signature   Date

Figure 5.8.1 A sample circular letter

SUMMARY QUESTIONS

1 State three reasons for which a circular letter may be sent.

2 Briefly describe two ways in which a circular letter can be personalised.

3 Outline five guidelines that should be followed when preparing a circular letter.

4 a What is the purpose of a cut-off slip?

  b Give three guidelines that should be followed when preparing a cut-off slip.

5.9 Mail merge

You can use a mail merge to easily personalise circular letters. The basic information such as sender's address, body and complimentary close will be the same, but the recipient's address and salutation will be different for each letter. You can also use this word-processing tool to prepare labels and address envelopes.

Elements of a mail merge

Mail merge is a very useful tool because any number of letters can be produced quickly and easily. When you are doing a mail merge, you actually work with three different elements, as outlined in Table 5.9.1.

LEARNING OUTCOMES

At the end of this topic you should be able to:

• integrate information to produce complete documents for dissemination by performing a mail merge and using a data source.

Table 5.9.1 Elements of a mail merge

Element	Description
Main document	• The **form letter** (see Figure 5.9.1 as an example) or circular letter you want to send out. The letter contains specially identified placeholders into which the recipient information will be placed.
Data source	• Information, such as names and addresses, which you use to merge into the main document: – Businesses often maintain a **mailing list** that contains the names and addresses of customers, suppliers and other people of interest. – Sometimes the contact data can be compiled from external data sources, such as the telephone directory. – The mailing list can be a special word-processed document that contains only a table, a database table or a spreadsheet file.
Merged documents	• A finished set of personalised documents.

You will also be working with a **task pane**, an area for commands that may require more information or options than a toolbar can provide. A task pane is a section of the word-processing window that opens up to offer a set of options for a specific task.

Performing a mail merge

The following are general instructions for performing a mail merge:

1 Use a database program or spreadsheet to create a data table with names and addresses. Save and close the data table.

2 Open the word-processing program and start a mail merge using the mail merge wizard. (Use the Help feature of your software if necessary.)

3 Select document type by clicking **Letters** in the **Mail Merge** task pane.

4 Select **Use the current document**.

EXAM TIP

It is essential that you learn how to do a mail merge. Practice! Practice! Practice!

5 Select **Use an existing list** from the **Mail Merge** task pane to open the data file and select the recipients.

6 Type the form letter, using the **Merge Fields** from the **Mail Merge** task pane to insert the necessary placeholders.

7 Click **Next: Preview your letters** to see the personalised form letters.

8 If you are satisfied with the results click **Next: Complete the merge**. If you wish to make changes click **Previous: Write your letter** and make the desired changes.

Fimgar Office Furnishings Limited
Vallaha Street
LA ROMAINE

23 June 2014

<<**Position**>>
<<**Company**>>
<<**Address Line 1**>>
<<**Address Line 2**>>

Dear <<**Recipient**>>

Fimgar Office Furnishings Limited is pleased to announce the arrival of our new range of executive office furnishings. We are offering <<**Company**>> a special 33% discount off all items in store. This offer is for a limited time only.

Please visit our store or email marketing@fimgar.net.tt to request a brochure. Our courteous and efficient staff will be happy to help you satisfy your office furnishing needs.

Yours sincerely

Veron Gooding-Rawles
Marketing Manager

Figure 5.9.1 | An example of a form letter

Figure 5.9.2 | A mail merge ribbon in a word-processing program

SUMMARY QUESTIONS

1 a Create a data source called Donors with the following table:

Title	First_Name	Surname	Address_Line_1	Address_Line_2	Amount
Mr	Anthony	Garvin	22 New Street	VANCE RIVER	$350
Mrs	Mariah	Bentley	87B Apple Street	LA PLAISANCE	$500
Mr	Prakash	Ramkaran	66 Main Street	POINT FORTIN	$250
Ms	Kellee	Chen	13 Harding Haven	GUAPO	$1000

b Use mail merge to prepare personalised appreciation letters for all donors on A5 paper from Natasha Abraham, the principal of Tiny Tots Kindergarten, Building 23, New Settlement, Point Fortin. Use the current date. The draft body of the letter is shown below:

We deeply appreciate your contribution of λ towards our Playground Reconstruction Project. As a result of your ~~generous~~ kind support we have been able to achieve our target. Consequently, work will begin during the first week of next month.

λ
Typist: Please insert donor's amount

Check your work by viewing the files named **5.9 Mail merge form letter** and **5.9 Completed mail merge** on the CD.

Letters with insets

At the end of this topic you should be able to:

• produce letters with an inset.

An **inset** is a portion of text that is typed at a greater distance from the margin than the rest of the document. Insets are used for several purposes, such as:

• to emphasise a section of text
• when typing bulleted or numbered lists
• for long quotations or to quote lines of poetry.

Typing insets

Observe the guidelines below when typing insets:

• Type the inset using single-line spacing.

TRY IT!

Prepare the following circular letter with an inset in blocked format. Make sure you observe all manuscript correction signs.

Grantley Secondary School
23 Federation Avenue
New Grant

Typist:
Insert current date

Dear Parent/Guardian

You are warmly invited to participate in a consultation with all ~~interested parties~~ stakeholders on **Student use of mobile handheld communication devices** in the School Auditorium at 3:30 pm on 23 May 20xx. In view of the increased availability and use of mobile hand-held communication devices, our administrative team has decided seek your input in revising our school's policy. We draw your attention to two key questions raised in the Policy Statement issued by the Ministry of Education:

uc

Use current year

From an educational perspective, the question that begs is *how are the mobile electronic technologies affecting the learning environment, pedagogy and school life?* More specifically the question is *how should these technologies be allowed to affect/influence school life, since banning them from schools would be pointless?* (Retrieved from http://www.moe.gov.tt)

We look forward to your input as we seek to resolve this issue in a way that will be in the best interest of our students.

∧ valuable

Marie Claire Jameison
PRINCIPAL

- Leave a clear line space before and after the inset portion.
- In a full-blocked or semi-blocked letter, type the inset text at 1.27 cm (0.5 inches) from the left margin. The text should extend to the right margin.
- In an indented letter, type the inset text at 1.27 cm (0.5 inches) from both the left and right margins so that it appears to be centred.
- Do not use quotation marks (inverted commas) unless they appear within the text you are quoting.
- Remember to return to the left margin when typing the paragraphs after the inset.

Figure 5.10.1 is an example of how insets can be used.

CDZ Fitness Centre
Jessame Street, CODRINGTON.
Telephone: 268 555 0099.

Insert current date

Dear Member,

ACCELERATE YOUR FITNESS PROGRAM WITH ACCELEREV!

The product that you have been asking for is finally here!

We are pleased to announce the arrival of the revolutionary new ACCELEREV! range of fully organic weight loss supplements that has taken the Health Care and Fitness World by storm.

ACCELEREV! is specially formulated from a unique blend of extracts from twelve proven fat-burning fruits. This delicious, highly nutritious drink can be used as a meal replacement, energy booster or as a between-meal snack. With only 60 calories per bottle, ACCELEREV is the ideal complement to your weight-loss and fitness programme.

Please read the enclosed brochure to see what eminent doctors, fitness experts and nutritionists have to say about ACCELEREV! Here are just two samples:

ACCELEREV! is packed with essential vitamins and minerals. It is rich in antioxidants that boost the body's immune system. It is free from artificial sweeteners, colouring and flavours. *Dr Benjamin Flame, Medical Doctor.*

After just three weeks, the results are clear. One of my clients was able to lose 10 pounds by using ACCELEREV! to replace coffee, fruit juices and carbonated beverages. Since I began using ACCELEREV! my energy level is at an all-time high. *Haydyn Skeete, Athletic Trainer.*

As a member of CDZ Fitness Centre, you automatically qualify for a 20% discount on our already low introductory price. This is a limited offer, so please place your orders without delay.

Carlin Horsford,
Manager.

Figure 5.10.1 Advertisement letter with an inset in indented format

TRY IT!

Prepare the sample advertisement letter (Figure 5.10.1) with an inset in indented layout on A4 paper.

SUMMARY QUESTIONS

1 a What is an inset?
  b State three purposes for which an inset is used.

2 List four guidelines for typing an inset.

Letters with enumeration

An **enumeration** is a set of numbered lines or paragraphs. Enumeration is used for lists that are in a required order, such as the sequence of steps followed to do a task. Word-processing programs usually have preset numbering styles from which you may choose. Alternatively, you may choose to manually enumerate the list.

Typing enumeration

You should observe the following guidelines for typing enumeration in a document.

Spacing

• Type each entry in the numbered list in single-line spacing.

• Use a clear line space before and after the enumerated list. You can also insert a clear line space between each enumerated item.

• If you are enumerating manually, type the enumeration first, then move two or three spaces consistently to begin the text. Alternatively, you can set a tab stop or a first line indent at the desired position (see 4.2).

• If you are using the full-blocked or semi-blocked letter format, type the enumeration against the left margin. If you are using the indented letter format, type it 1.27 cm (0.5 inches) from the left margin.

• Use hanging line indents in an enumerated list. This will mean that the second line of a list item begins under the first letter of the sentence above it rather than under the number.

Numbering

• You can use Arabic or Roman numerals or letters for enumeration. The letters may be either upper or lower case.

• Use letters to identify a sub-list within an enumerated list. Indent the sub-list by an additional 1.27 cm (0.5 inches). The letters may be in upper case or lower case as long as they are consistent (see Figure 5.11.1).

Punctuation

• Do not use a single parenthesis after the numbers in an enumerated list, for example 1), 2) and so on.

• Do not use full stops after the numbers when typing with open punctuation. Use full stops after the number when you are typing with full punctuation.

• Depending on the structure of the list, the punctuation at the end of the items can be a comma, semicolon or full stop. The last listed item should be a full stop.

Subject: Undergraduate Business Degrees

Reference: JK/23-1

Sender: Benita Perez, Assistant Registrar, Institute of Business and Technology, 345-9 Frederick Street, Port of Spain, Trinidad.

Recipient: Jacynth Karemba of Apartment 23C, Building 12, Seaview Housing Complex, San Fernando.

Thank you for enquiring about the undergraduate Degree in Business Administration that is offered at our institution. This letter briefly outlines our programmes and the application procedures. The enclosed Prospectus provides a detailed description of each course.

All our programmes are approved for Government Assistance for Tertiary Education (GATE) for nationals of Trinidad and Tobago. Students from other Caribbean countries may qualify for specially reduced CARICOM rates.

For your application to be considered, please do the following:

1 Complete the Online Application available at http://www.IBT.edu or complete the enclosed paper Application Form.
2 Pay a $100 application fee to Account Number 123-456-7890 at any branch of the Caribbean Commercial Bank.
3 Bring the following documents to our Admissions Office by 30 May of the year in which you wish to begin your studies:
A Completed paper application form (enclosed) or a print-out of your completed online application
B Application payment receipt
C Birth certificate - original and photocopy
D Valid Photo Identification - National Identification Card or Driver's Permit or Passport
E Academic Certificates and Transcripts - original and photocopy
F A letter of reference from your previous educational institution.

If you have any questions, please call me at 868 555 4383 or send an e-mail to admissions@ibt.edu. I will be happy to provide any further information that you require.

Encs: Prospectus and Undergraduate Application Form

Figure 5.11.1 An example of a letter containing enumeration

TRY IT!

Prepare the letter in Figure 5.11.1 with lists in blocked format, on an appropriate letterhead, using the current date.

SUMMARY QUESTIONS

1 State six guidelines that should be followed when typing an enumerated list.

2 Identify and correct six errors that were made in typing the following enumerated list in block format:

Steps in performing a mail merge:
1) Create a data table.
  2) Open a word-processing program and start the mail merge?
3. Select the document type.
4. Select the starting document by clicking on either:
    A Use the current document,
    b Start from a template, or
    C Start from existing document
5. Select the recipients.
6 Type the letter, inserting merge fields where required.
7 Preview the letters
8 Complete the merge

5.12 Letters with tables

LEARNING OUTCOMES

At the end of this topic you should be able to:

• produce letters with tables.

TRY IT!

Using your knowledge of spreadsheets and databases, review the basic concepts of a table by defining the features illustrated in Figure 5.12.1.

DID YOU KNOW?

You can convert typed text to a table if the items are separated by tabs, commas or paragraphs. Use the Help feature of your word-processing program to learn how to do this.

A table is used in a business letter to communicate a large amount of information effectively and concisely. They can help to present complex information in an easy-to-understand format. A table can also be used to compare, contrast or show trends over a period of time.

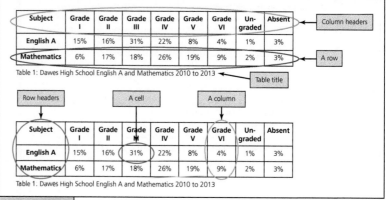

Figure 5.12.1 Features of a table

Creating a table

You can create a table in a word-processing document as well as in a spreadsheet (Figure 5.12.2).

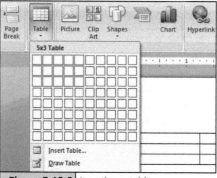

Figure 5.12.2 Inserting a table

The instructions in Table 5.12.1 show you how to do this in Microsoft Word.

Table 5.12.1 How to create a table in Microsoft Word

1	Position your cursor where you want the table to be inserted.
2	In Word 2003, click **Table** on the menu bar, then point to **Insert**, and click **Table**... In Word 2007, select the **Insert** tab, click the **Table** button and move your cursor over the grid to select the desired number of rows and columns. Alternatively, click on the **Insert Table**... option to open the **Insert Table** dialogue box.
3	Use the **Table size** section of the **Insert table** dialogue box to select the number of columns and rows.
4	Use the **AutoFit behavior** section to determine the width of the columns.
5	Click **OK** to close the dialogue box.

Preset table formats

Some word-processing programs offer several built-in table formats that use a variety of colours, borders and fonts. To access this feature in Word 2003, click the **Table AutoFormat...** button on the **Insert** menu. The preset formats in Word 2007 can be accessed from the **Design** section of the **Table Tools** ribbon that becomes available when you click on a table. Note that this ribbon will not be visible if you have not clicked on the table.

Preparing a letter with a table

When typing tables in letters, ensure that:

- you leave a clear line space before and after the table
- tables in an indented letter are horizontally centred on the page; however, in a blocked or semi-blocked letter the table is typed flush with the left margin
- tables have equal spaces between the columns and equal margins
- column headings start at the left margin of the column in the blocked style; they may be centred in the indented style
- column headings are typed in all capital letters or in initial capital letters with underscoring
- the width of a column is at least 2.54 cm (1 inch) – it may be more depending on the information it contains
- unless you have been given other instructions, you type the table in Times New Roman, size 12.

EXAM TIP

Always follow the instructions given with the table in an examination question. If no specific instructions are given, then follow the layout that is shown in the copy.

SUMMARY QUESTIONS

1 State three reasons why a table might be used in a letter.

2 List five guidelines that should be followed when typing a table in a letter.

3 Outline the steps that should be followed in order to create a table in a word-processing document.

4 Type the following letter in indented format from Samantha Sanderson, the Principal of Northern Academy, Tango Drive, Arnos Vale to Kathleen Grant, School Inspector II, 172 Granby Street, Kingstown. The letter, which has a reference of 19/2/NE, is in response to a circular with a reference number of SP-32-8. Create an appropriate subject line and use the current date. Show all relevant notations.

¶ In keeping w. your ~~Circular No. SP-32-8~~ request for a summary of my school's performance in English A and Mathematics, I wish to supply the data shown in Table 1 below:

Typist: Insert the table shown in Figure 5.12.1

Overall, there has been a pass rate of 62% in Eng A and 41% in Maths. As you will see in the enclosed 2013-2015 Action Plan, we have initiated a no. of strategies aimed at inc. our pass rates to at least 75% in both subjects in the short term, and at least 95% within the next five years.

I will be happy to provide further details on our progress towards achieving total quality education for all our students.

Envelopes and labels

At the end of this topic you should be able to:

• prepare envelopes and labels.

Envelopes

When preparing envelopes:

• Ensure that the envelope is large enough to accommodate the letter and any enclosed items. Table 5.13.1 summarises the international standard sizes of envelopes and the paper size for which each is appropriate. You should review this table so that you will be able to select the appropriate envelopes for your assignments.

• Unless you are using a mail merge, it is best to type the envelope for each letter immediately after typing the letter.

Figure 5.13.1 shows the formatting guidelines you should follow.

Table 5.13.1 Envelope sizes

Name	Measurement in mm	Measurement in inches (approx.)	Content format
C3	324 × 458	$12^{3}/_{4} \times 18$	A3 sheet flat; A2 sheet folded once
C4	229 × 324	$9 \times 12^{3}/_{4}$	A4 sheet flat; A3 sheet folded once
C5	162 × 229	$6^{3}/_{8} \times 9$	A5 sheet flat; A4 sheet folded once
C6	114 × 162	$4^{1}/_{2} \times 6^{3}/_{8}$	A6 sheet flat; A5 sheet folded once; A4 sheet folded in quarters
C5/6	114 × 229	$4^{1}/_{2} \times 9$	A4 sheet folded in thirds
C7/6	81 × 162	$3^{1}/_{4} \times 6^{3}/_{8}$	A5 sheet folded in thirds
C7	81 × 114	$3^{1}/_{4} \times 4^{1}/_{2}$	A6 sheet folded once; A5 sheet folded in quarters
B4	250 × 353	$9^{7}/_{8} \times 13^{7}/_{8}$	C4 envelope, A4 flat sheet
B5	176 × 250	$7 \times 9^{7}/_{8}$	C5 envelope, A5 flat sheet
B6	125 × 176	5×7	A4 folded in quarters
DL	110 × 220	$4^{1}/_{4} \times 8^{3}/_{4}$	A4 sheet folded in thirds, A5 sheet folded in half lengthwise (this envelope is similar in size to the C5/6)

Manually addressing envelopes

To manually address an envelope in your word-processing program:

1 Enter the dimensions of your envelope in the **Page layout** or **Page setup** dialogue box. For example, for a C5/6 envelope set the paper height to 11.4 cm (4.5 inches) and the width to 22.9 cm (9 inches).

2 Set the top margin to one-half the height of the envelope, and the left margin to one-third its width. For example, for a C5/6 envelope, set the top margin to 3.9 cm (1.5 inches) and the left margin to 7.6 cm (3 inches).

Automatically address an envelope to Danika Housen of 23 Railway Road, Siparia. Use your home address as the return address.

3 Type the recipient's address on the first line of the document.

4 If you are including the sender's address, type this in the header section of the document.

5 Print the envelope, using the manual feed tray of your printer.

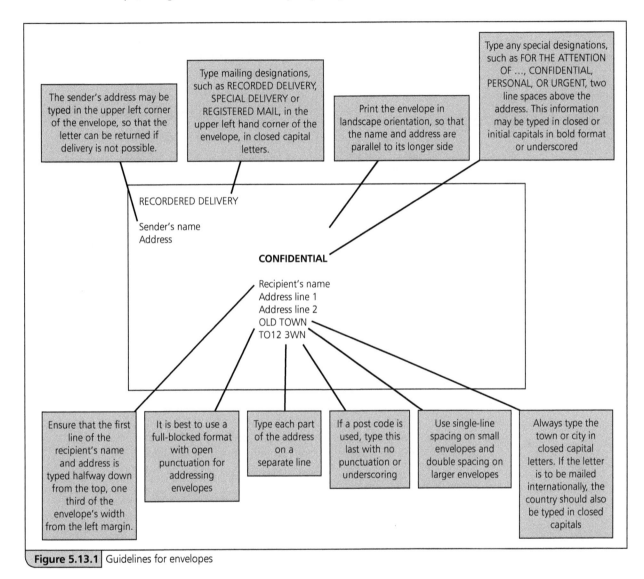

The sender's address may be typed in the upper left corner of the envelope, so that the letter can be returned if delivery is not possible.

Type mailing designations, such as RECORDED DELIVERY, SPECIAL DELIVERY or REGISTERED MAIL, in the upper left hand corner of the envelope, in closed capital letters.

Print the envelope in landscape orientation, so that the name and address are parallel to its longer side

Type any special designations, such as FOR THE ATTENTION OF ..., CONFIDENTIAL, PERSONAL, OR URGENT, two line spaces above the address. This information may be typed in closed or initial capitals in bold format or underscored

RECORDERED DELIVERY

Sender's name
Address

CONFIDENTIAL

Recipient's name
Address line 1
Address line 2
OLD TOWN
TO12 3WN

Ensure that the first line of the recipient's name and address is typed halfway down from the top, one third of the envelope's width from the left margin.

It is best to use a full-blocked format with open punctuation for addressing envelopes

Type each part of the address on a separate line

If a post code is used, type this last with no punctuation or underscoring

Use single-line spacing on small envelopes and double spacing on larger envelopes

Always type the town or city in closed capital letters. If the letter is to be mailed internationally, the country should also be typed in closed capitals

Figure 5.13.1 Guidelines for envelopes

Automatically addressing envelopes

Most word processors enable you to automatically address envelopes. In Microsoft Word the sender's and recipient's addresses are automatically copied from the letter and inserted into an envelope template. However, you may make any desired changes to these entries.

To automatically address an envelope, type the letter then:

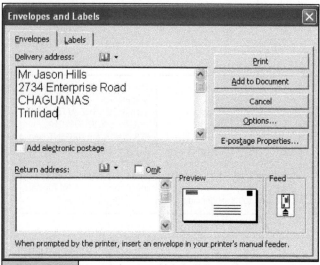

Figure 5.13.2 An envelopes and labels dialogue box

1 In Word 2003, click the **Tools** menu, point to **Letters and Mailings**, and then click **Envelopes and Labels...**, then click the **Envelopes** tab.

   In Word 2007, click on the **Mailings** tab and then click the **Envelopes** button in the **Create** section. The **Envelopes and Labels** dialogue box will appear (similar to that shown in Figure 5.13.2).

2 Ensure that the **Envelopes** tab is selected.

3 Enter or edit the addresses.

4 Insert the envelope into the printer as shown in the **Feed** box and click **Print**. If you do not want to print the envelope immediately, click **Add to Document**. The envelope will be added to the document in a separate section with its own formatting.

Labels

A label is a piece of paper, with an adhesive on one side, on which information such as an address is printed (see 5.1). The ISO sizes for labels are A7, A8 and A9. However, labels are often sold in letter-sized sheets so that they can be easily loaded into a printer. The sheets are scored or perforated to make it easier to detach each label.

Creating labels

To create a single label, type the letter then use the **Envelopes and Labels** dialogue box as described above. This time ensure the **Labels** tab is selected before you enter the address details.

When printing, choose one of the following options under **Print:**

- Click **Single label** to print a single label, then type or select the row and column number on the label sheet for the label you want to print.
- Click **Full page of the same label** to print the same information on a sheet of labels.
- Click the **Options** button to select the label type, the type of paper feed and other options and then click **OK.**

Using mail merge for envelopes and labels

By now you should have mastered performing a mail merge (see 5.9). You may also use this feature to create and print envelopes and labels.

EXAM TIP

Candidates often have problems applying mail merge when preparing envelopes. Make sure you practise until you have mastered this skill.

1 Create and save a data source called **Customers** as shown below:

Title	Name1	Name2	Company	Position	Address	City
Mr	Vishan	Lall	AMD Marketing Ltd	Manager	47 Park Street	GEORGETOWN
Mrs	Cyretha	Allan	A1 Image Makers	Director	123 Main Street	NEW AMSTERDAM
Ms	Johanna	Ravello	Ravello and Sons Ltd	Safety Supervisor	7th Avenue	BARTICA
Mr	Bernard	Apin	Ni-Nu Solutions	Manager	85 Nelson Street	GOED FORTUIN

2 Type and save the following form letter, inserting merge fields as indicated:

Safety Technologies Limited
Lahama Street
GEORGETOWN

(T: Use current date)

<<Title>> <<Name1>> <<Name2>>
<<Position>>
<<Company>>
<<Address>>
<<City>>

Dear <<Title>> <<Name2>>

LAUNCH OF OUR NEW WEBSITE

We are pleased to announce the launch of our new website at https://www. safetytechnologies.gy.

This fully secure website will enable you to browse our entire range of ISO Certified Safety Equipment and Supplies. You may place orders with the assurance that they will be delivered within three days.

Online orders automatically qualify for a 10% discount off our list prices, so we urge you to use this convenient new facility.

Our Customer Service Representatives are standing by to offer any assistance you might require. Please do not hesitate to call our toll-free number at 000-555-1111.

Yours sincerely

Anthony Le Blanc
Manager

---

3 Perform a mail merge to create personalised letters and envelopes for each record in the data file.

4 Print the letter and envelope for Ms Johanna Ravello.

5.14 Composition of business communication

LEARNING OUTCOMES

At the end of this topic you should be able to:

- prepare correspondence from skeleton notes and various media.

Skeleton notes outline the key ideas that should be expressed in communication, such as a letter, note, memorandum or audio message. Skeleton notes can assist you in preparing effective communication for a variety of purposes.

Skeleton letters

Many letters used by businesses contain similar information and have a similar structure. It is usually feasible to type and save skeleton letters that contain the unchanging information. Words in parentheses or ellipses may be used to indicate the places in which text should be added. The typist can then select and delete these placeholders and insert the relevant information. Below are some examples of when skeleton letters can be used.

Application letter

Figure 5.14.1 is a skeleton job application letter suitable for a recent graduate.

I wish to apply for the position of ... as advertised in ...

I have recently graduated from ... with passes in ... I am particularly interested in becoming a ... with you. Research has shown that your company is ... Being accepted as a ... will allow me the opportunity to apply my training and education in ... I am confident that my ... will enable me to be an excellent addition to your team

Further information may be obtained from my resume which is attached.

Please contact me at ... to arrange an interview.

I deeply appreciate your consideration.

Figure 5.14.1 Example of a skeleton job application

DID YOU KNOW?

A résumé and a curriculum vitae (CV) both present details such as qualifications, work experience and interests in tabular form. A résumé is typed on a single sheet of paper. A CV is more detailed, and consequently longer than a résumé.

TRY IT!

Find a job advertisement in a newspaper and compose a letter of application by filling in the relevant places in the skeleton letter (Figure 5.14.1).

Other types of letters

Skeleton notes can be composed for other types of business letter, including enquiries, response letters, sales letters and complaints.

Preparing notes from skeleton notes

The ability to construct notes from an outline is an essential skill. It is important to respect the intellectual property of others and avoid plagiarism (see 9.1 and 9.2). You should therefore research from a variety of sources, write down the key points in your own terms, arrange the points in a logical order and then write out supporting details. You will thereby ensure that the final document is entirely your own work.

Use the following outlines to create your own skeleton notes. You can refer to Table 5.2.1 for additional guidance.

1 Enquiry
- State your purpose.
- List your questions or requested action.
- Encourage a prompt response.

2 Response to enquiry
- Answer the questions clearly and concisely, preferably in the same order in which they were asked.
- If you cannot provide the requested information, explain the reasons and offer to assist with alternate methods.
- End by indicating your willingness to assist where possible.

3 Sales
- Use a subject line that will capture the recipient's attention. However, avoid exaggerated or untrue statements.
- Name the product or service and briefly state its value to the recipient.
- Outline the key features and invite the reader to examine the enclosed brochure or leaflet.
- State the guarantee that your business is offering.
- Offer an incentive for the reader to respond, such as a special discount or a free gift.
- Clearly state how the order should be made, for example on an enclosed form, by calling a specific number, or by visiting a website.
- Invite the reader to contact you for further information.

4 Complaint
- State the issue briefly but clearly.
- Identify the product or service, including date of purchase, serial number, model or any other information that will help the recipient to determine the issue.
- Explain the problem.
- Propose a solution, such as a refund or replacement.
- End the letter respectfully.

5 Response to a valid complaint
- Express your regret about the situation.
- State the correction you will make.
- End on a positive note by encouraging future business with your company.

6 Response to an invalid complaint
- Thank the customer for bringing it to your attention.
- Express regret (not an apology).
- Clearly and concisely explain why your company is not at fault.
- Clearly state that your company is denying the request, and supply reasons for this denial.
- End on a positive note. Try to create goodwill for future business transactions. For example, you may offer a special discount on the next transaction.

Entrepreneur – person who organises business venture →comes up with ideas →arranges funding – from personal resources

  – from loans from banks, credit unions etc.

→assumes the risks for the business

Entrepreneurship def'n:

– 'the act and art of being an entrepreneur' (check source);

– the capacity and willingness to develop, organise and manage a business venture along with any of its risks in order to make a profit (source: Business dictionary.com).

– Entrepreneurship is the pursuit of opportunity beyond resources controlled (Professor Howard Stevenson, as quoted in Entrepreneurship: A Working Definition by Thomas R. Eisenmann, http://blogs.hbr.org/hbsfaculty/2013/01/what-is-entrepreneurship.html)

| **Figure 5.14.2** | Skeleton notes |

The skeleton notes in Figure 5.14.2 were prepared from a combination of lectures and additional research from a variety of sources.

Figure 5.14.3 is a note constructed from the skeleton.

Entrepreneurship

Professor Howard Stevenson, defines entrepreneurship as 'the pursuit of opportunity beyond resources controlled' (Eisenmann, 2013). This definition indicates that an entrepreneur is a person who recognises and goes after a business opportunity with the aim of making a profit. The entrepreneur invests personal resources, such as time, money and labour. Where additional funding is required, this is obtained, usually at the entrepreneur's own risk, from external sources. These sources include bank or credit union loans. Entrepreneurship requires creativity, courage, determination and good organisational skills.

References

Eisenmann, T. R. 2013. Entrepreneurship: A Working Definition. Retrieved from http://blogs.hbr.org/hbsfaculty/2013/01/what-is-entrepreneurship.html

| **Figure 5.14.3** | Example of a note constructed from skeleton notes |

Audio messages

You might be required to compose an **audio message** based on an outline. Ensure that your message is clear, concise and contains all the essential information. You should also be polite, while at the same time ensuring you make clear what you want the listener to do. For example an employer might say the following:

'Mr Barton: I am too swamped with work now. I think I will have to call and ask Mr Peters to come in next week instead. (*Employer consults diary.*) I see that I am available on Wednesday at ten and on Thursday at two. Find out which he will prefer.'

An appropriate audio message would be:

'Good Morning, Mr Peters. Mr Barton regrets that he will be unable to meet with you tomorrow morning as scheduled. However he is available next Wednesday at ten in the morning and on Thursday at two in the afternoon. Would you like to reschedule your appointment for one of those times?'

SUMMARY QUESTIONS

1 Gracelyn Seldon, the Human Resource Manager of Cre-A-Tiv Advertising Company Limited, Building 27, Room 6A, Barrington Courts, Grande Coutain, has assigned Jerome Davis to interview the following applicants for the position of Trainee Copy Writer:

   a Cherise Hansen of 12 Victoria Avenue, New Grant on 12 November at 9:45 am.

   b Vincent Xavier of Apartment 7A, Freedom Place, Pottstown on 12 November at 10:45 am.

   c Desiree Bellamy of 34 Carrington Crescent, Gowers Road, Trincity on 13 November at 9:15 am.

Prepare appropriate response letters from the following skeleton note:

   Thank you for your application for the position of ...

   You are invited to come in to our office at this address for an interview on ... at .... Please go to ... and ask for ....

   You are required to bring the originals of all your certificates, valid photo identification and two reference letters.

2 Prepare skeleton notes for the following business situations:

   a response to an enquiry in which you are unable to provide the requested information

   b response to a valid complaint.

3 State three principles that should be followed when composing notes from an outline.

4 Compose an appropriate audio message for the following situation:

   The office photocopier has stopped functioning five days after it was last serviced. You are in the process of copying a significant amount of material for a meeting to be held in two days' time. The company usually has a wait time of three days for service calls.

TRY IT!

Prepare skeleton notes on the topic 'How to compose effective business letters'.

Compose and type a note using the ideas you have outlined.

LEARNING OUTCOMES

At the end of this topic you should be able to:

- produce memoranda in various styles using appropriate stationery
- prepare memoranda from skeleton notes.

DID YOU KNOW?

The formatting and design of a memo may vary from one organisation to another.

Table 5.15.1 Elements of memoranda

1	The heading: Memorandum.
2	To: followed by the name or job title of the addressee.
3	From: followed by the name or job title of the sender.
4	The date.
5	A reference (optional).
6	Subject heading.
7	The message.
8	Authentication initials or signature (used when the memorandum requires official approval or authorisation).
9	Enclosure notification (if there is an attached document).
10	Postscript (optional).

Purpose of memoranda

A memorandum, called a memo for short, is a specially formatted document that is used for communicating within a business. A memorandum is an efficient means of conveying information because it can be circulated to a large number of people. It can be used to eliminate the need for a meeting, particularly if the matter communicated does not require discussion. A memo is not normally used for private or confidential information.

A memo is usually concerned with a specific topic and can be used for a variety of purposes, such as to:

- make announcements
- disseminate information
- request information
- give instructions or suggestions
- discuss policies or procedures
- report on an activity.

The tone of a memorandum is usually less formal than that of an official letter. However, all rules of spelling, grammar, sentence construction and proper word usage must be observed.

All memoranda consist of the elements as shown in Table 5.15.1.

Preparing memoranda

Follow the guidelines below when preparing memoranda:

- Type the heading 'Memorandum' at the top of the page. It may be typed in close or expanded capital letters, with or without underscoring. It may be in bold font and larger than the text in the rest of the document (for example, size 16).
- Keep the message simple and direct. Only include information that is directly related to the subject.
- Prepare short memoranda on A5 paper in either portrait or landscape orientation. Use A4 paper for long memoranda.
- Prepare a continuation sheet if a memorandum is longer than one page. The page number, addressee and date should be typed 1 inch from the top. The layout of TO and DATE should be the same as the first page and the paper should be of the same size, colour and quality.
- Never type an address, salutation, complimentary close or signature block in a memo.

Layouts for memoranda

A memorandum can be typed in blocked or indented layout. In the **blocked format** the heading 'memorandum' may be centre- or left-aligned. All other elements are left-aligned. All paragraphs begin at the left margin.

In the **indented format** the reference is set to the right of the centre on the same line as TO, and the date is set to the right of the centre on the same line as FROM. The SUBJECT line is centred. The first line of each paragraph is indented approximately 1.27 cm (0.5 inches) from the left margin.

EXAM TIP

Remember that a memo is not a letter. The address, salutation and complimentary close or signature block are never used in a memo.

MEMORANDUM

TO	All Staff
FROM	Human Resource Department
DATE	1 March 20xx
REF	ADV-1/03

SUBJECT Submission of Updated TD1 Forms

You are reminded to submit your completed Tax Declaration Forms (TD1) to this department on or before 15 March. This is necessary for us to update our records before the start of the new fiscal year. For your convenience, blank forms have been placed at the reception desk.

Please remember to fill out the forms in **BLOCK LETTERS**, using **black** or **dark blue** ink only.

Figure 5.15.1 Example of a memo using the blocked format

MEMORANDUM

TO:	All Staff	**REF:**	ADV-1/03
FROM:	Human Resource Department	**DATE:**	1 March 20xx

SUBJECT: Submission of updated TD1 Forms

You are reminded to submit your completed Tax Declaration Forms (TD1) to this department on or before 15 March. This is necessary for us to update our records before the start of the new fiscal year. For your convenience, blank forms have been placed at the reception desk.

Please remember to fill out the forms in **BLOCK LETTERS**, using **black** or **dark blue** ink only.

Figure 5.15.2 Example of a memo using the indented format

ACTIVITY

Apply the skills you have developed for skeleton notes to prepare a memorandum from the Principal to all teachers informing them that the District Nurse will be visiting the school in two weeks from today to discuss lifestyle diseases with the fifth- and sixth-form students. Use the current date.

DID YOU KNOW?

Word-processing programs usually contain a variety of memo templates. However, these templates do not always follow the above guidelines, so you may need to modify them to meet professional standards.

SUMMARY QUESTIONS

1 List at least four purposes for which memos may be written.

2 Give at least five guidelines for the composition of a memo.

3 Give at least three differences between the indented and blocked memo styles.

4 Prepare a continuation sheet for a memo with the heading shown below:

TO:	All Security Personnel
FROM:	The Manager
DATE:	(Use current date)
REFERENCE:	SD-23-7

SUBJECT: CHANGES IN STAFF PARKING ARRANGEMENTS

EXAM TIP

Ensure that you know the correct placing of the parts of a memo. This is an area in which many candidates have difficulty.

At the end of this topic you should be able to:

- prepare notices for meetings
- prepare agendas for meetings
- prepare a chairman's agenda.

Your school's Parent Teacher Association is holding a meeting at the school auditorium four weeks from today, at 3.30 pm. Type a notice and save it as **PTA notice.**

Four documents are commonly used in connection with meetings. They are:

- **notice of meeting**
- **agenda**
- **chairman's agenda**
- **minutes**.

These items are sometimes collectively referred to as **committee documents**. This topic focuses on notices, agendas and the chairman's agenda, whereas 5.17 will discuss minutes.

Notice of meeting

A notice of meeting is a formal, written announcement that is prepared according to specific guidelines. A notice of meeting is usually sent no fewer than 14 days in advance to all people who are entitled to attend. It communicates the following information:

- name of organisation
- date and time of meeting
- venue
- type and purpose of meeting.

Table 5.16.1 provides guidelines for typing notices of meetings.

Notices may be typed in either blocked style with open punctuation or indented style with full punctuation (Figure 5.16.1).

Table 5.16.1 Guidelines for notices of meetings

✓	Notices are usually brief, so they are typed on A5 paper in landscape orientation.
✓	They are usually centred vertically on the page, so that there are equal top and bottom margins.
✓	The left and right margins are usually 2.54 cm (1 inch).
✓	The salutation and complimentary close are not used.
✓	Four or five clear line spaces are left before the signatory's name.

BAYVIEW FISHING COOPERATIVE SOCIETY

Notice is hereby given that a General Meeting of the Bayview Fishing Cooperative Society will be held at the Bayview Community Centre on 4 April, 20XX, beginning at 7 pm.

Please be advised that the agenda will be circulated later.

Bartholomew Hernandez
Secretary

Figure 5.16.1a An agenda in blocked layout

```
       BAYVIEW FISHING COOPERATIVE SOCIETY

        Notice is hereby given that a General Meeting of the Bayview
    Fishing Cooperative Society will be held at the Bayview Community
    Centre on 4th April, 20XX, beginning at 7:00 p.m.

        Please be advised that the agenda will be circulated later.




    Bartholomew Hernandez,
    Secretary.
```

Figure 5.16.1b | An agenda in indented layout

Agenda

An agenda presents a sequential list of the items that are to be discussed in a meeting. It is sent out in advance to all the people who should attend the meeting. Ideally, the agenda should be distributed with the notice, so both documents may be combined on a single sheet of paper.

Guidelines for preparing a combined notice and agenda

When preparing a combined notice and agenda follow these general guidelines:

- If the notice and agenda are short use A5 paper in portrait orientation. If they are long use A4 paper in portrait orientation.
- Type the word **AGENDA** flush with the left margin or centred in capital letters, either emboldened or in spaced capitals.
- Leave at least one clear line space between the notice and the agenda.
- Present the agenda items as an enumerated list.

A sample combined notice and agenda is shown in Figure 5.16.2 on p94.

Agenda for Annual General Meetings

An Annual General Meeting (AGM) is a public, yearly gathering of the directors, executives and shareholders of an official organisation. Public limited companies are legally required to hold an AGM within six months of the end of the organisation's financial year. Written notice of an AGM must be circulated at least 21 days in advance. Table 5.16.2 shows the typical agenda for an AGM.

DID YOU KNOW?

Sometimes a draft agenda is circulated to the members who can then propose changes such as the inclusion of other items.

ACTIVITY

Amend the file **PTA Notice** to include an agenda. New Matters are:

Introduction of a mentorship programme

Career Guidance seminar

DID YOU KNOW?

Organisations such as credit unions, clubs, sporting bodies and charities may have constitutions that state that AGMs must be held, although these are not required by law.

Table 5.16.2 An AGM agenda

1	Opening remarks (or Welcome)
2	Apologies
3	Minutes of previous Annual General Meeting
4	Matters arising from the Minutes
5	Presentation of Annual Report
6	Adoption of Annual Report
7	Presentation of Accounts (or Treasurer's Report)
8	Adoption of Accounts
9	Appointment of Auditors
10	Election of Officers
11	Motions to be put to the AGM
12	Any other business
13	Closing remarks

BAYVIEW FISHING COOPERATIVE SOCIETY

Notice is hereby given that a General Meeting of the Bayview Fishing Cooperative Society will be held at the Bayview Community Centre on 4 April, 20XX, beginning at 7 pm.

AGENDA

1 Welcome and opening
2 Apologies
3 Minutes of the previous meeting
4 Matters arising from the minutes
5 Correspondence
6 Matters arising from the correspondence
7 New matters
  i Plans for fundraising fiesta
  ii Proposed workshop series
8 Any other business
9 Date for next meeting

Bartholomew Hernandez
Secretary

Phone:	868 555 0088
Fax:	868 555 1321
Email:	bfcs@cooperative.org

Enclosure: Minutes of meeting held on 5 March, 20XX

Figure 5.16.2 A combined notice and agenda

The chairman's agenda

The chairman is the person who is responsible for opening, conducting and closing a meeting. He or she seeks to put people at ease and ensure that each person has an opportunity to speak.

The chairman's agenda is different from the agenda that is distributed to meeting attendees. It contains the same items as the normal agenda. However, there is space at the right of each item in which notes may be written. Additional details that help the chairman to manage the meeting more effectively may be typed on the chairman's agenda (Figure 5.16.3), including:

- apologies for absence
- resolutions and motions
- information to be taken into account before reaching a decision.

Guidelines for typing a chairman's agenda

When preparing the chairman's agenda ensure that:

- it contains all the text from the agenda that is circulated to all members
- the typed text of the chairman's agenda occupies the left side of the page

- one half or more of the page is left blank for the writing of notes
- numbers are typed in the blank area, in the same order and spacing as the agenda
- notes are typed to the right of the dividing line
- a clear line space is left between each item.

BAYVIEW FISHING COOPERATIVE SOCIETY

A General Meeting to be held at the Bayview Community Centre on 4 April, 20XX, beginning at 7 pm.

CHAIRMAN'S AGENDA

1 Welcome and opening	1
2 Apologies	2
3 Minutes of the previous meeting	3
4 Matters arising from the minutes	4
5 Correspondence	5
6 Matters arising from the correspondence	6
7 New matters i Plans for fundraising fiesta	7 i
ii Proposed workshop series	ii
8 Any other business	8
9 Date for next meeting	9 Suggest 6th May as the 5th is a public holiday

Figure 5.16.3 A chairman's agenda

EXAM TIP

To properly align the items in a chairman's agenda when using word-processing programs, use tabs. For example, to prepare Figure 5.16.3 you will need a left tab and a bar tab. The bar tab will draw the vertical line seen in the agenda.

SUMMARY QUESTIONS

1 Outline at least three guidelines that should be followed when preparing each of the following documents:

   a notice of a meeting

   b a combined notice and agenda.

2 Prepare a combined notice and agenda for the 7th AGM of Towering High Manufacturing Company Limited, to be held at the Starcove Conference Centre on 21 July of this year at three o'clock in the afternoon.

3 Discuss the purpose of a chairman's agenda.

4 Describe three ways in which the chairman's agenda differs from the agenda that is circulated to other members.

ACTIVITY

Type out the sample chairman's agenda, paying close attention to the spacing and tabs.

TRY IT!

Locate an agenda in a textbook or from the Internet. Prepare a corresponding chairman's agenda.

Minutes of meetings

Purpose of minutes

The minutes are a written record of all official proceedings, from the start of the meeting to its conclusion. The minutes are vital because they:

• document the discussions held at the meeting
• provide a permanent record of the decisions and activities of the organisation
• identify the actions taken or that should be taken, and by whom
• record whether the organisation's goals have been achieved
• assist in organising future meetings
• inform members who were unable to attend about what transpired in the meeting
• help to remind members of assigned duties and deadlines
• serve as a valuable reference when planning and coordinating activities.

Preparing minutes

The format, style and content of minutes vary depending on the type of meeting and the practices of the organisation. However, most minutes must contain the following information:

1 date, time and venue of the meeting

2 name of the chairman

3 names of all who are present

4 apologies for absences, if given

5 type and/or purpose of the meeting

6 issues discussed, usually in the order indicated on the agenda

7 decisions taken

8 the date, time, venue and purpose of the next meeting.

A sample of minutes of a meeting is presented in Figure 5.17.1.

Table 5.17.1 lists some tips to follow when preparing minutes.

Table 5.17.1 Tips for preparing minutes

✓	You should only offer your opinions if they were stated as part of the discussion in the meeting.
✓	Your report should not be biased.
✓	You should follow the order of the items on the agenda.
✓	Notes should be concise but ensure they record all the necessary information.
✓	It is a good idea to prepare the minutes as soon as possible after the meeting so that your memory is fresh.

BAYVIEW FISHING COOPERATIVE SOCIETY
Bayview Avenue
PORT TOWN
Minutes

A General Meeting of the Bayview Fishing Cooperative Society was held at the Bayview Community Centre at 7 p.m. on 4 April, 20XX.

Presiding: Mr Anil Ramdewar, Chairman

Present: Mr Nathan Knowles
                Mr Victor Charles
                Mr Allan Chen
                Ms Ann Marie Jaimungal
                Mr Bartholomew Hernandez, Secretary

Absent: Mr Harold Stevens
                Mr Hezekiah Henry

1 Welcome and opening
After ascertaining that there was a quorum, the meeting was declared open by the Chairman at 7:08 p.m.

2 Apologies
The Chairman communicated apologies from Mr Stevens and Mr Henry for their unavoidable absence from this meeting.

3 Minutes of the previous meeting
The minutes of the meeting held on 5 March, 20XX were approved and duly signed by the Chairman.

4 Matters arising from the minutes
Mr Raymond reported that the laying of the foundation for the Cooperative's headquarters was well underway, and that Phase 1 of the project was expected to be completed in the next six weeks.

5 Correspondence
The cooperative has received an invitation to send three representatives to a consultation on Maritime Safety, to be held by the Fisheries Division of the Ministry of the Environment, at the Hodgetown Community Centre on 18 May at 6:30 p.m.

6 Matters arising from the correspondence
Mr Knowles, Mrs Charles and Mr Bartholomew have volunteered to represent the Cooperative at the consultation on Maritime Safety.

7 New matters
  i Plans for fundraising fiesta
        An ad hoc committee consisting of Mr Ramdewar, Ms Jaimungal and Mr Bartholomew was formed. The first meeting will be held on 12 April at Mr Ramdewar's home.

  ii Proposed workshop series
        Mr Ramdewar proposed that the Cooperative should hold a series of workshops on topics such as aquaculture, sustainable fishing techniques and small engine repairs. This motion was seconded by Ms Jaimungal and unanimously approved. Mr Charles has agreed to prepare a draft proposal for presentation at the next meeting.

8 Any other business
It was decided by majority vote that a farewell function for the Stevens will be held on 28 April at the Chen residence at 7:30 p.m. A budget of $2200, including the cost of a gift, was approved.

9 Date for next meeting
It was decided to hold the next General Meeting on 6th May at 7:00 p.m.

There being no other matter, the meeting was brought to a close at 8:45 p.m.

Anil Ramdewar   Bartholomew Hernandez
Chairman   Secretary

Figure 5.17.1   Sample minutes of a meeting

DID YOU KNOW?

You can change the colour and add effects such as shadow or 3D to your shape or WordArt. In Word 2007, these options are displayed in the **Drawing Tools** tab when the WordArt object is selected. In Word 2003, you can change the colour of the object by right-clicking on the graphic and using the **Format** menu.

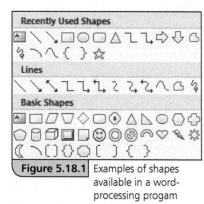

Figure 5.18.1 Examples of shapes available in a word-processing progam

You already know how to insert clip art and pictures from another file. You should now also be able to resize graphics and use text wrapping to control the behaviour of text in relation to your graphics (see 5.3). These skills will be necessary as you work with other graphics, including WordArt, shapes, graphs and charts.

This topic focuses on using graphics in a word-processing program to enhance your business documents where appropriate. However, the skills can also be applied in other software, including spreadsheet and presentation programs. Table 5.18.1 provides instructions for working with graphics in Microsoft Word.

WordArt

WordArt is a feature that allows you to create text with a variety of shapes and effects. WordArt can be rotated, stretched, shadowed and coloured. Use WordArt for single words or short phrases, not for large blocks of text.

AutoShapes

In Word the AutoShapes tool includes lines, connectors, basic shapes, flowchart symbols, stars, banners and callouts. These features are available from the **Insert** menu or ribbon. Once you have selected the shape you want from the shapes menu (such as that shown in Figure 5.18.1), click and drag your cursor, which will now look like a plus sign, to the size you want your shape.

Charts and graphs

It is possible to insert a new chart or graph into a word-processing document without opening the spreadsheet program. Follow the instructions in Table 5.18.1. A chart with sample data will be displayed, along with a related datasheet. Enter your information on the datasheet and the changes will be shown on the chart.

Table 5.18.1 Instructions for working with graphics using Microsoft Word

Task	Method
Add WordArt	1 In Word 2003, click **Insert,** point to **Picture**… and click **WordArt**…. In Word 2007, select **Word Art** from the **Insert** ribbon. The **WordArt Gallery** will appear. 2 Click on the WordArt style that you want to use and click **OK**. 3 Type in your text in the **Edit WordArt Text** box (in Word 2010 you can just type your text in the placeholder). 4 Make any changes you want to the font, font size and whether the text is bold or italic. Click **OK**.

Task	Method
Change the text in WordArt	In Word 2003: **1** Double-click the WordArt object you want to change. **2** In the **Edit WordArt Text** dialogue box or toolbar, change the text, and then click **OK**. In Word 2007: **3** Click the WordArt object and select **Edit Text** from the ribbon. In Word 2010: **4** Click the WordArt object to bring the placeholder up again and edit the text.
Rotate or flip an AutoShape	**1** Click on the shape. **2** Click **Draw** in Word 2003. In Word 2007 the **Drawing Tools** tab will open automatically. **3** In Word 2003 point to **Rotate or Flip** and select the option you want to use. In Word 2007 click on **Rotate** then select the option from the drop-down menu. **Note:** You can also freely rotate the object at any time. When you click on the object a green circle will appear on one of the edges. Click and drag this circle to rotate the picture to the desired angle.
Insert a chart or graph	In Word 2003: **1** Click the **Insert** menu, select **Object...**, and then click the **Create New** tab. **2** Click **Microsoft Graph Chart** in the **Object type** box, and then click **OK**. **3** You will see a chart and sample data in a table. This is where you can edit the data from the chart. In Word 2007: **1** Click on the **Insert** menu and then click on **Chart**. **2** Select the type of chart you want from the **Insert Chart** box. **3** Click **OK**. A datasheet will open in a separate window. This is where you can edit the data for the chart.
Change the chart to another chart type	In Word 2003: **1** Double-click on the chart. **2** On the chart toolbar that appears, select the chart type you want to use from the **Chart Type** drop-down list. In Word 2007: **1** Click on the chart to select it. **2** On the chart menu, click **Change Chart Type**. **3** Choose a chart type from the options that are displayed and click **OK**.

SUMMARY QUESTION

Create the sign as displayed below:

DID YOU KNOW?

You may use the Freeform and Scribbles options in the **Lines** section of the **Shapes** menu to draw freehand shapes.

TRY IT!

Open a word-processing program and create a bar graph to represent statistical data taken from any of your textbooks.

There are several reasons for using columns when producing creative displays. For example:

• you can often fit more text onto the page
• a long list of words is more effectively displayed by using three or four columns
• the document is easier to read because the reader's eyes travel a shorter distance across the page
• the use of shorter lines usually makes comprehension easier
• the layout can be more visually attractive.

Working with columns

Observe the guidelines below when using columns in business documents:

• There should be a significant space between columns, usually 1.27 cm (0.5 inches). If the page is to be folded, for example if you are preparing a booklet, then leave at least 2.54 cm (1 inch) between columns.
• If the space between columns is small, then you should add a line between the columns to make reading easier.
• If the entire document is in columns, it is more efficient to set the columns before starting to type.
• If columns will only be used in a section of the document, type the entire document before setting up columns. Select the text for which you want to change the layout and change the column format as shown below.

How to create two or more columns

Columns can usually be created using the page formatting tools in your word processor. For example, in Microsoft Word 2003, click **Format**, then **Columns**. A **Columns** dialogue box will appear, similar to that shown in Figure 6.1.1. Choose the desired number of columns under **Presets**.

In Word 2007, select the **Page Layout** tab, click the **Columns** button and select the desired number of columns from the drop-down menu.

How to change the column settings

You can also alter the settings of your columns. In Word, the **Columns** dialogue box allows you to change the width of the columns, the size of the spaces between columns and whether or not there should be a line between. In Word 2007, click on **More Columns...** from the **Columns** drop-down menu on the **Page Layout** ribbon to activate the dialogue box.

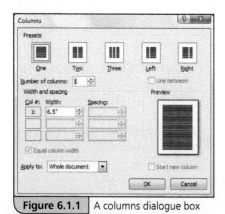

Figure 6.1.1 A columns dialogue box

Type the following passage and then set a two-column layout for the second and third paragraphs only.

Good Writing is Essential!

Although the telephone is now used more frequently than a letter, effective writing skills are still essential in the business world. All letters must be free of errors in spelling, pronunciation, word usage and grammar.

A dictionary is a vital reference book for office workers. A good dictionary contains more than the spellings and meanings of words. It gives information on grammar and usage, including sample sentences. It also provides guidance on how the word is used in context, for example whether it is formal or informal. Ensure that the dictionary you use is up to date.

A thesaurus provides the synonyms and sometimes antonyms of words. A thesaurus is very useful when trying to find alternatives for words that are used too frequently.

Depending on the software you are using, columns will only be visible if your document is in a certain view, such as Print Layout. If you are not able to see the columns you have added, check the view you are in.

SUMMARY QUESTIONS

1 State at least three reasons why a document may be prepared in multiple columns.

2 Prepare the following document as shown below. Set three columns for the listed words only.

Words of Latin Origin — Header: Times New Roman, size 16, bold

Most people consider Latin to be a 'dead language' because there are no native speakers of the language. However, it is still alive in the business world as many Latin words are commonly used in speech and writing. A wise business student will learn the correct spellings of these words, their meanings and the context in which they are used. — Subheader: Times New Roman, size 14, bold

Latin terms used in business —

The following are some examples of Latin terms that are used in business:

Ad hoc	Ex gratia	Prima facie
Bona fide	Ex officio	Pro bono
Caveat emptor	Modus operandi	Pro forma
Curriculum vitae	Per annum	Pro rata
De facto	Per diem	Status quo
Et cetera	Per se	Verbatim

Subheader: Times New Roman, size 14, bold

The meanings of Latin terms —

It is fairly easy to find out the meanings of these terms. Do an Internet search, using the keywords *Latin words business use*. You will find that there are many websites with a wealth of information on these and other terms.

Creative displays 1

At the end of this topic you should be able to:

• produce effective and creative displays including notices, cards, menus and invitations.

NOTICE
Closure of Computer Lab
The computer lab will be closed for essential maintenance work from
18th to 20th February
Scheduled classes will be accommodated in the
Audio Visual Room
We apologise for any inconvenience

Figure 6.2.1 A notice

TRY IT!

Prepare and print Figure 6.2.1 on a sheet of A4 paper using appropriate font sizes so that the paper is utilised effectively.

To produce effective and creative displays that incorporate a variety of design elements follow the general guidelines in Table 6.2.1.

Table 6.2.1 Guidelines for creative displays

✓	Centre the document horizontally and vertically
✓	Ensure that all design elements are well aligned with each other, as well as with the page
✓	Avoid very wide borders and unnecessary clutter such as irrelevant pictures
✓	Use sufficiently large margins (at least 2.54 cm or 1 inch) with adequate spacing between the design elements
✓	Use only one or two fonts: a more decorative but readable font for headlines and a plainer font for all other text
✓	Size the fonts to effectively use up the printable area of the page
✓	Proofread your work to ensure that there are no errors

Notices

A **notice** is a document that clearly and concisely presents urgent or important information to its readers. It is arranged so that attention is drawn to the most important information (see Figure 6.2.1). Short notices may be prepared on A5 paper, but for longer notices use A4 paper. Notices for display on a wall or board should be printed on larger paper, such as A3, A4, legal or tabloid (17 inches × 11 inches).

Notices are prepared for business purposes, such as to announce a special event or advertise vacancies.

Cards

Small documents such as postcards, compliment slips and business cards are usually printed on A4 sheets and then cut to size. The Activity below focuses on the preparation of business cards. However, the instructions can also be followed when preparing other small documents.

ACTIVITY

Use the appropriate layout, fonts and graphics to design and print a business card with your contact information. You may use a fictitious business if you wish. There are several ways to create a business card in a word-processing program, but one of the easiest ways is to use a text box:

1 Set a new blank document to A4 with 1.27 cm (0.5 inches) margins and two columns.

2 Insert a text box and format its size so that it measures 5.1 cm × 8.9 cm (2 inches × 3.5 inches).

3 Type all the information and place all graphics within the text box.

4 Copy and paste the text box, positioning them so that there are five cards in each column.

5 Print the page and cut to size.

Business cards

A **business card** is a small rectangle (approximately 5.1 cm × 8.9 cm or 2 inches × 3.5 inches) that displays the contact information of an individual or an organisation.

Invitations and menus

Invitations contain information on the date, time, venue and nature of the event. Mail merge can be used to insert the names of the invitees.

A **menu** is an attractively presented, organised listing of the meals that are served at a restaurant or event. Sometimes an invitation and a menu are printed as a single document.

How to prepare invitations and menus

Follow the guidelines below when preparing invitations and menus:

- Use a single border to enclose all text.
- Use large and/or expanded text for the organisation's name and event.
- Use initial capitals for each menu item. Underlined or bold font may be used.
- Type each menu item in a separate line.
- Divide the meal options into courses such as appetisers, main course, dessert, beverages. Use a symbol or small picture as the divider between each course. Leave a clear line space before and after each divider.

SUMMARY QUESTIONS

1 List at least six guidelines that should be followed when designing display work such as notices or invitations.

2 a Create a data source with the names and addresses of at least three people.

 b Create the invitation with the menu shown in Figure 6.2.3 on A5 paper. Save it as **Invitation**.

 c Use mail merge to create personalised invitations and envelopes for all invitees and save it as **Merged**.

 d Print one invitation and envelope.

Dele's Professional Typing Services
35 Sweet Briar Street, Georgetown
Telephone 555 9898 Email delepro@mailers.org

We design professional layouts for all documents
✓ Black-and-white and colour printing
✓ Photocopying
✓ Document scanning
✓ Digital photography

Contact us for all your document preparation needs

| **Figure 6.2.2** | A business card |

DID YOU KNOW?

Desktop publishing programs such as Microsoft Publisher also offer a variety of business card templates.

Brooksfield High School

Cordially invites

<<Title>> <<First Name>> <<Surname>>

To our
Christmas Concert and Dinner

At the School's Auditorium
On 17th December 20xx, 6:00 pm

Menu
Spicy Seafood Cocktails
Savoury Ham Rolls

Salmon Fillets with Angel Hair Pasta
Or
Baked Turkey with Almond Stuffing
Served with your choice of Rice,
Mixed Vegetables and Salads

Traditional Fruit Cake
Sorrel Ice Cream

Price $300 all-inclusive

| **Figure 6.2.3** | An invitation with a menu |

DID YOU KNOW?

Simple, uncluttered layouts are usually more attractive than displays that are crowded with graphics and many different font types.

6.3 Creative displays 2

Flyers

A **flyer** is an announcement printed on a single sheet of paper that is designed to be widely distributed, usually in a public place or by mail. A flyer is typically printed on A4 paper but A5 paper can also be used. Flyers are used to advertise or provide information about products, services or events.

How to prepare flyers

Follow the guidelines below when preparing a flyer:

• Attract the reader's attention by using a bold header.
• Create a desire to obtain your product or service by featuring its unique attributes, or making a special promotional offer such as a discounted price.
• Do not add too much information.
• Include a statement of action, such as 'Please visit our store today' or 'Call us to place your order'.

Programmes

A **programme** is a sequential list of activities that are scheduled to take place at an event. Programmes may be displayed on a single sheet like a flyer. Longer programmes can be prepared on two pages, and printed on both sides of a single sheet of paper. If they are longer, or consist of several sections, they may be folded to make leaflets.

Leaflets

A **leaflet** is a sheet of paper, usually printed on both sides, that is folded to create pages. Figures 6.3.1 to 6.3.3 show the folding options for four-, six- and eight-page leaflets.

A4 paper in landscape orientation is used for four-page leaflets. Six-page and eight-page leaflets are better displayed on legal paper.

It is best to plan out your leaflet with pen and paper before creating it on the computer. Fold a sample piece of paper to the intended size, number the pages and write out the layout for each page. Then open the sheets of paper. You may need to check your printer settings to ensure your leaflet is printed correctly.

Figure 6.3.1 | How to fold a four-page leaflet

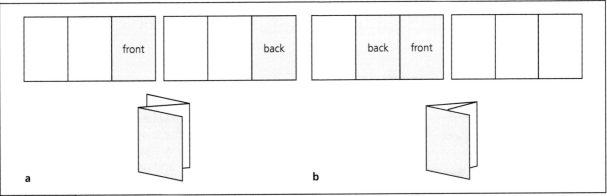

Figure 6.3.2 Two ways to fold a six-page leaflet

ACTIVITY

a Create a four-page leaflet for your school sports day by following these steps:

1 Open a new document and change the paper to A4 in **Landscape** orientation.

2 Format the page with 1.9 cm (0.75 inch) margins and two columns with a space of 3.8 cm (1.5 inches) between the columns.

3 Design the back page of your leaflet by typing either the Athlete's Oath or your school's motto.

4 In Microsoft Word 2003, click **Insert** then **Break...** then **Column Break** to get to the second column. In Word 2007, select **Column** from the **Breaks** section of the **Page Layout** tab.

5 Create the front cover of your leaflet to show the name, date, time and venue of the event, with an appropriate graphic.

6 To get to the next page in Word 2003, click **Insert** then **Break...** then **Page Break**. In Word 2007, select **Page** from the **Breaks** section of the **Page Layout** tab.

7 Design the first inside page of your leaflet by entering a list of events for the first half of the day.

8 Insert a column break and design the second inside page by entering a list of events for the second half of the day.

9 Print the leaflet on both sides of a single sheet of paper.

b Apply your knowledge of page layouts and breaks to set three columns and create a six-page leaflet.

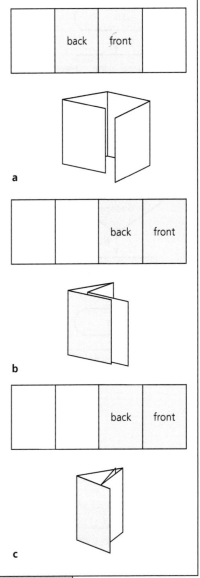

Figure 6.3.3 Three ways to fold an eight-page leaflet

SUMMARY QUESTIONS

1 a Define the term **flyer**.

b State at least four guidelines that should be followed when designing flyers.

2 Outline the steps that should be followed to create a four-page programme for an event.

6.4 Flow charts

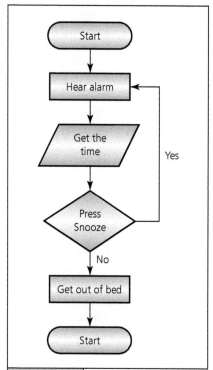

Figure 6.4.1 | A simple flow chart

A **flow chart** is a pictorial representation of the steps, sequence and relationship of the various operations involved in a process, such as how to send a fax or how to change the toner cartridge in a laser printer. Figure 6.4.1 shows a simple flow chart. You will observe that arrows are used to show the direction and order of the process steps.

Each shape or **process symbol** in a flow chart has a specific meaning. Table 6.4.1 lists commonly used flow chart symbols.

Table 6.4.1 Commonly used flow chart symbols

Terminator	An *oval* that is used to show the beginning and end of the process.
Process	A *rectangle* that indicates each operation in the process.
Data or I/O	A *parallelogram* that is used to show inputs to and outputs from the process.
Decision	A *diamond* that represents the point at which a choice is made that leads to different processing steps.
Connector	A *circle* that depicts a jump from one point in the process flow to another.

Preparing effective flow charts

There is no single way to prepare a flow chart. However, the following guidelines will help you to create flow charts that effectively communicate your message:

• List every stage in a logical order.
• Use the same size symbols.
• Maintain even spacing around symbols and ensure that they line up neatly.
• Use arrows as connectors to link each process symbol.
• Ensure that only one line goes into a decision symbol; however, two or three lines can come out of this symbol – with the following exception:

   – only one line should come out of a *process symbol*.

• Avoid very colourful symbols as they are distracting.
• Use short, clear statements in your process symbols.
• Ensure that your text is readable.

How to create a flow chart

You can insert a flow chart into your word-processing document in the same way you would insert a shape. Revise the steps for this in 5.18.

To line up your shapes evenly:

1 Hold the **Shift** key on the keyboard and click on each shape to select them all.

2 If you are using Microsoft Word 2003, click **Draw** on the drawing toolbar and point to **Align or Distribute**. If you are using Word 2007, select the **Align** drop-down on the drawing toolbar.

3 Click **Align Left**.

4 Repeat step 2.

5 Click **Distribute vertically**.

Connectors are lines that link shapes in a flow chart. You must add connectors between each of the shapes.

To add a connector:

1 In Word 2003 select **AutoShapes** and point to **Connectors**. In Word 2007 select **Shapes**; you will then be able to see the **Lines** available for connectors. Click the connector line you want.

2 Point and click to where you want to anchor the connector e.g. under the first shape.

3 Point to the other shape, and then click where you want the connector to end. In some programs you will need to click and drag the connector.

Note: You should usually insert a text box to place text near to a line or connector to indicate what the connection refers to, for example *yes* or *no*.

ACTIVITY

Create the flow chart shown below:

Troubleshooting a light

SUMMARY QUESTIONS

1 a Define a flow chart.

  b Name and explain the purpose of at least four flow chart symbols.

2 Marcie the receptionist tells her trainee the following: 'When the phone rings, this is what you should do: Answer the telephone. Find out the purpose of the call. If it is an order, take the customer's name and telephone number. Inform the customer that a sales representative will return the call. Then thank the customer and hang up. If it is not an order, transfer the call to the relevant department'.

Construct a flow chart entitled *Telephone Procedures* to represent Marcie's instructions.

An **organisation chart** or *organisational chart* is a diagram that represents the structure of an organisation in terms of levels of authority, lines of responsibility and reporting relationships. The organisation chart usually shows the managers and sub-workers who make up an organisation. It provides a quick, easy-to-understand view of the formal relationships in the organisation. It can also be used as a planning tool when developing or restructuring an organisation.

Creating organisation charts

An organisation chart is created using blocks and lines. Although a horizontal layout can be used, a vertical layout is more common. In the vertical layout, the chart is read from top to bottom, whereas in the horizontal layout it is read from left to right.

• A block is used to represent a single position such as *Accountant* or a department such as *Human Resources*.

• The topmost block represents the position with the highest level of authority.

• The other positions are arranged in descending order of authority with the exception of secretaries or administrative assistants.

• Positions having the same authority or importance are normally placed at the same level on the chart. However, where there is not enough space, they may be typed on different horizontal lines.

• Administrative assistants or secretaries are placed subordinate to their supervisors but to the side. They are not represented in the main vertical structure.

• Where there are many members holding the same position, you can simply list the title with the number of people assigned to that title in that department (for example, Sales Representative 12).

• Use a solid line to represent a formal, direct relationship. Use a dashed line to show an indirect relationship, such as where one employee or department advises but does not have direct authority over another.

Practise inserting and modifying organisation charts. You can create these manually by using the same tools used for flow charts.

Some word-processing programs have preset layouts that can be used (Figure 6.5.1). In Microsoft Word 2003, you can find the option to add an organisation chart in the **Diagram Gallery** which is available in the **Insert** menu. Word 2007 uses **SmartArt**, which can be found on the **Insert** ribbon. You can then add and edit relationships as needed. Use the Help function if you are unsure about how to use the different options.

Figure 6.5.1 Examples of hierarchical chart layouts available in a word-processing program

Example

Let us see how these principles can be applied to produce an organisation chart.

Tropical Fusion Limited is led by a managing director who is supported by her administrative assistant. There are five departments:

1 research and development (R&D) with six workers

2 production with 40 factory workers

3 health and safety (H&S) with four health and safety officers

4 marketing with 16 workers

5 finance with five workers.

Each department is led by a manager, with the exception of the finance department, which is led by the chief accountant. The chief accountant has the same level of authority as the four managers. The health and safety manager is expected to advise all departments. Examine the organisation chart shown in Figure 6.5.2 to see how these relationships are represented.

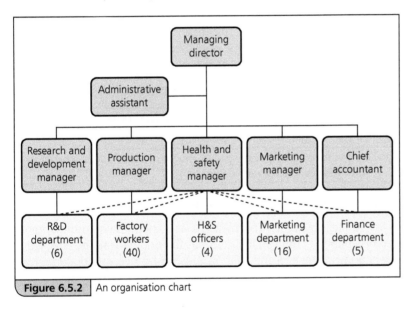

| **Figure 6.5.2** | An organisation chart |

You can produce a document containing a variety of charts and graphs, for example pie charts, histograms, line graphs and area charts. Leave a clear line space before and after a graph or chart.

Creating embedded and linked charts and graphs

Charts or graphs can be created in both word-processing (5.18) and spreadsheet (4.6) programs. You can also create the chart or graph in a spreadsheet program and then paste it into a word-processing document. This may be a more useful method if you are working with a lot of data that is already stored in a spreadsheet program. You can paste an existing chart or graph as either an **embedded** or a **linked object**.

How to paste an embedded chart or graph

An embedded chart is *static*. This means that it does not change when changes are made to the original file from which it was copied. Table 6.6.1 shows you how to create an embedded chart or graph.

Table 6.6.1 How to create an embedded chart or graph

1	Open the spreadsheet program, enter data and create a graph or chart.
2	Click on the graph or chart, and **Copy** it.
3	Go to the word-processing document, position the cursor where you want the chart to appear and **Paste** it.

How to paste a linked chart or graph

A linked file is *dynamic*. This means that it changes when the original data is changed. You can instruct that the original data be checked for changes whenever the chart in the word-processing document is opened. Table 6.6.2 shows you how to create a linked chart.

Table 6.6.2 How to create a linked chart or graph

1	Open a spreadsheet program and create and save the spreadsheet containing the data and graph or chart. **Copy** the graph or chart.
2	Go to the word-processing document and position the cursor where you want the chart to appear.
3	You will need to select the paste option that will allow you to paste the link (see Figure 6.6.1 as an example of the options that might be available). In Microsoft Word 2007, this is done by clicking **Paste Special...** from the list of options.
4	Click **Paste link** and then select **Microsoft Office Excel Chart Object**.
5	Click **OK**.

Figure 6.6.1 Paste options

Adding a chart title

It is good practice to have a title for your chart. To do this you first need to select the chart.

In Microsoft Word 2003:

1 Click **Chart**, and then **Chart Options...** on the menu bar. The **Chart Options** box will be displayed.

2 Type the title in the **Chart title** box.

In Word 2007:

1 Click the **Chart Tools** tab that appears when the chart is selected.

2 Ensure you are under the **Layout** tab of the **Chart Tools** ribbon and select the option you want from the **Chart Title** drop down list.

Note: The row and column headings in the datasheet are used to label the values on the vertical and horizontal axes. To change these labels, you must change the headings on the datasheet.

SUMMARY QUESTIONS

1 Explain the difference between a linked and an embedded chart.

2 a Create a pie chart to represent the following data in Excel and save the file as **Exam Grades**.

				Grade				
	I	II	III	IV	V	VI	UNG	ABS
	16	23	45	29	18	7	3	2

b Type the following memorandum from the Principal of South-Central Secondary School to the Mathematics department, on A5 paper, using the current date:

> The following ch. represents the performance of our maths students in the most recent csec exam. Please prep. a list of suggestions for the improvement of our school's performance in this subject for presentation in the Strategic Planning session to be held on Sept. 25 at 1:00 pm in the audio-visual room.
>
> (stet)

c Insert the chart at the end of the memorandum as a **linked** object, with the title *CSEC Mathematics Results*, and print the memo.

d The Principal had entered an incorrect figure for Grade V. Adjust the 18 to 28 and print the corrected memo.

e The Principal has decided that a column chart will be more effective. Print a memo with the new chart type.

Newsletters

At the end of this topic you should be able to:

- produce creative and effective newsletters using appropriate formatting.

DID YOU KNOW?

Serifs are the slight projections that finish off the strokes of letters in some font types. Fonts with serifs, such as Times New Roman, Baskerville and Garamond, are generally easier to read than those without serifs.

DID YOU KNOW?

Desktop publishing programs such as Microsoft Publisher contain attractively designed newsletter templates.

A **newsletter** is a short, regularly published bulletin that is distributed to interested people, such as members of an organisation, business clients or the general public. It is a simple version of a newspaper. A newsletter is published to:

- inform
- instruct
- advise
- advertise
- announce
- remind
- build relationships.

Newsletters enable you to apply many of the word-processing skills you have already developed, such as:

- formatting font, including spacing, colour, size and effects
- paragraph formatting such as spacing, indents and alignment
- page layouts such as margins, columns and borders
- inserting and modifying graphics, including WordArt, photographs, graphs and charts.

Preparing newsletters

Table 6.7.1 lists the guidelines you should follow when preparing a newsletter.

Table 6.7.1 Guidelines for preparing newsletters

✓	Use a relatively short nameplate (newsletter title) that can be displayed across the top of the page in large font.
✓	Display the issue number and date of publication under the title, in small font.
✓	Keep your layout clear and uncluttered. One way to do this is to use sufficiently large margins and spaces between columns.
✓	You can vary the appearance and add interest by using two or three columns in some sections of the newsletter.
✓	Use a single distinctive easy-to-read font for headlines. Leave a clear line space before and after headlines.
✓	Use an easy-to-read font such as Times New Roman for the body text.
✓	Ensure that your writing is free of errors in spelling, grammar, punctuation, sentence construction and word usage.
✓	Avoid overly long sentences. It is better to break a long idea into two shorter sentences.
✓	Make sure that your articles are informative, interesting and entertaining.

See Figure 6.7.1 for an example of a newsletter. Note the instructions on how to introduce **drop caps** into your documents.

Tips and Tricks

in Electronic Document Preparation

Issue 2 Volume 1   **Use current date**

Colour Matters

My teachers have frequently told me that I should not write my assignments with my favourite red, orange or hot pink gel pens. I could not see their reasoning. Don't they use their red ink pens to scrawl comments all over my essays and examination scripts? I decided to do some research on the issue, and discovered that the colour red may not be as rosy as I thought.

 Red ink is normally used by accountants to indicate that there is a deficit. That is why *in the red* is used to describe a business that is spending more than it earns.

Have you ever had to wait an unusually long time to have a matter processed by a government office? Then it was probably tied up in *red tape*. This term refers to the many rules and regulations that often slow down the rate at which an official matter is handled. Such delays can make a busy person *see red*.

The colour red is believed to stimulate aggression. That is why matadors wave a *red flag* at a bull. However, scientists have now proven that bulls are colour-blind, so they might be equally provoked if the matador waves the white flag of peace.

It was also interesting to discover that in many Asian countries, the colour red is used to write the names of dead people, never the living. In other countries, it is considered an insult to write a letter or card in red. Ignorance of these cultural standards can leave a business professional *red in the face*.

Positive meanings of red

If you are a red lover though, do not despair. There are also positive meanings associated with the colour. Red hearts and roses are associated with love. We roll out *the red carpet* to welcome and honour a special guest. Holidays on a calendar are printed in red, so a special occasion is called a *red letter day* and might be a time for a celebrant to *paint the town red* with some friends. My research showed me that I should not indulge my love for red when preparing business documents and class assignments. In addition to all the negative connotations and cultural taboos, it is more difficult to read. Instead, I should use dark blue or black ink. That information is enough to give me *the blues*!

Draw Attention with Drop Caps

Have you ever wondered how to get those large decorative letters that start off the first paragraph in some publications? That effect is called *drop caps*. While it might look complicated, it is quite easy to do. To add a drop cap:

1 Click in the paragraph in which you want to apply the drop cap.
2 In Word 2003 or earlier, click **Format** then **Drop Cap....** The **Drop Cap** dialogue box will appear.
3 Select the drop setting you want to use.
4 Select the font you want to use for the drop cap.
5 Select the number of lines by which you want the cap dropped and the distance from the text. Click **OK**.
In Word 2007 to 2010, click **Insert** and then **Drop Cap**. You can set the font and number of lines by selecting **Drop Cap Options...** to display the **Drop Cap** dialogue box as above.
After inserting the drop cap, you can format the text by changing its font, colour and effects.

Figure 6.7.1 | A newsletter

SUMMARY QUESTIONS

1 Reproduce the newsletter shown in Figure 6.7.1. Use WordArt for the title text and Arial Rounded MT Bold in size 18 for the subtitle. Use Arial Rounded MT Bold size 16 for headlines and Times New Roman, size 12 for all other text. You may use a different graphic.

2 Navin, the secretary of your school's book club, has asked you to guide him in creating a newsletter. Explain to Navin:

a at least four reasons why a newsletter might be published

b at least six guidelines he should follow when preparing a newsletter.

Reports and proposals

At the end of this topic you should be able to:

• prepare reports and proposals using appropriate formatting.

A company's annual financial report

An investigation into a complaint made by an employee

The outcome of a study on the feasibility of opening a new branch

A health and safety officer's report on an accident

The analysis of data gathered from a customer survey

Figure 6.8.1 Examples of reports in business situations

Reports

A report is a document that communicates information, usually observations or the findings of an enquiry. It is used to present facts, figures and data analyses accurately, clearly and logically. The report should be concise, and focus only on information that relates to its purpose.

Reports are prepared in many business situations, as shown in Figure 6.8.1.

The layout of a report

If you are not given specific instructions, you may use the following layout for a report.

Table 6.8.1 Layout of a report

1	**Heading or title page** – shows information such as the writer's name and department; the name and department of the person or people for whom the report is written; the reference number for the report, if there is one; and the title of the report.
2	**Table of contents** – lists the sections of the report and the corresponding page numbers. This is not necessary in a short or informal report.
3	**Terms of reference** or **abstract** – states why it is necessary for the report to be compiled and what it aims to achieve.
4	**Body** – this section consists of an introduction that states the reasons for the report; a description of the methodology used to gather the information; a description of the research undertaken and details of the findings; a **conclusion and recommendations** section that summarises the findings and suggests an appropriate course of action; and a list of **references** showing the sources of information taken from books, websites and other publications.
5	The report might also contain an **appendix** that provides the detailed statistical data or other pertinent information that was analysed.

Sometimes you are given a word limit for reports. If you find that your report is too short, do additional research or further analysis of your statistical data. If the report is too long, you should delete any information that is not crucial.

Proposals

A proposal is a detailed and persuasive presentation of an idea that is used to gain the interest and support of the reader. Proposals are written for a number of different purposes, such as to:

• offer a solution to a problem or a course of action in response to a need

• describe in detail the programme for a proposed investigation

• request to engage in business with another company

• ask for financial support for a project.

The layout of a proposal

There are no set rules for the layout of a proposal. However, the ideas should flow in a logical order. Table 6.8.2 lists one suggested layout.

Table 6.8.2 Layout of a proposal

1	**Title** – this is a clear and unambiguous statement that identifies the proposal.
2	**Project overview** – this presents a summary of the main details of the proposed project.
3	**Project details** – this section presents information on the goals and objectives, anticipated benefits, methods, background information on the people involved, available resources and needed resources, including a budget.
4	**Evaluation plan** – this outlines how the project's effectiveness will be determined.
5	**Appendix** – this contains supporting documents such as testimonials and survey questionnaires.

EXAM TIP

Always proofread your documents to identify and correct errors in spelling, grammar, word usage, punctuation and sentence construction.

Preparing reports and proposals

The following are some general guidelines for the preparation of reports and proposals:

- Unless otherwise instructed, use Times New Roman, size 12, with double line spacing, a clear line space between paragraphs and 2.54 cm (1 inch) margins.
- The tense should be consistent; preferably past tense should be used for reports and future tense for proposals.
- Reports and proposals should not be written in the first person (*I* or *we*).
- Headings should be used for each section of the document. Long sections should be divided with appropriate subheadings.
- Figures such as charts and graphs should be clearly represented, preferably with white backgrounds. They should be numbered consecutively and should be given appropriate captions.

DID YOU KNOW?

To make report writing easier, you can write or type the outline first. Then insert the details under each heading.

ACTIVITY

1 **a** Use the Internet to search for the keywords **sample report**. Observe the structure and layouts of the samples you find.

  b Do a survey of your classmates to determine their viewpoints on the use of cellphones as a tool for teaching and learning. You may use questions such as:

   Would you like to receive messages on your phone from your teachers, about things such as class notes, projects and assignments? ☐ Yes ☐ No

  c Prepare a report of your findings.

2 The students of Form 4 want to raise funds to have their classrooms air-conditioned. Prepare an appropriate project proposal for the school's principal.

SUMMARY QUESTIONS

1 Outline at least three essential differences between a proposal and a report.

2 Summarise the formatting and layout that should be used for:

  a a report

  b a proposal.

Press releases

A **press release** is a concisely written document that contains information and is sent to a media house in the hope that it will be published. Other names for a press release include news release, media release and press statement.

Types of press release

Table 6.9.1 lists some types of press release and their purpose.

Table 6.9.1 Types of press release

Type of news release	Purpose
General news release	Used to disseminate information that is of interest, such as the merging of two companies.
Launch release	Used to stimulate interest in a new development, such as the introduction of a website, the opening of a new branch, or the introduction of a new product or service.
Product release	Used to give information about a product, such as innovative features or the winning of an award for excellence.
Executive or staff news release	Used to give information about a newly hired or promoted individual.
Event release	Used to give information about an event such as a seminar, exhibition, health screening, community sports day or a school bazaar.
Public service advisory	Used to provide information that is for the safety or welfare of the general public, such as what to do in the event of a hurricane or earthquake or how to eradicate insect pests.

Preparing a press release

When preparing a press release you should:

- be concise, while providing sufficient details to communicate the information effectively
- use an attention-grabbing headline to capture interest
- use the first paragraph to briefly summarise the main news of the release
- always write in the third person; do not use *I* or *we* unless it is in a direct quote
- type in double line spacing, with a clear line space between paragraphs.

Press release format

There is no single format for press releases. However, they should contain the items listed in Table 6.9.2.

Table 6.9.2 Contents of a press release

1	A cover page or heading that displays: **a** the sender's address and telephone number (a letterhead may be used) **b** the heading 'News Release' or 'Press Release' **c** the embargo or terms of the release – usually the date after which the release may be published **d** the writer's name and position (if sent from an organisation)
2	The date the release is created
3	The subject of the release
4	The information for publication
5	The word **end** or three crosshatches ### to signify the end of the information for publication

SUMMARY QUESTIONS

1 Describe at least four types of press release.

2 Outline at least six guidelines for the preparation of a press release.

3 Compose and type a press release for a school or community event.

A news release may be prepared in full blocked format, as is shown in Figure 6.9.1.

Southwark Secondary School
437 Coral Street, Castries, St Lucia
Phone 1 717 171 7171-2 Email admin@southwarksec.org

To Learn is to Change

PRESS RELEASE

Embargo   For Immediate Release

From   Verniece Anderson, Coordinating Teacher

CARIBBEAN YOUTH E-RALLY TO SAVE THE ENVIRONMENT

(Castries, 13 May 20XX) -- Southwark Secondary School will be hosting the first ever Caribbean Youth E-Rally on 27 May 20XX, by using Internet-based videoconferencing to bring together students from throughout the region.

Entitled **Our Earth, Our Future**, this rally is the collaborative effort of students of Environmental Studies, Information Technology and Electronic Document Preparation and Management.

According to **Verniece Anderson**, coordinating teacher of the **Our Earth, Our Future Initiative**, "This E-Rally will showcase the dynamism, commitment and creativity of our youth. The students are eager to meet with their Caribbean neighbours to develop viable solutions to environmental issues that are affecting out region."

Southwark students have been using email and Skype to communicate with peers from several Caribbean countries over the past few months. They have been discussing issues such as environmental degradation, global warming and sustainable development. The overwhelming success of these discussions has led to this initiative to create what is expected to be the largest ever video conference in the region.

Southwark Secondary School is committed to providing total quality education that will produce young leaders who have the knowledge, skills, aptitudes and attitudes to make valuable contributions to their national, regional and global communities. Consequently the school emphasises the importance of collaborative problem solving, technological competence and the development of a strong social conscience.

End

For more information please contact **Verniece Anderson** at **1 717 171 7171** or **v.anderson@southwarksec.org**.

Encl: Videoconference programme

Figure 6.9.1 | A press release

6.10 Legal documents

LEARNING OUTCOMES

At the end of this topic you should be able to:

- outline the general guidelines for preparing legal documents, including endorsements
- use appropriate formatting to create these documents.

A **legal document** is used to officially record an agreement that is intended to be enforceable in a court of law. Table 6.10.1 lists some terms you will come across in legal documents.

Table 6.10.1 Terms associated with legal documents

Party: each person or organisation involved in a legal agreement.
Draft: a copy of the document that is sent to each party for approval or amendments. The draft is returned with either the statement 'approved as drawn', or with changes written in red print.
Engrossment: final copy of a legal document for signature.
Counterpart: a duplicate copy of the legal document for signature.

The endorsement

An **endorsement** is a brief statement of the nature of the business document and is printed on the outside of the envelope into which the document is placed. An endorsement can also be typed on the outside of a document, positioned so that it will be visible after it has been folded into thirds or quarters.

The following are typed in the endorsement:

- date of signature
- name and description of document
- names of parties
- name and address of solicitor.

01 April 20XX
This sealed packet contains the
Last Will and Testament of

Jericho Teesdale
of Apartment 2A, Building 4,
Dickens Housing Complex,
Portmore

whereof

Vincent Teesdale
of 1900 Columbus Heights,
Ocho Rios

and

Kentwood Charles, Solicitor of
1345A Caledonia Avenue,
Kingstown

are appointed executors, and the
same are brought into the
Registry of the Supreme Court
in Kingston by me for safe
custody, there to remain
deposited until after my death.

Figure 6.10.1 An endorsement

DID YOU KNOW?

People skilled in document preparation can undergo further training to become legal assistants (also known as paralegals).

Preparing legal documents

The guidelines, samples and exercises that are presented here are to help you to become familiar with the general principles that govern the preparation of legal documents (see Table 6.10.2). They should not be used to prepare official documents, because different countries have specific instructions for the preparation of each legal document. It is therefore advisable to have legal documents prepared or reviewed by qualified lawyers.

Table 6.10.2 Guidelines for the preparation of legal documents

Paper size and layout	Print on A4 or legal-sized paper in portrait orientation. Revise 4.3 so you know what margin sizes to use.
Paragraph formatting	Ensure that paragraphs are left-aligned or fully justified, in double-line spacing, and in full block format. Short lines should be filled in with a series of unspaced hyphens. This is done by setting a right tab with a leader at the right margin of the document.
Use of upper case	Use upper case for the names of people when they are first stated or stated in the attestation clause. Traditionally, upper case is used for terms that have a specific and important meaning within the legal document (e.g. HEREBY and BETWEEN).
Construction	Do not use abbreviations. Type out numbers, such as dates and currency amounts, in full. For example, the date 22/09/2015 should be typed as: The twenty-second day of September, Two Thousand and Fifteen. However, numerals are used for numbers in addresses such as street or apartment numbers and postal codes. Use simple, unambiguous sentences. Do not use legal terms unless you are certain of their meaning and correct usage. Break a lengthy document into sections with clear headings. Proofread the document to ensure that it is free of all errors.
Corrections or changes	Ideally the document should be checked and corrected before it is printed. If the document has already been printed, draw a single neat line through the text to be changed, ensuring that the text is still visible. The person(s) signing the document should initial all changes made. Do not erase or use liquid paper.

Folding

A legal document is folded in either three or four equal parts.

Trifold: Place the sheet face up on the table. Turn the bottom third up and crease flat. Turn the top third down and crease flat.

Quarter fold: Place the sheet face up on the table. Turn the bottom edge up to meet the top. Crease flat. Take the folded edge, turn upwards to meet the top and crease flat again.

TRY IT!

Type the endorsement shown in Figure 6.10.1 on legal paper in landscape orientation by doing the following:

1 Set your document in landscape orientation.

2 Set three columns of equal width.

3 Insert a column break so that your cursor is in the middle column.

4 Type the endorsement, such as is shown in Figure 6.10.1.

SUMMARY QUESTIONS

1 Differentiate between an engrossment and an endorsement.

2 What is the difference between a draft and a counterpart?

3 State at least six general guidelines that should be followed when preparing legal documents.

6.11

Wills

At the end of this topic you should be able to:

• prepare wills using appropriate formatting.

A **will** is a legal declaration that clearly states the way in which a person's assets should be distributed after his or her death. Table 6.11.1 provides the definition of some key terms associated with wills.

Table 6.11.1 Terms associated with wills

Term	Definition
Assets	Property such as land, a building, automobile or piece of equipment.
Estate	Assets are collectively called the estate.
Testator (male); **testatrix** (female)	The owner of the assets, whose will is being prepared.
Beneficiaries	The people or organisations to receive the assets.
Executor (male); **executrix** (female)	The person responsible for ensuring that the terms of the will are carried out.

Preparing a will

The layout of a will is determined by the laws and customs of the country in which it is to be executed. However, the following are some general guidelines for preparing a will:

• The first paragraph should begin with the words **Last Will and Testament of** followed by the name and address and of the testator/testatrix (see Figure 6.11.1).

• The rest of the will should be laid out in paragraphs numbered in sequence.

• The first words of each paragraph should be in block capitals and underlined.

• Each paragraph should consist of a single unpunctuated sentence.

• All names should be typed out in full and in block capitals.

• The first words of each new statement and connecting words such as HEREBY, WHEREAS, BETWEEN should be capitalised.

• Sums of money should be stated in words in block capitals followed by the sum in figures in brackets.

• The will must end with an **attestation clause** that states the conditions under which the document was signed and the names and signatures of the testator/testatrix and witnesses.

• A closing parenthesis is used at the end of each line of the attestation clause. Alternatively, a single vertical line may be used.

This is the Last Will and Testament

- of me - CARYN JAMES-HERNANDEZ

of 89 Eversley Court

Point Fortin

1 I HEREBY REVOKE all former Wills and testamentary dispositions made by me under the law of the Republic of Trinidad and Tobago and declare that the proper law of this my Will shall be the law of the Republic of Trinidad and Tobago

2 I APPOINT my husband VINCENT HERNANDEZ to be the Executor and Trustee of this my Will (hereinafter called 'My Trustees' which expression shall include the Trustee or Trustees for the time being hereof) AND in case the aforesaid shall die in my lifetime or shall refuse or be unable to act in the office of Executor and Trustee then I APPOINT STEPHON DE CRUZ, of De Cruz and Clark, 8928 Court Street, Point Fortin to fill the vacancy in the office of Executor and Trustee hereof

3 I GIVE the following legacies:

   i   I give to my son VINCE HERNANDEZ absolutely and free of tax the sum of <u>FIFTY THOUSAND</u> dollars ($50 000)

   ii I give to my daughter JACYNTH HERNANDEZ absolutely all of my jewellery PROVIDED THAT if the said Jacynth Hernandez shall predecease me or fail to survive me by thirty days then I GIVE the said legacy absolutely to my goddaughter NELINE DAWES

4 I GIVE DEVISE AND BEQUEATH the residue of my estate both real and personal of whatsoever nature and wheresoever situated to my husband VINCENT HERNANDEZ PROVIDED THAT if the said Vincent Hernandez shall predecease me or fail to survive me by 30 days then I give the residue of my estate or the part of it affected equally to those of my children who survive me

Signed by the said CARYN JAMES-HERNANDEZ)
as and for her last Will and Testament)
in the presence of us both and we in her presence)
and in the presence of each)
have hereunto subscribed our names as witnesses:-)
)
....)
Signature of witness)
)
....)
Signature of witness)
)
....)
CARYN JAMES-HERNANDEZ)

Figure 6.11.1 A will

SUMMARY QUESTIONS

1 Define the following terms as they relate to a will:

   a testator   c estate

   b beneficiary   d executrix.

2 Outline at least five guidelines that should be followed when preparing a will.

3 Type and print the will shown in Figure 6.11.1 on legal paper in double-line spacing with appropriate margins.

Leases

At the end of this topic you should be able to:

• prepare leases using appropriate formatting.

A **lease** is an agreement by which one person conveys to another party the rights to possess and use an asset for a specified period of time. Table 6.12.1 provides the definition of some key terms associated with leases.

Table 6.12.1 Terms associated with leases

Term	Definition
Lessor	The owner of the asset. In the case of land or buildings, the lessor is also called the landlord.
Lessee	The person or organisation receiving permission to use the asset.
Tenant	A person or group who pays rent to use or occupy property owned by another.
Security deposit	A sum of money that a tenant must pay in advance to the lessor to cover the cost of damage to the property.

A lease is meant to protect the rights of both the lessor and the lessee. It is legally enforceable, so it must be prepared according to the laws of the country in which it is to be executed. The lease is no longer binding if either the lessor or the lessee fails to comply with any of its terms. The person who breaks the lease may be subject to legal action and a financial penalty.

Preparing a lease

There is no single way to prepare a lease. However, a well-prepared lease will usually have the following elements:

• a specific description of the asset, such as:
  - the type, size and address of a building, apartment or parcel of land
  - the name, model and serial number of an automobile or piece of equipment
• the duration, start date and end date of the agreement
• required payments such as rent and security deposit, when it is due and the person(s) responsible for its payment
• conditions under which the asset may be used, including the specific rights and responsibilities of the lessor and the lessee
• terms and conditions under which the lease may be renewed.

Two copies of the lease should be prepared. Both copies should be signed by all parties. One copy remains with the lessor and the other is given to the lessee.

Figure 6.12.2 shows an example of a lease.

Lease agreements are also prepared for the rental of vehicles and equipment.

Figure 6.12.1 What essential information should a lease contain?

PARAMARIBO, SURINAME

1 **Parties:** This lease is made on (Insert today's date) between AVERIL JOSEPH of Mozart Street, Paramaribo, hereinafter called Landlord, and hereinafter called Tenant.

2 **Properties:** Landlord hereby lets the 10 000 square feet commercial property known as Level One, Building 2372, Corona Street, Paramaribo, to Tenant for the terms of this Agreement.

3 **Term:** The term of this Agreement shall be for one year beginning on (Insert today's date) and ending on (Insert date one year from today).

4 **Rent:** The total rent for said property shall be TWENTY-FOUR THOUSAND dollars ($24 000), to be paid by Tenant monthly in amounts of TWO THOUSAND dollars ($2000) due and payable on the first day of each month.

5 **Security Deposit:** Tenant shall deposit with the Landlord FOUR THOUSAND dollars ($4000) to be held as security deposit.

This deposit will be returned in full when this lease expires if, after inspection by the Landlord, the premises are in good condition (normal wear and tear excepted) and Tenant owes no back rent.

6 **Subleasing:** Tenant shall not lease or sublease nor assign the premises without the written consent of the Landlord (but consent of the Landlord shall not be unreasonably withheld).

7 **Access to Premises:** Landlord may enter premises at reasonable times for the purposes of inspection, maintenance or repair, and to show the premises to buyers or prospective tenants.

8 **Notice of Access:** In all instances, except those of emergency or abandonment, the Landlord shall give 24-hour notice prior to such an entry.

9 **Maintenance of Premises:** Tenant agrees to occupy the premises and shall keep same in good condition, reasonable wear and tear excepted, and shall not make any alterations without the written consent of the Landlord.

10 **Use of Premises:** Tenant agrees not to use the premises in such a manner as to disturb the peace, quiet, security and safety of other tenants in the building and the immediate neighbours.

Tenant further agrees not to maintain public nuisance and to conduct strictly legal activities on the premises.

11 **Termination:** Tenant shall, upon termination of this Agreement, vacate and return the premises in the same condition that it was received, less reasonable wear and tear, and other damages beyond the control of the Tenant.

12 **Renewal:** This lease will automatically renew for a period of TWELVE months if neither party ends the Lease at the end of the original term or the end of any renewal term and if Landlord does not send a renewal notice.

SIGNED SEALED AND DELIVERED
by the within named AVERIL JOSEPH
in the presence of

....
WITNESS   AVERIL JOSEPH

SIGNED SEALED AND DELIVERED
by the within named CARISSA NEALE
in the presence of

....
WITNESS   CARISSA NEALE

Figure 6.12.2 A lease

SUMMARY QUESTIONS

1 Define the following terms as they relate to a lease:

   a asset   b lessor   c lessee.

2 Outline at least four details that should be included in a lease.

3 Prepare and print the lease shown in Figure 6.12.2 in double-line spacing on legal paper.

Conveyance documents

A **conveyance document**, also called a deed of conveyance, is a legal document that transfers the ownership of property from one party to another. The deed of conveyance shows the person or organisation that has the legal right to possess the property. Table 6.13.1 provides the definition of some key terms associated with conveyance documents.

Table 6.13.1 Terms associated with conveyance documents

Term	Definition
Grantor or vendor	The recorded owner of the property to be conveyed.
Grantee or purchaser	The recipient of the property.
Consideration	The price paid for the property.

Preparing a conveyance document

The laws of each country specify the content and format of conveyance documents. These must be prepared by a qualified legal practitioner. The following are general guidelines for conveyance documents:

- The document must be formatted according to the general guidelines presented in 6.10.
- The entire document must be clearly set out in logical order.
- The deed must name the grantor and the grantee.
- There must be clear description of the property to be conveyed, so that it can be unmistakably identified. This includes its size, nature and specific location.
- The document must clearly state the conditions under which the grantor or vendor presently holds the property.
- It must clearly state the terms under which the grantee or purchaser is receiving the property, including:
  - the sale price (consideration), amount of advance payment if any and the remaining balance to be paid on the execution of the sale deed
  - the mode of payment, such as by a certified cheque.
- The deed must be witnessed by two people, one for each party. The full name and address of each witness must be included.

See Figure 6.13.1 as an example of a conveyance document.

DEED OF CONVEYANCE

ST JOHN'S, ANTIGUA AND BARBUDA

This DEED is made (*insert date, spelled out in full*) BETWEEN KESHAN HARAN of 23 Hastings Heights, Temple Street, St John's ('the Vendor') of the one part and DELBY JAYMES of Lionel Hurst Street, St John's ('the Purchaser') of the other part.

WHEREAS:

1 The Vendor is the Estate owner in respect of the property HEREBY assured for his own use and benefit absolutely free from encumbrance.

2 The Vendor has agreed with the Purchaser to sell to him the said property free from encumbrances for the price of THREE HUNDRED AND TWENTY THOUSAND dollars ($320 000).

NOW THIS DEED WITNESSES:

THAT in consideration of the sum of THREE HUNDRED AND TWENTY THOUSAND dollars ($320 000) now paid by the Purchaser to the Vendor by certified cheque (the receipt of which the Vendor HEREBY acknowledges) the Vendor as Beneficial Owner HEREBY conveys to the Purchaser ALL THAT land thereto described hereunder written:

That parcel of land two hundred and fifty metres by three hundred metres having a frontage to Keith Lane to the North, and bounded by Lot Number 457 to the West, and bounded by Lot Number 459 to the East and having a frontage to Industry Street to the South, as delineated and coloured pink on the plan annexed to this Deed.

TO HOLD unto the Purchaser DELBY JAYMES

IN EXECUTION WHEREOF the parties to this deed have hereunto set their signatures on the day and year first above written.

SIGNED AND DELIVERED by the said KESHAN HARAN

as and for his act and deed in the presence of

....

WITNESS   KESHAN HARAN

Of ....

....

SIGNED AND DELIVERED by the said DELBY JAYMES
as and for his act and deed in the presence of

....

WITNESS   DELBY JAYMES

Of ....

....

Figure 6.13.1 A deed of conveyance

SUMMARY QUESTIONS

1 State at least four details that must be included in a conveyance document.

2 Type and print the conveyance document shown in Figure 6.13.1, using appropriate page, paragraph and font formatting.

Agreements

An agreement is a document that states the relative rights and duties of two or more parties. One common example is a hire purchase agreement.

A **hire purchase agreement** is made when a buyer wishes to immediately use a product but does not have enough money to pay the full purchase price. Under this agreement the buyer pays specified portions of the cost over a period of time. The seller remains the owner of the goods, until the cost of the good plus agreed interest and charges are paid off in full. Ownership is transferred to the hirer when the final payment is made.

Table 6.14.1 explains some key terms used in hire purchase agreements.

Table 6.14.1 Terms associated with hire purchase agreements

Term	Definition
Goods	Those products that are identified in the agreement, such as a car, furniture or appliance.
Owner	The person or organisation that is selling the goods under the agreement.
Hirer	The customer who enters into the agreement with the owner.
Hire purchase price	The total sum payable over the duration of the hire purchase agreement in order to complete the purchase of the goods.
Hire purchase instalment	The portion of the hire purchase price, also called the rent, that is paid at a specified interval to allow ownership of the goods to pass to the purchaser.

Preparing a hire purchase agreement

Unless you are otherwise instructed, follow the guidelines in 6.10. A hire purchase agreement must contain the information shown in Table 6.14.2.

Table 6.14.2 Contents of a hire purchase agreement

✓	The words **Hire purchase agreement** prominently displayed
✓	The description of the goods
✓	Where the goods are to be kept
✓	The date when the hire purchase commences
✓	The cash price of the goods, that is, the cost paid if it had been a cash purchase
✓	The deposit required, if any
✓	The number of instalments the hirer has to pay
✓	The frequency of the instalments, such as weekly, monthly or quarterly
✓	The amount of each instalment
✓	The hire purchase price (the total of all instalments plus fees) that the hirer must pay to own the goods
✓	The costs and penalties the hirer is liable to pay if he/she cannot meet the hirer's repayments

VALUE CITY ENTERPRISES LTD
Hire Purchase Agreement

DATE OF THIS AGREEMENT...

FULL NAME OF HIRER...

RESIDENTIAL ADDRESS...

Telephone Number Work .... Home .... Cellphone...............................

ITEMS PURCHASED...

<u>PAYMENTS</u>

Cash Price of Goods Including Taxes	$ . . . .
Add Hire Purchase Charges	$ . . . .
Hire Purchase Price	$ . . . .
Less Initial Cash Instalment	$ . . . .
BALANCE OF HIRE	$ . . . .

TERMS AND CONDITIONS OF HIRE

An agreement made this (*Insert current date*) between **VALUE CITY ENTERPRISES LTD** (hereinafter called the Owner), of the one part and **LASHEY JUBIN** (hereinafter called the Hirer), of the other part, WHEREAS it is agreed as follows:

1 The Owner will let and the Hirer will take on hire the goods mentioned, for the term of....... weeks/months/years from the date hereof, at a weekly/monthly rent of $ ....

2 The Hirer shall, upon the making of this agreement, pay the initial instalment specified in the Schedule and shall punctually pay the several instalments of the balance as specified in the Schedule.

3 The Hirer shall, until and unless all instalments of rent are paid, keep and maintain all the said goods in good order and condition (reasonable wear and tear only excepted).

4 The Hirer shall at all times allow the owner, his agents or servants to inspect the same whenever demanded.

5 In the event of the goods being damaged or destroyed beyond repairs or replacement or lost by fire, theft or any other cause, the Hirer shall pay the owner all remaining instalments due on the goods.

6 The Hirer shall not, without the owner's previous written consent, remove or permit removal of the said goods and effects from the above residential address of the Hirer stated in the schedule.

7 For the duration of this Agreement, the Hirer shall not sell, assign nor encumber or otherwise dispose of the goods.

8 If the Hirer fails and/or neglects to carry out any of the terms of this agreement, the owner may terminate the hiring and retake possession of the said goods.

9 The Hirer may at any time put an end to this agreement by returning the goods at his own expense to the Owner in good working order and condition.

10 In the event that the goods are returned to the Owner, the Hirer must pay any instalment that is in arrears.

11 The Hirer may, at any time during the term of hiring, become the absolute owner of the goods by paying to the owner the outstanding balance of the hire amount less a 5% discount.

In witness whereof the said parties have placed their signatures:

....
Hirer   For and on behalf of   Witness
                               Value City Enterprises Ltd

Figure 6.14.1 A hire purchase agreement

SUMMARY QUESTIONS

1 Define the following terms as they pertain to a hire purchase agreement:
   a hirer
   b good
   c instalment.

2 Prepare and print the hire purchase agreement shown in Figure 6.14.1 on two sides of a sheet of legal paper.

Contracts

A contract is a legally enforceable agreement between two or more parties. Contracts are prepared for a wide variety of purposes including employment, the supply or purchase of products or services, and the rental of equipment. Unless you are otherwise instructed, you should follow the general formatting guidelines for legal documents presented in 6.10.

Table 6.15.1 defines some terms associated with contracts.

Table 6.15.1 Terms associated with contracts

Term	Definition
Remuneration	The money that is paid for work done.
Grievance arrangement	The step by step procedure that the employee must follow if he/she has a complaint against the employer.

Information included in employment contracts

A contract for employment usually contains: the names of both the employer and employee; the starting date of the employee; job title and description; and the address of the place at which the employee will be working.

Table 6.15.2 shows the items of agreement it should also contain.

Table 6.15.2 Items of agreement in a contract

1	Requirements of the job, including details on equipment to be used, the level of risk, provision of safety equipment if necessary, and so on
2	Details of remuneration (hourly rate or salary) and when it is paid (weekly or monthly)
3	Hours worked each week
4	Holiday entitlement
5	Sickness entitlement
6	Details of any pension schemes and insurance
7	Grievance arrangements
8	Termination of Contract Notice
9	Redundancy
10	Disciplinary procedures
11	Signatures of both the employer and employee

Preparing a contract

While there is no set format for a contract, the following principles should be observed:

- The title **Employment Contract** or **Employment Agreement** should be prominently displayed, in block capitals or emboldened with initial capitals.
- Each item of agreement should begin in a separate line with appropriate headings. Marginal or paragraph headings may be used.
- Items of agreement should be displayed in numbered sequence.
- If the contract is prepared as a form, then sufficient space should be left for the writing of required information.
- Item labels are usually typed in block capitals, or bold with initial capitals.

Figure 6.15.1 shows an example of an employment contract.

WeSee Tours and Travels Limited
Employment Contract

This Employment Contract is HEREBY entered into BETWEEN **WESEE TOURS AND TRAVELS LIMITED** whose principal place of business is 456 Atlantic Avenue, Scarborough, Tobago, hereinafter called 'the Employer' and **NADIA PIERRE** of 34 Western Street, Anyville, hereinafter called 'the Employee', with effect from the 1st day of September, 20xx.

WHEREAS the Employer desires to obtain the benefit of the services of the Employee, and the Employee desires to render such services on the terms and conditions set forth, the parties agree as follows:

Job Title:	Receptionist
Job Description:	The Employee is hired to be the first point of contact between the organisation and the public, creating a favourable impression of the organisation to clients and customers; and any other duties that can reasonably be required in the management of a reception office.
Level of Risk:	The Employee will be required to use a diverse range of equipment including, but not limited to: computer, photocopier, risograph, guillotine, binder, shredder.
Work Address:	456 Atlantic Avenue, Scarborough, Tobago.
Remuneration:	The Employer agrees to pay a wage of $23.50 per hour worked, to be paid weekly. Statutory payment such as Taxes and National Insurance shall be deducted from the Employee's wages.
Hours of work:	Monday to Friday – 7:30 a.m. to 4:30 p.m. with one (1) hour paid lunch break from 12:00 noon to 1:00 p.m.; Saturday – 7:30 a.m. to 12:30 p.m. The Employee is not required to work on public holidays.
Vacation Leave:	The Employee is entitled to ten (10) working days paid vacation leave per year after the first year of work, to be increased in increments of two days per year worked to a maximum of twenty (20) working days per year.
Sick Leave:	If the Employee is ill and unable to attend work, the Employee should inform the Employer as soon as possible to enable other arrangements to be made. The Employee is allowed a maximum of ten (10) days' paid sick leave per year.
Pension/Insurance:	The Employee has the option to participate in the subsidised group health insurance and pension plan offered by BCV Insurance Company Limited.
Grievance/Discipline:	Please consult the Employee Handbook for the established Grievance and Disciplinary Procedures.
Termination Notice:	This contract may be terminated by either party with seven (7) days' notice in writing. Notwithstanding this, the Employer reserves the right to immediately terminate employment in the case of gross misconduct as listed in the Employee Handbook.
Redundancy:	Employment may be terminated with five (5) days' pay if the position becomes redundant.

....
Employee Signature   For WeSee Tours and Travels Limited

....
Date   Date

Figure 6.15.1 An employment contract

6.16 Specifications

LEARNING OUTCOMES

At the end of this topic you should be able to:

- prepare builder or architectural specifications using appropriate formatting.

DID YOU KNOW?

Architectural or builder specifications are used in the construction industry. They enable the architect, builder, customer and independent inspectors to determine whether the work that is done matches the design.

A **specification** is a precise statement of the exact material, method, process, service, and/or work for every aspect of a proposed project.

Information included in specifications

Specifications should include detailed descriptions of:

- the type and quality of every product required for the project
- the requirements for each stage of the project
- the quality of workmanship required
- any essential codes and standards that are pertinent to the project
- descriptions and procedures for substitute materials, products, processes or services if required.

Preparing a specification

Some countries have precise guidelines for the formatting and layout of specifications. If you are not given specific instructions follow the guidelines in Table 6.16.1.

Table 6.16.1 Guidelines for typing a specification

Formatting	• Use text that is clear and easily read. It is recommended that you use Times New Roman, size 12 and double-line spacing. • Use top, left and right margins of 2.54 cm (1 inch) and bottom margins of 1.27 cm (0.5 inches) on letter-sized or A4 paper. • Avoid leaving only one line of a paragraph at the bottom of a page, or at the top of the next page. • If the document is longer than one page, insert page numbers centred in the footer.

Heading	• Type a heading beginning with the word **SPECIFICATION** in spaced capital letters at the top of the page. This may be in full block format or aligned to the right of the centre. The heading is typed in 1.5 or double-line spacing. The heading consists of:
	  1 an introductory paragraph that summarises the work to be done and the location of the site
	  2 the name and address of the architect or contractor, typed two line spaces below the introductory paragraph
	  3 the date typed at the left margin two clear line spaces below the name and address of the architect or contractor.

Body	• Type the body of the specifications, divided into sections that identify in logical sequence the materials and work processes for the project. Side or shoulder headings should be used for each section. • Avoid large blocks of text on a page. These should be divided into appropriate subsections. • Number sections and subsections. It is best to use multilevel numbering style (1.1. 1.1.1, and so on) as is shown in Figure 6.16.1.

130

Figure 6.16.1 shows an example of a builder's specification.

SPECIFICATION of work to be carried out and materials to be used for the construction of a retaining wall at 45 Brewster Street, VALENCIA for FRS Realtors Ltd to the satisfaction of:

Gabriel Architectural Enterprises
8 Kelly Street
SANGRE GRANDE

12 June 20XX

1 GENERAL CONDITIONS

1.1 Visit to Site
The contractor is required to thoroughly inspect the site and surrounds, accompanied by the Architect before the initiation of the project.

1.2 Environmental Impact

1.2.1   The contractor must ensure that all procedures and processes conform to the standards laid out by the Environmental Management Agency.

1.2.2   The contractor must ensure that there is no damage to the area surrounding that designated for the retaining wall.

1.2.3   The contractor will be held liable for any damages incurred to the surrounding area that is incurred in the process of constructing the retaining wall.

1.2.4   The contractor shall be responsible for the removal of all excavated material, rubble or other waste produced in the construction of the retaining wall.

2 SITE PREPARATION

2.1 Clearance

2.1.1 Remove vegetation, roots and any surface debris in the area identified for the construction of the retaining wall.

2.2 Excavation

2.2.1   Excavate a 3' wide trench in the area identified for construction of the retaining wall.

2.2.2   Existing soils must be removed to the bottom of the levelling pad elevation for the retaining wall.

2.3 Laying of levelling pad

2.3.1   The levelling pad shall consist of crushed stone of a 2.5 cm or smaller diameter.

2.3.2   The levelling pad shall be laid, compacted and levelled to a minimum thickness of 15 cm.

3 CONSTRUCTION OF THE RETAINING WALL

3.1 Laying of 32K Blocks

3.1.1   The 32K Blocks shall be laid according to the manufacturer's specifications contained in Appendix 1.

3.1.2   Ultra High Density 10 cm SP Steel Grid shall be used for the entire length of the wall, as per specifications contained in Appendix 2.

3.2 Backfill

3.2.1   The area behind the retaining wall shall be filled with a suitable, easily drained material.

3.2.2   As far as possible site-excavated material may be used.

Figure 6.16.1 Builder specifications

ACTIVITY

Use the Internet to find sample architectural specifications. Observe their layouts. Practise typing at least one of the specifications that you find.

DID YOU KNOW?

Specifications are prepared as part of a contract document for building construction. Consequently the terms in a specification are legally enforceable.

SUMMARY QUESTIONS

1 Explain three reasons why specifications should be prepared for a project.

2 Name four items of information that are contained in a builder's specification.

3 Type and print the specifications shown in Figure 6.16.1, ensuring that you observe all guidelines presented in this topic.

Bills of quantity

At the end of this topic you should be able to:

- prepare bills of quantity using appropriate formatting.

The customer can hire a quantity surveyor to prepare the bill of quantities. Each contractor will then be asked to fill in the bidding prices for the project.

EXAM TIP

Ensure that you use consistent formatting and alignments when preparing tabular work, such as bills of quantities.

A **bill of quantity** or bill of quantities is a document that lists the quantities, descriptions and prices of the items of labour, materials and parts that are required to complete a project. Bills of quantity are commonly used in the construction industry.

A bill of quantity is important because it:

- provides a clear and detailed statement of the work to be carried out
- helps a **contractor** to accurately estimate the costs involved in a project since it lists all the materials and equipment to be used and the work to be done
- enables the customer to select from a number of contractors who are competing for the project
- can be used to manage the expenditure during the venture, such as in determining when funds will be needed.

Preparing a bill of quantity

Bills of quantities are best prepared in a spreadsheet. This allows for the use of formulae and functions to perform necessary calculations. The following guidelines should be observed when preparing bills of quantities, unless you are otherwise instructed:

- A bill of quantity should provide a full, accurate description of the work to be done and the associated costs.
- The items are usually presented in the order in which they will be used, based on the architect's or builder's specifications.
- Text should be aligned to the right of the column, while currency figures should be left-aligned. Headings may be centred or left-aligned consistently.
- Text such as item names and descriptions should not be entered into the same cell as figures to be used for calculation.
- Prices and total costs should be presented in currency format.
- Format the cells so that all borders in the header row, the vertical borders between columns and the outside borders will be printed.

Figure 6.17.1 shows an example of a bill of quantities.

CSL CONTRACTING COMPANY LIMITED

4323 Freeling Street, CUREPE.

BILL OF QUANTITIES for work to be carried out and materials to be used for the expansion and paving of a 600 m^2 parking area at 18 Utopia Heights, Caroni for and to the satisfaction of:

Abraham and Sons Consultants,
97 Festival Street, Point Fortin.

REF	DESCRIPTION	QUANTITY	UNIT	RATE	$
	SITE PREPARATION				
SP1	Excavate 600 m2 area to required subgrade level	170	m3	320.00	54,400.00
SP2	Remove surplus excavated material from site	170	m3	235.00	39,950.00
SP3	Grade and roll surface of excavation to required level	600	m2	69.00	41,400.00
SP4	Spread, level and thoroughly compact a 15 cm base with crushed stone with a diameter of 2.7 cm or smaller	600	m2	264.00	158,400.00
SP5	Grade and roll surface of base course to specified angle finished to receive asphalt	600	m2	67.00	40,200.00
	PAVING				
P1	Prepare and apply two tack coats primer and 4 cm thick asphalt laid and rolled to specification	600	m2	590.00	354,000.00
	FINISHING				
F1	Painting of lines for parallel parking as depicted in Drawing No. 371/1AD	1800	m	10.00	18,000.00
F2	Remove refuse from site.	2	trip	1800.00	3,600.00
	TOTAL COST OF WORK				709,950.00

Figure 6.17.1 A bill of quantities

SUMMARY QUESTIONS

1 What is a bill of quantity?

2 State at least three reasons why a bill of quantity would be important in the construction industry.

3 What guidelines should be followed when preparing a bill of quantity?

4 Prepare the bill of quantity that is shown in Figure 6.17.1.

Scope of works

LEARNING OUTCOMES

At the end of this topic you should be able to:

- prepare a scope of works using appropriate formatting.

A **scope of works** is a document that sets out the requirements for performance of work so that the objectives of a project will be achieved. It describes the work to be performed or the services to be provided. It is part of the contract for the project.

For example, your school's administration might want to buy new computers for the lab and create a network for the sharing of resources, including Internet access. The scope of works for this project will include a clear statement of the equipment, software and warranty period and frequency of maintenance that will be required (Figure 6.18.1).

Table 6.18.1 defines some key terms you may come across in a scope of works.

Table 6.18.1 Terms associated with scopes of works

Term	Definition
Project deliverables	The items of work that are to be delivered to the customer.
Applicable standards	The quality of work and materials that is required, according to the law of the country and the standards of the industry.

Preparing a scope of works

The scope of works should provide clear details on the:

- **purpose** of the project
- **location** where the work will be performed
- **deliverables schedule**, which is a listing of project deliverables and the due date
- **allowable time for projects**, such as start time, duration, and number of hours per week or month
- **applicable standards** or specifications that need to be adhered to in fulfilling the contract
- **payment schedule** that outlines the specific arrangements for payment, whether in advance, phased during the project, or upon completion.

There is no single layout for a scope of works. Where no specific instructions are given, you may use the layout shown in Figure 6.18.1.

DID YOU KNOW?

A scope of works is a legally binding agreement. It should therefore be meticulously prepared.

SCOPE OF WORKS

AAK COMPUTER SUPPLIES AND SERVICES LIMITED
87A GRANDBY STREET
PORTSMOUTH
TELEPHONE/FAX 1 767 555 3443
EMAIL serv@aakcomp.org

CUSTOMER: PORTSMOUTH COMMUNITY COLLEGE

SUMMARY

AAK COMPUTER SUPPLIES AND SERVICES LIMITED is a provider of computer hardware, software and maintenance services for governmental organisations, educational institutions and business organisations. With more than twenty years' experience in information and communication technology, AAK COMPUTER SUPPLIES AND SERVICES LIMITED is committed to delivering total value to our customers through our professional solutions and services.

Project Overview

This Scope of Works is in response to a request from PORTSMOUTH COMMUNITY COLLEGE for pricing on the supply and maintenance of equipment for their computer room to create a networked environment with Internet access.

Deliverables

Schedule 1 and Schedule 2 details the deliverables for this project, to be supplied and installed within six (6) weeks of the signing of the project contract.

Schedule 1: Hardware to be supplied and installed

Quantity	Item	Specifications
1	Server	Dell PowerEdge 2950 2U Processors: Two (2) Intel Xeon E5440 2.83 GHz quad-core Memory: 16 GB of DDR2 Fully Buffered Motherboard: Intel 5000X chipset Hard drives: Six (6) 146 GB 15,000 RPM SAS 3.5-inch
25	Desktop computers	Power Supply: 500W Processor: INTEL CORE i3 2120 (3.3GHZ) SKT 1155 Memory: 2 X 2 GB DDR3 Hard Disk Drive: 500GB Sata 3 with 16MB cache Optical drive: DVD+RW Sata 2
1	Wireless router	Cisco Wireless Network Security Firewall Router

Schedule 2: Software to be supplied and installed

Quantity	Item	Specifications
1	Server OS	Microsoft Windows Server 2012
25	Desktop OS	Microsoft Windows 8 Professional

Verification

PORTSMOUTH COMMUNITY COLLEGE shall appoint a suitably qualified representative to verify that equipment and software are delivered and installed as specified.

Maintenance and Support Services

Upkeep and maintenance of the hardware installed for a period of **two (2) years** as detailed in the attached service agreement (Appendix 1).

Exclusions

This Scope of Works does not include the wiring for or provision of Internet Services.

This Scope of Works does not include problems that result from:
1. Usage that is not in agreement with product instructions.
2. Accident, misuse, abuse or issues with electrical power.

Pricing

Please see Appendix 2 for detailed item pricing.

Delivery schedule

All products are to be delivered and installed within **six (6) weeks** of the signing of the project contract.

Payment schedule

Payment of the full contract price by certified cheque is due immediately upon completion and verification of the equipment and software installation.

Figure 6.18.1 A scope of works

SUMMARY QUESTIONS

1 Define a scope of works and list at least four sets of information it should contain.

2 Prepare and print the scope of works displayed in Figure 6.18.1 using the following formatting: 3.8 cm (1.5 inch) left margins, all other margins 2.54 cm (1 inch); 1.5 line spacing; header font Times New Roman size 16 bold; subheader font Times New Roman size 14 bold; table text Arial size 10 with single-line spacing and no spacing between paragraphs; body text Times New Roman size 12.

Literary work

At the end of this topic you should be able to:

• prepare poetry, plays for radio, theatre and television, actors' scripts and index cards using appropriate formatting.

ACTIVITY

Follow the guidelines presented above to type the following poem, entitled *The Arrow and the Song*, written by Henry W. Longfellow.

I shot an arrow into the air,
It fell to earth, I knew not where;
For, so swiftly it flew, the sight
Could not follow it in its flight.

I breathed a song into the air,
It fell to earth, I knew not where;
For who has sight so keen and strong
That it can follow the flight of song?

Long, long afterward, in an oak
I found the arrow, still unbroke;
And the song, from beginning to end,
I found again in the heart of a friend.

Literary work is any piece of composition or creative writing such as a play, poem or short story. In this topic you will learn the guidelines for correctly formatting poetry, plays and actors' scripts and index cards.

Poetry

Follow these general rules when you are typing poetry:

• Type the title in closed capitals and centre align it.

• Type verses in single-line spacing, with one or two clear line spaces between verses.

• Ensure that each line begins with a capital letter.

• If the poem is the only item on the page centre it vertically and horizontally.

• The indentation of lines is determined by the rhyming pattern of the poem.

  – Poems that do not rhyme or those in which all lines rhyme are typed in block format, so that each line begins at the left margin.

  – Alternate rhyming lines should be indented two or three spaces.

  – If the lines are of significantly different lengths they may be centred.

  – Choruses should be indented by at least 1.27 cm (0.5 inches).

• Align the poet's name with the longest line of the poem, one clear line space below the last line. To do this set a right tab in line with the last word of the longest line.

• Punctuate and capitalise the poem exactly as given in the copy.

Plays and actors' scripts

Table 6.19.1 lists formatting guidelines for typing plays and actors' scripts.

Theatre

When typing plays for theatre, the name of the character speaking is typed as a side heading, such as in the Macbeth extract in the Activity on p138. To do this:

1 Set a tab stop and hanging line indent at 3.8 cm (1.5 inches) from the left. If the character names are long, the tab and indent may be set at 5.1 cm (2 inches).

2 Type the character's name in upper case.

3 Press tab and then type the dialogue.

Television

• When preparing scripts for television, the character's name is typed in upper case, centred, above the dialogue. The dialogue is also centred.

Table 6.19.1 Guidelines for typing plays and scripts

Formatting guidelines	
Initial preparation	• Plays for radio, theatre or television are usually typed on single-sided A4 paper, in Courier font size 12, with single- or 1.5 line spacing. Two spaces should follow the punctuation at the end of each sentence. • If the document is to be stapled or bound, use left margins of 2.9 cm (1.1 inches). All other margins should be 2.54 cm (1 inch). Unbound work should have equal margins of at least 2.54 cm (1 inch).
Introductory pages (title page, synopsis and list of characters)	• The title page displays the title and type of play and author's name, typed in capitals and centred vertically and horizontally. • The synopsis of acts and scenes is centred vertically and horizontally. Acts are typed in capital letters. • The list of characters is typed in upper case, in double-line spacing, centred horizontally and vertically. If the names of the cast are included, the characters are in initial capitals and the cast in full capitals. The list of costumes may be included on this page.
First page of script	• The first page of the play is not numbered. However, all subsequent pages are numbered 1.27 cm (0.5 inches) from the top, aligned with the right margin, in Arabic figures and followed by a full stop. • The title should be placed 5.1 cm (2 inches) from the top of the first page, in spaced capitals, centred and underscored. • The name of the act should be typed two line spaces below the title, in all capitals and centred.
Script	• Start each new scene of an act on a new page. Scenes are left-aligned in underscored initial capital letters with small Roman numerals e.g. <u>Scene iv. In the Market. Miss Maisie and Gwendolyn.</u> • Unspoken words, such as instructions, are typed with a clear line space before and after, underscored or bold and in brackets.

Radio

The dialogues in scripts for radio are usually numbered consecutively in the left margin (see Figure 6.19.1).

1. MUSIC CHORUS OF BOB MARLEY'S *ONE LOVE*. FADE UNDER
2. DYLAN Remember when the village was like one big family?
3. MARIE Remember when yuh could ah trus' yuh neighbor, an' if yuh doin' sumtin' wrong any big person could da straighten yuh out?
4. FABIO Remember long time, when current gone an' moonlight bright, how all de village children used tuh play in de road?
5. MUSIC FADE IN. NAPPY MYERS' *OLD TIME DAYS*

Figure 6.19.1 An excerpt from a radio script

Figure 6.19.2 An actor's script is specially formatted

Actors' scripts

An **actor's script** is formatted so that the character's dialogue and instructions are distinctive from the rest of the play and therefore it is easier for the actor to see their lines. The individual's dialogue is typed in double-line spacing in a font colour that is different from the rest of the play.

ACTIVITY

Type and print the following play for theatre prepared for the character the FIRST WITCH. Observe the guidelines provided above and on pp136–7.

MACBETH
ACT I

Scene iii. A Heath Near Forres.

(Thunder. Enter the three Witches.)

FIRST WITCH	Where hast thou been, sister?
SECOND WITCH	Killing swine.
THIRD WITCH	Sister, where thou?
FIRST WITCH	A sailor's wife had chestnuts in her lap,
	And munch'd, and munch'd, and munch'd:--
	'Give me,' quoth I:
	'Aroint thee, witch!' the rump-fed ronyon cries.
	Her husband's to Aleppo gone, master o' the Tiger:
	But in a sieve I'll thither sail,
	And, like a rat without a tail,
	I'll do, I'll do, and I'll do.
SECOND WITCH	I'll give thee a wind.
FIRST WITCH	Thou'rt kind.
THIRD WITCH	And I another.

Index cards

Index cards are typically used in a manual filing system, for example to type the names and related information of clients, employees, patients and stock. In addition, these cards may be used for literary purposes, such as to learn the lines of a play. Index cards may also be used to plan a script. Each scene can be outlined on a separate card. The cards may then be rearranged as necessary.

To create and print index cards it is more efficient to print on letter-sized sheets of card stock and then use a guillotine to cut them to size.

To create index cards in a word-processing document:

1 Enter the orientation, width and height of the card you want to create.

2 Type the cards.

3 Depending on the size of the cards, select four or six pages per sheet from the **Pages per sheet** selector on the **Print** dialogue box.

DID YOU KNOW?

You can also create index cards by using the Labels feature of your word-processing program (see 5.13).

SUMMARY QUESTIONS

1 Outline at least six guidelines that should be followed when typing each of the following:

a poems

b plays.

2 Type and print the following dialogue as:

a a radio play

b a television script.

THE ANGEL INTRUDES

by Floyd Dell

NARRATOR: Washington Square by moonlight. A stream of Greenwich Villagers are hurrying across to the Brevoort before the doors are locked. In their wake comes a sleepy policeman. The policeman stops suddenly on seeing an Angel with shining garments and great white wings, who has just appeared out of nowhere.

THE POLICEMAN: Hey, you!

THE ANGEL: *(haughtily, turning)* Sir! Are you addressing me?

THE POLICEMAN: *(severely)* Yes, an' I've a good mind to lock you up.

THE ANGEL: *(surprised and indignant)* How very inhospitable! Is that the way you treat strangers?

THE POLICEMAN: Don't you know it's agen the law of New York to parade the streets in a masquerade costume?

THE ANGEL: No. I didn't know. You see, I've just arrived this minute from Heaven.

THE POLICEMAN: Ye look it. *(Taking his arm kindly)* See here, me lad, you've been drinkin' too many of them stingers. Ye'd better take a taxi and go home.

THE ANGEL: What! So soon?

THE POLICEMAN: I know how ye feel. I've been that way meself. But I can't leave ye go traipsin' about in skirts.

THE ANGEL: *(drawing away)* Sir, I'm not traipsing about. I am attending to important business, and I must ask you not to detain me.

THE POLICEMAN: *(suspiciously)* Not so fast, me laddie-buck. What business have you at this hour of the night? Tell me that.

Trial balances and balance sheets

Trial balances and balance sheets are used to summarise the financial position of a business.

Both trial balances and balance sheets are prepared in table format. If you are given a copy of a trial balance or balance sheet to type, you may use a table in your word-processing program to apply the skills you acquired in 4.5 to 4.7 and 6.1. Ensure that you know how to perform these actions before attempting to create each financial statement.

If you need to perform calculations, it is best to use a spreadsheet. If your trial balance or balance sheet is to be presented as part of a larger text document, then it can be created as a spreadsheet object within the word-processing program.

Typing a trial balance

Look at the layout of the trial balance in Figure 6.20.1. You should observe the following details:

• The trial balance table consists of four columns.
• The heading of the trial balance states the name of the organisation and is centred. If you are using a spreadsheet, then cells A1 to D1 can be merged before you type this information.
   • The words **Trial Balance as at**, followed by the date, are typed in the next line and centred. You can merge cells A2 to D2 for this.
• You may create a clear line space by leaving row 3 empty.
• The header row of the trial balance table contains the following words in cells A4 to D4 respectively: Particulars Folio Debit Credit.
• The **Particulars column** containing the information relating to the account is the widest and left-aligned.
• The **Folio column** containing the page number of the ledger on which the account was recorded is narrowest, as the page number is generally no more than four digits long.
• The **Debit** and **Credit** columns are equal in size, and should be wide enough to accommodate the largest figure from the accounts. They should be right-aligned.

Something Sweet Candy Shoppe			
Trial Balance as at 12 June 20XX			
Particulars	**Folio**	**Debit**	**Credit**
Equipment	96	4,800	
Cash	103	3,480	
Accounts receivable	108	575	
Stock	117	1,000	
Accounts payable	119		2,355
Bank loan			3,000
J Blessed, capital			4,500
		9,855	9,855

Figure 6.20.1 A trial balance

Typing a balance sheet

Figures 6.20.2 and 6.20.3 show two layouts for a balance sheet. The principles governing their preparation are very similar to those for the trial balance.

- Ensure that the widths of the columns are equally balanced. For example, in the horizontal layout, columns 1 and 3 should be of the same width. Similarly, the widths of columns 2 and 4 should be the same.
- Format the cell borders as displayed. For example, a double line is used for the bottom border of the final cells in columns 2 and 4.
- Use bold font for section headings.
- If the balance sheet is the only item on the page, centre it vertically and horizontally.
- Use a consistent format for expressing currency.

Something Sweet Candy Shoppe
Balance Sheet as at 12 June 20XX

	$
Assets	
Current Assets	
Cash	3,480
Accounts receivable	575
Inventories	1,000
Total Current Assets	5,055
Fixed Assets	
Equipment	4,800
Total Assets	**9,855**
	$
Liabilities & Owner's Equity	
Current Liabilities	
Accounts payable	2,355
Bank loan	3,000
Total Current Liabilities	5,355
Owner's Equity	4,500
Total Liabilities and Equity	**9,855**

Figure 6.20.2 A balance sheet in vertical layout

Something Sweet Candy Shoppe
Balance Sheet as at 12 June 20XX

Assets	$	**Liabilities & Owner's Equity**	$
Current Assets		Current Liabilities	
Cash	3,480	Accounts payable	2,355
Accounts receivable	575	Bank loan	3,000
Inventories	1,000		
Total Current Assets	5,055	Total Current Liabilities	5,355
Equipment	4,800	Owner's Equity	4,500
Total Assets	**9,855**	**Total Liabilities and Equity**	**9,855**

Figure 6.20.3 A balance sheet in horizontal layout

TRY IT!

Create and print the balance sheets shown in Figures 6.20.2 and 6.20.3.

EXAM TIP

Ensure that you can create tables with a wide variety of formats. This skill is frequently examined.

SUMMARY QUESTIONS

1 Outline at least six principles that should be followed when typing financial statements such as trial balances or balance sheets.

2 The ledger of Dress with Flair Garment Shop shows the following balances:

Page 12	Equipment: $2,000;	Page 89	Accounts payable: $3,451;
Page 67	Accounts receivable: $1,690;	Page 70	Cash: $4,575.00;
Page 55	Bank Loan: $8,600.00;	Page 5	R Le Flair, capital $12,000.
Page 113	Inventory: $15,786	Debit total: $24,051.00	Credit Total: $24,051

   a Prepare and print a trial balance.
   b Prepare and print a balance sheet in vertical layout.
   c Prepare and print a balance sheet in horizontal layout.

6.21 Income and expenditure statements

LEARNING OUTCOMES

At the end of this topic you should be able to:

• prepare income and expenditure statements (also known as profit and loss statements) using appropriate formatting.

An **income and expenditure statement** is a summary of the sales and expenses of a business over a specific period of time. They are also called **income statements** or **profit and loss statements**.

Typing an income and expenditure statement

The layout of an income and expenditure statement can be simple or more complex depending on the detail required.

Single-step statements

Figure 6.21.1 shows a simple layout for the income and expenditure statement.

You should observe the following details about the layout:

• An unruled table is used to display the statement. Top and bottom borders are applied to cells containing totals. There is a double-line bottom border for the final cell, indicating the end of the statement.

• The first line of the heading of the statement states the name of the organisation, in block capitals or in initial capitals, bold and centred.

• The second line contains the title 'Income Statement', with initial capitals, centred.

TRY IT!

Prepare and print the statement of income and expenditure that is shown in Figure 6.21.1.

Cha-Tec Trading Company Limited
Income Statement
For the Six Months Ended June 30, 20XX

Revenues & Gains	
Sales Revenues	$160,500
Rent Revenues	15,000
Gain on Sale of Assets	5,500
Total Revenue & Gains	181,000
Expenses & Losses	
Cost of Goods Sold	64,500
Wages Expense	25,000
Office Supplies Expense	4,800
Office Equipment Expense	1,500
Advertising Expense	3,290
Utilities Expense	2,000
Total Expenses & Losses	101,090
Net Income	**$79,910**

Figure 6.21.1 A single-step income statement

- The third line states the precise period of time being covered, for example, Year Ended September 30 or Six Months Ended December 31 or Month Ended February 28, 20XX. This is typed with initial capitals and centred.
- One or two clear line spaces are left before typing the financial information.
- Section headings of the income statement use bold font.

Multi-step statements

Look at the statement displayed in Figure 6.21.2. You will observe that it is very detailed, showing how to calculate figures such as net sales, net purchases, gross profit and net profit. This format is called a multi-step income statement.

The table consists of four columns:

- The first column should be wide enough to accommodate the longest line of text.
- The other three columns should have equal widths, and should be wide enough to accommodate the longest figure.

TRY IT!

Prepare and print the statement of income and expenditure that is shown in Figure 6.21.2.

DID YOU KNOW?

Accountants use double lines in financial statements to indicate major totals. See the major total at the end of the statement in Figure 6.21.2.

Exclusively Yours Beauty Services and Supplies
Trading and Profit & Loss Statement
For the Three Months Ended March 31, 20XX

	$	$	$
Sales		69,836	
Less Return Inwards		799	
Net Sales			69,037
Cost of Goods Sold			
Purchases	37,800		
Less Return Outwards	1,250		
Net Purchases		36,550	
Less Closing Stock		1,900	34,650
Gross Profit			34,387
Add Revenue			
Discount Received		1,895	
Rent Received		11,000	12,895
			47,282
Less Expenses			
Electricity		1,298	
Telephone		1,500	
Office Supplies		2,850	
Depreciation		800	
Wages		5,000	11,448
Net Profit			35,834

Figure 6.21.2 A multi-step income statement

SUMMARY QUESTIONS

Over the last month, Dhanraj Business Solutions earned revenues totalling $27,000 from $24,000-worth of sales and a commission of $3,000. During that time the business expenses totalled $10,790, consisting of $8,500 cost of goods sold, $400 for utilities and $1,890 for office supplies. The net income was $16,210.

Prepare and print a statement of income and expenditure using **either** the single-step **or** multi-step layout.

Bank statements and receipts

At the end of this topic you should be able to:

- prepare bank statements and receipts using appropriate formatting.

Bank statements

A **bank statement** is a printed listing of all deposits to and withdrawals from a banking account within a period of time. The statement is prepared by the bank and issued to the customer, usually by mail.

Figure 6.22.1 illustrates the typical layout of a bank statement.

TRANS-CARIBBEAN BANK OF COMMERCE
2908 JAMES-SMITH STREET
SAN FERNANDO

CHEQUING ACCOUNT STATEMENT
Page: 1 of 1

	Statement period	Account No.
	2014-01-01 to 2014-01-31	109-98-781

CUSTOMER: NAVIN JAGESSAR
67 CARRINGTON STREET
FYZABAD

Date	Description	Ref.	Withdrawls	Deposits	Balance
2014-01-01	Previous balance				1,255.00
2014-01-05	ATM Withdrawal - USLID	3978	640.00		615.00
2014-01-07	Payroll Deposit - KRD SPECIALS			2,750.00	3,365.00
2014-01-07	Point-of-Sale W/D - SUPERMARKET	2908	587.87		2,777.13
2014-01-09	Web Bill Payment - ELECTRICITY	4772	96.00		2,681.13
2014-01-14	Pre-Auth. Payment - CABLE		112.95		2,568.18
2014-01-15	Loan Repayment		380.14		2,188.04
2014-01-22	ATM Withdrawal - USLID	4889	800.00		1,388.04
2014-01-25	Cheque No. - 288		350.99		1,037.05
2014-01-27	Web Funds Transfer - From SAVINGS	5001		660.00	1,697.05
2014-01-30	Monthly Service Charges		25.00		1,672.05
2014-01-31	**Closing balance**				1,672.05
	Totals		2992.95	3410.00	

Figure 6.22.1 A bank statement

How to prepare a bank statement

Each bank has its own style for its statements. However, all statements contain similar information:

1 the header that displays the bank's name and address, customer's name and address, account type and number, and the time period reported in the statement

2 a table with a header row with distinctive shading, border and font formatting. The column headings may be left-aligned or centred

3 one row of text for each transaction. Alternate rows may be shaded to make the statement easier to read.

When you are creating the bank statement you should:

- use a clear, uncluttered layout to ensure that the statement is easy to read
- use a plain font, preferably without serifs, such as Arial or Calibri
- use a consistent format for the dates

Prepare and print the bank statement shown in Figure 6.22.1.

- ensure that your columns are wide enough to display all the required information, without having the text wrap to the next line
- ensure that there is sufficient space between the text in adjacent cells
- use the same width for the columns containing withdrawals, deposits and balances.

TRY IT!

Create and print the receipt shown in Figure 6.22.2.

Receipts

A **receipt** is a written acknowledgement that a sum of money or something of value has been received. For example, when a customer makes a purchase, the business should issue a receipt.

There are usually two copies of a receipt. The original copy is given to the person who made the payment. The other copy is kept by the person who collected the money. A signed receipt is a legal document.

Sales receipts are usually prepared as shown in Figure 6.22.2.

Payment receipts as shown in Figure 6.22.3 are used when a payment is made, for example, a hire purchase instalment or rent.

If the customer is not paying immediately, then an invoice is prepared (see 4.7).

Artistic Designs Limited
SALES RECEIPT

Date: _____

Qty.	Description	Price	Amount

Subtotal: _____
Tax: _____
Total: _____

Payment by:
[ ] Cash
[ ] Debit Card
[ ] Credit Card
[ ] Cheque No. _____
[ ] Other: _____

Figure 6.22.2 A sales receipt

Vin & Cal Trading
23 Greenleaf Street, Speyside
Phone/Fax: 1 868 555 6745

Payment

Receipt #: _____   Date: _____

Received From _____
of _____
the sum of _____ dollars and _____ cents
for _____

For
Payment Received

Cash [   ]
Cheque [   ]
Other [   ]

Total Amount Due	
Amount Received	
Balance Due	

_____
Signed By

Figure 6.22.3 A payment receipt

SUMMARY QUESTIONS

1 Outline at least five guidelines that should be followed when creating a bank statement.

2 Create and print the payment receipt shown in Figure 6.22.3.

Forms

Organisations use **forms** to gather information for a variety of purposes. A club, for example, might require potential members to fill out a form. Banks and credit unions use forms to obtain detailed information from loan applicants. Businesses create application forms for people seeking employment.

You will need to apply the following skills when creating forms:

- inserting symbols such as check boxes
- setting tabs with leader dots
- inserting tables with more than the preset number of columns
- showing and hiding cell borders
- inserting shapes and text boxes.

Review the relevant topics to ensure that you know how to perform these actions.

Creating forms

Forms should be designed so that it is easy for the user to fill out the required information. If the form is too complicated, the user might become frustrated and leave it incomplete. The following guidelines will help you to design user-friendly forms:

- Avoid extra long forms. Create forms that are clear and concise, while obtaining all required information.
- Ensure that each field is labelled clearly.
- Provide instructions if information should be presented in a particular way. For example, indicate whether a date should be entered in the *dd/mm/yyyy* format.
- Create placeholders wherever possible. For example, to ensure that names are printed clearly, this field may be displayed as:

Surname   First Name   Other Names

- Leave sufficient space for information to be written legibly. If you are using lines, then type the document in 1.5 or double line spacing.
- Ensure that fields are evenly spaced.
- Group fields logically. For example, an employment form should first obtain personal information, such as name, address and date of birth. Next obtain information on education and training, then on previous work experience, and so on.
- Break complex forms into sections, leaving at least one clear line space before starting each new section.

Figure 6.23.1 shows an example of a membership application form.

BRIMAC YOUTH CLUB
MEMBERSHIP APPLICATION

Surname First Name Other Names

Address Line 1

Address Line 2

Date of birth (dd/mm/yyyy) Home Telephone Mobile

ATTACH
PHOTOGRAPH
HERE

Hobbies: _____
_____
_____

Signature: _____
Date: _____

Figure 6.23.1 A membership application form

Figure 6.23.2 Forms should be clearly presented so that the person filling it in understands what information he or she needs to provide

SUMMARY QUESTIONS

1 State at least six guidelines that should be followed when designing forms.

2 Create and print the form that is displayed in Figure 6.23.1 on A5 paper in landscape orientation.

DID YOU KNOW?

Many organisations now use online forms to collect information. You can view examples by doing a search with the keywords *web form design samples*.

A **wizard** is a tool that helps the user to perform a task by using dialogue boxes to present a series of clearly defined steps. Wizards have been replaced by a wider variety of templates in more recent word-processing programs.

A template is a preset design for a document that controls elements such as font, page layouts and paragraph formatting. A template consists of a pre-designed document with **placeholders**. Placeholders are sections that are replaced with the desired text. Simply select the placeholder and type the text you want to use.

The advantages of using a template are:

• it saves time because you do not have to apply formatting changes each time you type the document

• it protects the document from unwanted changes. Anyone can use the template; however, it can be write protected, so that the user must save changes as a new document

• it gives all documents from an organisation a standardised appearance.

Using a template

Many word-processing programs come with a number of templates. Some are saved on your computer, whereas others might be available online from the software provider's website. Table 6.24.1 shows you how to access a template.

Table 6.24.1 How to access a template

1	Open Word and then select **New** from the **File** menu. The **New Document** task pane will appear.
2	Select the category of template that you want to use from the pane on the left (e.g. **Installed templates**). The available templates will appear in the middle pane.
3	Click on the template you want to use, and then click the **Create** or **OK** button that is found at the bottom right of the task pane.

Creating your own template

It is more efficient to create templates with the formats for each type of document that you use on a regular basis. For example, you may create an indented letter template similar to the one shown in Figure 6.24.1.

It is usually best to start a new template from scratch. The instructions in Table 6.24.2 show you how to do this in a word-processing program.

```
Street Address
Town/City
Country

Date

Position
Company
Street Address
Town/City
Country

Dear Name

    Type a line that succinctly states the subject of the letter

        Paragraph 1: This paragraph will state the purpose of the letter
clearly and concisely. It usually consists of only one or two sentences.

        Paragraph 2: This paragraph gives supporting details related to
the main purpose of the letter. Do not include irrelevant or
unnecessary information.

        Paragraph 3: This paragraph indicates the action that you
expect the recipient to take.

Complimentary close

                                    Sender's name
                                    Sender's designation
```

Figure 6.24.1 A template for an indented letter

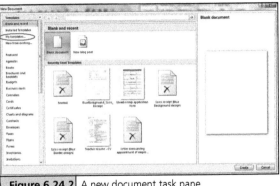

Figure 6.24.2 A new document task pane

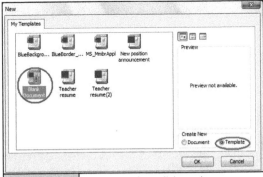

Figure 6.24.3 A new templates dialogue box

Table 6.24.2 How to start a new template

1	From the **File** menu, select **New**. The **New Document** task pane will appear (similar to that shown in Figure 6.24.2).
2	Under **Templates**, select **On my computer**... or **My templates**.... The **Templates** dialogue box will appear. Click on the **General** tab if you are using Microsoft Word 2003.
3	Ensure that you click on **Blank Document** (similar to that shown in Figure 6.24.3).
4	At the bottom right of the **Templates** dialogue box you will see **Create New**. Select **Template**.
5	Click **OK**. A new blank document will appear.
6	Put in the placeholders and apply the desired formatting.
7	Save the template with an appropriate file name in the **Templates** folder.

Using your templates

To create a new document based on a template you created, you need to open up a new file as before, ensuring that you select the **On My Computer** or **My Templates** link in the **New Document** task pane. You will then see a dialogue box containing your templates. Select the one you want to use, and then click **OK**.

Editing and saving this new document will have no effect on the original template.

TRY IT!

Create and save the indented letter template shown in Figure 6.24.1.

SUMMARY QUESTIONS

1 Define the term **template**.

2 State three advantages to using templates.

3 Outline the steps you should follow to:

  a use a preset template

  b create a new template.

7 Electronic communication

7.1   Types of electronic communication

Electronic communication refers to the transmission of messages that have been created in digital format. Electronic communication has become an integral part of the everyday lives of many people. Examples of electronic communication include:

• telecommuting
• teleconferencing
• electronic mail (see 7.4)
• social networks and social media
• the Internet (see 7.2)
• facsimiles (see 7.3)
• scanning to mail
• scanning to file.

Telecommuting

Telecommuting is defined as working at home or from another location by using a computer that is electronically linked to a central place of employment. Telecommuters are expected to perform the same task as their counterparts who work from the business place. However, they do not have to travel to work each day.

Telecommuting offers a number of advantages and disadvantages as presented in Table 7.1.1.

Table 7.1.1 Advantages and disadvantages of telecommuting

Advantages for employees	Advantages for employers
• Less time is spent travelling. • Telecommuters can coordinate their work schedule to accommodate family commitments such as caring for babies or elderly parents. • Workers do not have to invest in office clothes. • Employment opportunities for differently abled people increase.	• Employers are able to access expertise from any part of the world. • Unscheduled absences are reduced, such as for family emergencies; the telecommuter can make up for the lost time later in the day if necessary. • Less office space is required so the company saves money that would have been spent on real estate and utilities.
Disadvantages for employees	**Disadvantages for employers**
• There is a lack of social interaction with co-workers, resulting in feelings of isolation from the organisation.	• Workers can become distracted by home issues. • It is more difficult to foster collaboration and teamwork. • Not everyone is able to work without supervision.

Teleconferencing

A **teleconference** is a meeting between two or more people in different locations through the use of electronic communication technology. A teleconference can be either:

- an **audio conference** – the participants can only hear each other. Audio conferencing can be done by telephone, or on a computer with a microphone and speakers or a combination headset, or
- a **video conference** – the participants can both hear and see each other. Video conferencing requires a computer with a camera, as well as speakers and microphones (Figure 7.1.1).

Figure 7.1.1 | A video conference

Social networks

You may be familiar with **social networking** sites such as Facebook and Twitter that allow users to create profiles, link with other users, exchange messages and share a wide range of content, including photographs and videos.

Social media

Social media offers a range of easily accessible, user-friendly, interactive applications that are available on the Internet.

- **Wikis** are sites that allow users to collaboratively write information.
- **Weblogs** or **blogs** are online journals that allow users to regularly share information, opinions, photographs and other content.
- **Forums** are online discussion sites that are designed for readers to post brief messages related to a topic.
- A **podcast** is a digital audio recording that is distributed via the Internet, and can be downloaded to computers or portable media players. The term **Vidcast** is used for digital video files.

Scan to mail and scan to file

The software that controls the scanner (called the scanner's **driver**) can offer the options **Scan to mail** and **Scan to file**. Scan to mail allows you to email documents directly from the scanner. Scan to file enables you to save the document on a storage medium such as a hard disk drive or flash drive.

RESEARCH IT

Businesses now use social media for a wide range of purposes. Research and identify at least one business use for each type of social media.

DID YOU KNOW?

You might notice that many social media sites feature a link labelled RSS. This is a small program that allows users to conveniently access new media when they are uploaded.

SUMMARY QUESTIONS

1 Clearly explain the difference between:
   a teleconferencing and telecommuting
   b scan to mail and scan to file.

2 Discuss, with the use of examples, at least four ways in which electronic communication can be used for business purposes.

3 State the relative advantages and disadvantages of face-to-face conferencing, audio conferencing and video conferencing.

EXAM TIP

Ensure that you know the difference between teleconferencing and telecommuting. These terms are not interchangeable.

At the end of this topic you should be able to:

- discuss the Internet as a means of electronic communication
- discuss the advantages and disadvantages of the Internet as a means of electronic communication.

A **network** is created when two or more computers are linked, either by cables or wirelessly, so that they are able to share information and resources. The **Internet** is the largest existing computer network, linking individual computers and networks throughout the world via telephone lines, cables and satellites.

The most common use of the Internet is to access the immense number of websites that comprise the World Wide Web. Each website is made up of one or more webpages. A **webpage** is a document that can contain any combination of text, graphics, videos, sounds and content placeholders called frames.

Most websites contain **hyperlinks**. A hyperlink is specially formatted text or graphic that leads to another webpage when it is clicked.

Using web browsers

Figure 7.2.1 illustrates two important parts of a web browser: the **address bar** and the **search bar**. See Table 7.2.1 for their descriptions.

Figure 7.2.1 | An example of a web browser

DID YOU KNOW?

The **World Wide Web** is not the same as the Internet. Rather, it is one means of accessing information from the Internet. Other means of accessing information from the Internet include instant messaging and file transfer protocols.

TRY IT!

Search the Internet for *ecotourism* and observe the number of search results that are given. Now do a search for *ecotourism destinations in the Caribbean*. What effect did the additional keywords have on the results?

Table 7.2.1 Elements of web browsing

Address bar	If you know the specific name of a website, you can type it into the address bar and then press the **Enter** key on the keyboard.
Search bar	If you do not know the specific website, then you may type keywords into the search bar or search engine.
Search engine	A **search engine** is a program that is designed to search for information on the World Wide Web. Sometimes a keyword search will give thousands, or even millions, of results. It is therefore important to use keywords that are as specific as possible.

Uniform resource locator

A webpage is identified by its **uniform resource locator (URL)**. Figure 7.2.2 shows part of the website maintained by the Caribbean Examinations Council (CXC). If you look at the address bar, you will notice that the URL is **http://cxc.org**.

This URL consists of two main parts: the **protocol** (http) and the **domain name** (cxc.org).

Figure 7.2.2 | The URL

Communicating via the Internet

The Internet is a means of electronic communication because it allows digitally coded data and information to be sent from one computer to another. It has become one of the most commonly used communication tools for individuals and businesses.

Table 7.2.2 lists some advantages and disadvantages of using the Internet for communication. Most of the electronic communication mentioned in 7.1 relies on the Internet so these can be applied to other forms of electronic communication as well.

Table 7.2.2 Advantages and disadvantages of communication via the Internet

Advantages	
Cost	Most Internet Service Providers now offer unlimited Internet access at a relatively low cost. Some companies host websites at little or no cost, usually in exchange for advertising space. Many businesses now practice **e-commerce** by conducting a significant portion of their transactions online. This reduces the need for office and display space, hiring of many workers or storage of a large inventory.
Speed	Communication is instantaneous. For example, emails are received seconds after they are sent.
Versatility	It allows for different types of communication, including verbal, written and visual. The communication requires both sender and receiver to be on the Internet at the same time, such as in a live chat (called *synchronous* communication). It can also be asynchronous, which does not require both parties to be online simultaneously (e.g. email).
Capacity	It permits the exchange of large volumes of information (e.g. online encyclopaedias).
Timeliness	Information is easily updated. For example, news services are able to post reports of breaking news events as they occur.
Disadvantages	
Access	The Internet increases the risk of viruses and other harmful software. It also exposes people and businesses to new types of fraud (e.g. online scams, **phishing**, electronic eavesdropping). There is a danger that communication can be accessed by unauthorised people. Although many take it for granted, not everyone has access to the Internet.
Effect on social interaction	There can be a loss of human contact and increasing sense of isolation if used exclusively.

Facsimile and multifunctional devices

A **facsimile** (or **fax**) is an exact copy of a document that is converted to a code that is transmitted via telephone lines or the Internet. It is a form of electronic communication that enables documents to be sent faster, and usually more economically, than by mail or courier services.

A facsimile can be used when a copy of a document must be sent urgently to a recipient. Sometimes an individual or organisation will specifically request for documents to be sent by fax, for example when they do not have Internet access.

A fax may be sent from a fax machine like the one shown in Figure 7.3.1. However, some individuals and businesses prefer to purchase a **multifunctional device** that combines a scanner, printer, photocopier and fax machine in a single unit.

How a facsimile works

Figure 7.3.2 shows how sending a fax works.

How to use a fax or multifunctional machine

The instructions for using a fax machine or multifunctional machine vary according to the model, but you should always use a **fax transmission form** (Figure 7.3.3) or a cover letter to identify:

• the subject of document being faxed
• the number of pages
• the sender's name and fax number
• the name of the intended recipient.

How to send a fax via the Internet

You can also send a fax via the Internet. Table 7.3.1 provides instructions for sending a Microsoft Word document.

| **Figure 7.3.1** | A facsimile (fax) machine |

DID YOU KNOW?

The first fax machine, called a pantelegraph, was invented in 1843, 30 years before the telephone was patented. It made use of telegraph lines to transmit handwritten messages and signatures.

TRY IT!

Apply your previously learned skills to create the fax transmission form shown in Figure 7.3.3.

1 The document is scanned into the sending machine.

↓

2 The machine's sensor detects the marks on the paper and creates a code called a bitmap.

↓

3 The bitmap is sent via the telephone system or Internet to a receiving machine.

↓

4 The receiving machine uses the bitmap to reconstruct and print an image of the original document.

| **Figure 7.3.2** | How sending a fax works |

Table 7.3.1 How to send a fax using Microsoft Word

1	Choose the **Send** option in the **File** menu and select the option labelled **Internet Fax** or **Recipient Using Internet Fax Service** (this label may differ slightly depending on what version of Word you are using). **Note:** If you are using this feature for the first time, you will be prompted to sign up for the service. Click **OK** to open the Web browser, and then follow the on-screen instructions. Close the Web browser and return to Word and repeat step 1.
2	An email message will open in Outlook with your document attached as an image file.
3	Fill in the Fax Recipient, Fax Number and Subject sections of the message window.
4	Complete the fax cover sheet to ensure that the recipient can identify the sender and the purpose for which the fax is sent.
5	Click **Send**.

```
              [COMPANY NAME]
              [COMPANY ADDRESS]

       FACSIMILE TRANSMITTAL SHEET

TO:                        FROM:
   [Name]                     [Name]
COMPANY:  DATE:
   [Company name]             10/6/2013
FAX NUMBER:                 TOTAL NO. OF PAGES, INCLUDING COVER:
   [fax]                      [number of pages]
PHONE NUMBER:               SENDER'S REFERENCE NUMBER:
   [phone]                    [reference number]
RE:                        YOUR REFERENCE NUMBER:
   [subject of fax]           [reference number]

 ☐ URGENT  ☐ FOR REVIEW  ☐ PLEASE COMMENT  ☐ PLEASE REPLY  ☐ PLEASE RECYCLE

NOTES/COMMENTS:
```

Figure 7.3.3 | A fax transmission form

Another way to send a fax via the Internet is by using a **fax modem** that must be installed on your computer. Open the folder in which the document is saved, right-click on the document icon and select **Send to** then **Fax recipient** on the pop-up menu.

Disadvantages of fax

There are disadvantages and limitations of using fax as a form of electronic communication:

- For legal documents, the original is usually still required, so it would have to be sent as a hard copy anyway.
- It is not suitable for confidential documents because the intended recipient might not be operating the receiving machine.
- It can only work if the intended recipient has a fax machine.
- Documents do not pass through the fax machine if they are torn, heavily creased, printed on thick card stock, bound or stapled together.

SUMMARY QUESTIONS

1 Define the following terms:
   a facsimile
   b multifunctional device
   c fax transmission form.

2 You have been asked to fax a copy of your academic certificates to a potential employer.
   a Explain how to send a fax using a facsimile machine.
   b Outline two other methods for sending faxes.
   c What are two advantages of faxing a document?
   d What are two disadvantages of using fax as a means of communication?

Electronic mail (email) is a system for sending, receiving and storing messages via communication networks such as the Internet. Table 7.4.1 lists the advantages and disadvantages of using email.

Table 7.4.1 The advantages and disadvantages of email

Advantages of emails	Disadvantages of emails
They improve speed in that messages are sent and received instantaneously.	Destructive programs called viruses can be sent from one computer to another via email.
They reduce cost because there is no need to purchase stamps or stationery.	They cannot be signed. Therefore they are generally not used for legally binding business documents such as contracts.
They reduce the need for physical storage equipment such as filing cabinets for the keeping of correspondence.	Advertisers send out large volumes of unsolicited emails called **spam** which can crowd your inbox, making it difficult for you to locate important communications.
They are ecologically friendly because the consumption of paper is reduced.	They can only be read if the recipient has Internet access.
They can be sent on any day and at any time.	
They can be sent simultaneously to many recipients.	

Email accounts

You need an email account to send or receive email. Each email account is identified by a unique **email address** that is typed as a continuous string of letters, numbers and symbols.

Creating an email account

You can easily create free email accounts at several websites, such as outlook.com and gmail.com. Log on to the website of the email service provider and follow the on-screen instructions.

Using your email account

Take some time to familiarise yourself with the webpage of your email account. The appearance and labels will vary, depending on which service you use. You will notice the following:

- The **Inbox** represents a storage location (folder) for the mail you receive.
- The **Outbox folder** contains a copy of each email that you send.
- The **Drafts folder** contains any email that you started to compose but did not complete.

- The **Trash folder** temporarily holds any emails that you delete.
- **Contacts** stores an address book with the names and email addresses of people with whom you want to communicate.

Sending emails

Table 7.4.2 explains how to send an email.

Copying in recipients

To copy the email message to several people at the same time just for information purposes, type the additional addresses in the **Cc** box. To send copies without making the original recipient aware that these copies have been sent, type the additional addresses in the **Bcc** box.

Working with attachments

You may want to send a file from your computer, such as a photograph or a document. You can send this as an attachment to your email message (see Table 7.4.3).

Table 7.4.3 How to attach a file

1	Click the **Attach** button (see Figure 7.4.1 as an example).
2	Browse in the box that pops up to search for the file on your computer. You may have to select the type of file you want to attach first, e.g. **Picture**.
3	Click on the file you want to attach and click **Open**.
4	Repeat this process for each file that you want to attach.

Figure 7.4.1 Adding an attachment

File organisation

Your inbox may become crowded. You can delete unwanted files. However, you will want to keep important communication. You can add order and make files easier to find by creating folders to sort your mail by subject or by sender. The program will automatically order the email in these folders by date.

Contact list organisation

Email software automatically organises the contact list into alphabetical order. You can also organise contacts into groups such as friends, relatives and business associates.

To create a contact list:

1 Click on the appropriate link, such as **New Contact** or **People** and enter the required information such as the person's name and email address.

2 Click **Save and Add another contact**, and repeat this process until you have added all of the contacts.

Table 7.4.2 How to send an email

1	Click on the link that will allow you to compose a new mail message.
2	Type the recipient's email address (or recipients' email addresses if you are sending to more than one person) in the **To** box.
3	Type your message in the space provided.
4	Click **Send** and your email will be sent simultaneously to all recipients.

DID YOU KNOW?

You might have become used to shortening words when sending text messages, such as using U for you, or R for are. However, such 'text talk' should not be used in emails.

SUMMARY QUESTION

You have been asked to explain the use of email to a group of first-form students. Prepare a well-laid out presentation, using no more than 10 slides, outlining the following information:

- benefits and challenges of emails
- how to set up an account, including selecting an appropriate account name
- how to set up a contacts list
- how to compose and send an email with an attachment
- how to send emails to multiple recipients, including the difference between Cc and Bcc.

New communication technology

Information and communication technology is highly dynamic. New technologies are always being developed, and existing technologies change or become obsolete. Some examples are discussed below.

There have been dramatic increases in the capacity of mobile hand-held communication devices. Many now combine cellular phone service with a wide range of computer applications, including high-speed internet access and on-screen drawing. These **smart phones** can also be used for video conferencing.

You can create and store any file in a secure online location instead of on your personal computer. This is called **cloud computing**. This technology dramatically increases the storage potential of a computer system. Backup copies of important files can be made and stored in different locations.

Many academic institutions offer students the option to study from home through the Internet. Students and lecturers use a range of communication modes including collaborative whiteboards, live chat, emails, electronic portfolios and forum discussions.

As you have learned, many organisations offer employees the option to telecommute, resulting in considerable savings. For example, each year the CXC spends millions of dollars on travel and accommodation for teachers who mark their examinations. The organisation is now seeking to implement an online marking system that will enable teachers to remain in their home countries.

Selection of communication media

Throughout your studies of EDPM you were introduced to a wide range of communication media. Table 7.5.1 presents the factors that should be considered when choosing the medium or channel to be used for conveying a message.

Table 7.5.1 Factors to consider when selecting communication media

Urgency	Electronic communication media (e.g. fax or email) is best if a message needs to reach its recipient immediately. Less-urgent communication can be sent by conventional mail.
Genre	The genre or nature of the message influences the choice of media. Official or formal communication such as contracts or agreements must be typed, printed and signed, not emailed. An email or telephone call is often less formal. It is wise for businesses to follow up important email or telephone communication with a letter to confirm the details. Written communication should be used for long and complicated information. Shorter, simple messages may be communicated orally, face to face or by telephone.
Level of confidentiality	A sealed letter that is hand delivered to the recipient is one of the most confidential means of communication. Email and fax are less confidential, as they can sometimes be accessed by unauthorised people.
Location and time zone	Most internal communication in a business may be done face to face or by using memos. Telephone, letters, printed publications or electronic media can be used for external communication. Some organisations do business internationally, requiring that time zones be taken into consideration. For example, the time in London is approximately 4 hours ahead of Trinidad time. Thus, an email must be sent at 4 a.m. or earlier if a Trinidadian business person wants a recipient in London to access it at the start of the business day.
Cost	Some methods of communication are more expensive than others. Calls over the Internet have become popular because of their minimal cost. If the purpose of the communication is to inform and it is not time sensitive, a company's website can be used to post a wide range of information for workers and the general public at relatively low cost.
Efficiency	Efficiency involves achieving the desired goal with the least expenditure of time and effort. It might be more efficient to send out a memo rather than to call a meeting of all employees. It would be inefficient to rely on email communication if relatively few employees have access to the Internet.
Effectiveness	Effectiveness relates to the extent to which the desired outcome is achieved. For example, direct oral communication is usually most effective when seeking to persuade people or obtain their point of view. If the sender and recipient are far apart, telephone may be chosen. For larger audiences, a meeting or teleconference may be used if oral communication is preferred. The literacy level, language skills and previous knowledge of the recipient must also be considered. Use short, simple sentences to minimise misunderstanding. Define all unfamiliar terms. Where possible, support your words with visuals such as charts and photographs.

SUMMARY QUESTIONS

1 Compare at least three new or emerging communication technologies to the use of conventional mail and telephone, using the following headings:
   a versatility
   b accessibility
   c cost.

2 Discuss the advantages, disadvantages and situations in which each of the following forms of communication may be used:
   a email
   b teleconference
   c telephone call
   d face-to-face meeting
   e memorandum
   f letter.

3 Discuss how each of the following factors will influence your selection of a communication medium:
   a time zone
   b complexity of the message
   c confidentiality
   d cost.

4 Mellision Petroleum Services Limited operates in 12 countries around the globe. Select the means of communication that you consider most appropriate for each of the following situations. You must justify your choice.
   a To inform all employees about the appointment of a new chief executive officer.
   b To transmit signed contracts to the head office.
   c For the human resource managers of the 12 branches to collaboratively prepare a new employee handbook.

An individual or organisation creates and receives a significant number of documents while engaging in business activities. It is difficult and time consuming to locate documents if they are left in a disorganised collection. These files may be misplaced, lost or damaged. Proper file management allows for easy access to documents and helps to keep them clean and neat (Figure 8.1.1).

Each document in a filing system is called a **record**. Examples of records include: letters and memoranda, agreements, contracts, specifications, receipts, invoices, statements of income and expenditure, balance sheets and minutes of meetings.

Individuals and organisations keep records for various reasons, for example:

- as evidence that transactions were performed
- to provide information for the day-to-day operations of the organisation
- as a source of data that can be used to analyse past performance and plan the future direction of an enterprise
- to fulfil legal requirements such as government regulations for accounting or tax purposes.

Manual and electronic filing systems

A **filing system**, also known as an **information management system**, is a method of collecting, organising, storing, preserving and allowing the retrieval of information.

A **manual filing system** is used for the organisation and storage of hardcopy documents in fireproof and waterproof filing cabinets. An **electronic filing system** is used for electronic documents, and is normally stored on a computer system. Table 8.1.1 summarises the advantages and disadvantages of each filing system.

Figure 8.1.1   Records should be filed properly

Table 8.1.1 The advantages and disadvantages of manual and electronic filing systems

Advantages of manual filing systems	Disadvantages of manual filing systems
• Enable the organisation and storage of physical documents such as signed contracts. • Safe from unauthorised access by computer hackers. • Cannot be destroyed by viruses. • Files are safe in the event of failure of computer equipment. • Records can be accessed even when there is no electricity. • Employees can use the system with little or no specialised training.	• Occupy more physical space than electronic systems. • Records might be located in a centralised location that is far from the people who need to use them. • Records can be destroyed by fire or flood. • Records are normally available to only one user at a time. • It takes a lot of time to manually organise, find and retrieve documents. • It is easy for documents to be misfiled or lost.
Advantages of electronic filing systems	**Disadvantages of electronic filing systems**
• Reduce the physical space required for storing documents. • Information is immediately available online to workers and customers. • Reduce the number of staff that must be hired to manage records. • Increase the speed with which documents can be located and retrieved. • Records created in various departments are available throughout the organisation. • Enable documents to be available for viewing by different people at the same time. • Files can be password protected to ensure that only authorised people are able to access records. • Documents are less likely to be misfiled, misplaced, damaged or lost.	• Paper documents must be scanned into the computer system; this can be time consuming in organisations that have lots of written communications. • Staff must be trained in computerised records management. • Records cannot be accessed if there is a power failure. • Records may be lost if the computer system crashes. Hence there must be a schedule for the automatic backing-up of all records. • Some countries have not yet modified their laws to accommodate electronically stored documents. Hence the organisation may need to store paper documents, such as signed contracts. • Hackers can access, change or destroy records.

SUMMARY QUESTIONS

1 State at least three reasons why documents should be filed properly.

2 The principal of your school is seeking information on whether your school should change from a manual to an electronic filing system. Prepare a memorandum discussing the differences between manual and electronic filing systems, using the following headings:

  a main characteristics

  b examples of use

  c advantages

  d disadvantages.

Electronic filing systems

Table 8.2.1 File extensions and their meanings

File extension	File type
.txt	text documents such as those created with Microsoft Notepad
.doc and .docx	documents created in Microsoft Word
.jpg	photograph
.gif	graphic file
.bmp	bitmapped picture
.wav	sound file
.mp3	sound file
.mpg	movie file
.avi	video clip
.exe	executable file, a program

Data processing

Data processing involves entering records into an electronic filing system. The data can be obtained from source documents, turnaround documents and machine-readable documents.

Source documents are the records that are created whenever business is conducted, such as cheques, invoices, leases and contracts of work. Organisations use them as evidence to prove that the transaction occurred. These documents are entered into the computer system using magnetic ink character readers, bar-code scanners, optical mark readers (OMRs) and optical character readers (OCRs).

A **turnaround document** is a paper or electronic document that is sent to an external party, such as a customer or supplier, to gather data. The document is then returned and the data is added to the company's computer system as input. The tear-off slip on a circular letter is one example of a turnaround document.

A **machine-readable document** can be scanned directly into the computer and does not need to be manually typed in by a person. It is a fast, efficient and accurate method for inputting data. One example of a machine-readable document is the multiple-choice answer sheets that are used for examinations.

Electronic filing

The data and programs in your computer are saved as files. Each file in a location has a unique file name. The computer identifies each type of file by using a **file extension** after the file name. Table 8.2.1 summarises some commonly used file extensions and their meanings.

Hierarchical file structures

Like paper documents, electronic files should be sorted and stored properly. A **hierarchical file structure** organises files into folders and sub-folders, making it easier to locate them. The drive on which the files and folders are stored is called the **root directory**. For example, items

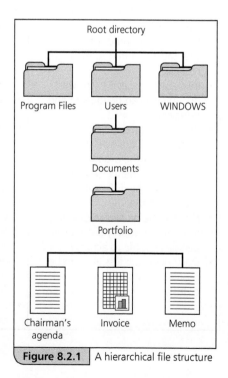

Figure 8.2.1 A hierarchical file structure

saved on the computer are normally placed in the Documents folder unless another is selected. The Documents folder is on the hard drive, within a folder called Users. You can create sub-folders within the Documents folder, as shown in Figure 8.2.1.

If you fail to keep your computer files organised, you may experience the following:

- You may have difficulty finding files because you may not remember the names under which they were saved.
- You may have to spend time searching through numerous files to find the one you want to use.
- Your computer may run out of storage space because you have saved too many unwanted documents.

Table 8.2.2 provides instructions to enable you to manipulate an electronic filing system. These may vary according to the software you are using, but the principles apply to most operating systems.

DID YOU KNOW?

You can also create a new folder by right-clicking a blank area in any folder window or on the desktop, pointing to **New**, and then clicking **Folder**.

Table 8.2.2 Electronic filing methods

Task	Method
Create a new folder	**1** Click on the **Start** menu and then click **Documents**. If **Documents** is not visible, this can be found in the **Libraries** section of **Computer**. **2** Under **File and Folder Tasks** or **Organize**, click **New folder**. A new folder will be displayed with the default name, **New Folder**. **Note:** in newer versions of Windows there is a **New Folder** button. **3** Type a name for the new folder, and then press the **Enter** key on the keyboard.
Move a file or folder	There are several ways to move an item. One of the easiest ways is to cut and paste. **1** Right click on the file or folder and select **Cut** from the pop-up menu. Note: If you want to leave a copy of the document in its original location, select **Copy** instead of **Cut** from the pop-up menu. **2** Open the new folder to which you want to move the item. **3** Right click a blank area of the folder window and select **Paste** from the menu that will appear.
Use 'Send to'	You can send a file or folder to **Documents**, to a removable storage device such as a flash drive or to another folder on your computer network. **1** Right-click on the item that you want to move. **2** Point to **Send to** and select the location to which you wish to send the item.
Move multiple files	If you want to move more than one file you may select them simultaneously. To select a consecutive group of files, click the first file, press and hold down the **Shift** key, and then click the last file. To select files or folders in non-consecutive order, press and hold down **Ctrl**, and then click the items you want. After the files have been selected, right-click to cut and paste.

SUMMARY QUESTIONS

1 Brenna and her family use the computer to create, save and download a large variety of files. They are all saved in the Documents folder and they never delete anything.

  a State three challenges that Brenna might experience when she wants to work with a document.

  b Explain how Brenna and her family can develop an effective electronic filing system.

2 Jayden has noticed that whenever he saves a document name the computer adds a full stop (period) followed by a few letters. He is puzzled by this phenomenon.

  a What are these additions to the document name called?

  b Explain the purpose of these additions to the document name.

  c State the meanings of the following:

    i .txt ii .bmp iii .wav iv .doc

File integrity and security

At the end of this topic you should be able to:

• discuss issues related to the integrity and security of files.

File integrity refers to maintenance of a file in the exact condition that it was originally stored.

File security refers to the protection of files from damage, destruction and unauthorised access, whether accidental or deliberate.

A number of measures can be taken in an attempt to protect the integrity and security of files. Table 8.3.1 shows the different ways you can protect files.

Table 8.3.1 How to protect different filing systems

You can protect files in an electronic system by:	You can protect files in a manual system by:
• keeping computers and storage media in a secure location, where they cannot be accessed by unauthorised people • using passwords and encryption to restrict access to confidential files • making files read-only access so that they are not easily changed • using **virus protection** (see 1.5) • using a **firewall**, a set of programs that protects a computer or a network from other users • developing and using disaster recovery strategies such as the frequent backing-up of files to an external storage medium.	• only allowing authorised people access to filing cabinets • locking away confidential files when they are not in use • storing files in waterproof, fireproof cabinets.

Password protection

Password protection gives documents a higher level of security. Users will be required to enter a password to open and/or make changes to the file. To password protect a file created with Microsoft Word:

1 Open the file.

2 For Microsoft Word 2003 on the **Tools** menu, click **Options**, and then click **Security**. For Word 2007, click the **Microsoft Office Button**, point to **Prepare**, and then click **Encrypt Document**.

3 Follow the on-screen instructions to enter and confirm the password. Note that the password will appear as a series of asterisks or some similar **placeholder** symbol. This prevents an onlooker from seeing your password.

4 Click **OK**.

You will be unable to open the document if you lose or forget your password.

Normal document

↓

Encryption
The code that makes up the file is scrambled so it is in a different pattern

↓

Encryted file
The text is impossible to read for users without the encryption key

↓

Encryption key
Unscrambles the code

↓

Document can be read as normal

Figure 8.3.1 The encryption process

Encryption

Figure 8.3.1 shows how **encryption** works. Word 2007 and 2010 automatically encrypts password-protected files. Encryption is used to protect sensitive information such as a customer's name, address, phone number and credit card number when business is transacted online.

Overwrite protection

Sometimes you may want to ensure that people do not change a file to which they have access. You can do this by making the file read only. Users will be able to open a read only document but if they make changes to it they will be prevented from saving those changes – they will have to save it as a new document with a new file name. To **write-protect** a file:

1 Open the folder in which the document is saved.

2 Right-click on the file you want to write protect.

3 Select **Properties** from the pop-up menu that appears.

4 Click on **Read-only** in the **Attributes** section of the **Properties** dialogue box (Figure 8.3.2) so that a check mark appears in the box.

5 Click **OK**.

System backup

You should prevent information from being permanently lost by creating a copy of the information stored on your hard disk. If the original data on your hard disk is lost or damaged, you can then use the copy to restore the information. The system backup utility on a computer helps you to do this. You will need an external hard drive, or a CD-RW or DVD-RW drive and several disks, to store the backup information.

Table 8.3.2 shows you how to complete a system backup in Windows.

Table 8.3.2 Instructions for a system backup

Windows Vista, 7 and 8	
1	Click on the **Start** button to open your **Start** menu.
2	Click on the **All Programs** menu option.
3	Click on the **Maintenance** folder.
4	Click on the **Backup and Restore** Center icon.
5	Follow the on-screen instructions in the **Backup and Restore Center** that will open.
Earlier versions of Windows (e.g. 98 and XP)	
1	Click **Start**.
2	Point to **All Programs**, and then point to **Accessories**.
3	Point to **System Tools**, and then click **Backup**.
4	Follow the on-screen instructions.

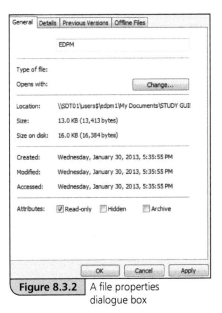

Figure 8.3.2 A file properties dialogue box

DID YOU KNOW?

You can also use the Backup and Restore utility to set up a schedule for the computer to automatically back up its files.

SUMMARY QUESTIONS

1 Outline at least three ways to protect the security and integrity of:

   a manual filing systems

   b electronic filing systems.

2 As an office worker you are expected to perform routine file maintenance tasks on the computer. Outline the steps you will follow to do a system backup.

3 Outline the key differences between write protection and password protection.

File retention and traceability

Figure 8.4.1 Effective file retention policies help to prevent overcrowding

Organisations maintain a vast number of records for administrative, legal, financial or historical purposes. Files that are useful for the organisation's current operations are termed **active** and must be kept in an easily accessible location. Records that are no longer useful for performing current activities are termed **inactive**.

File retention policy

It is beneficial for an organisation to have a **retention system** with a systematic method for dealing with outdated files. The benefits are:

• it is easy to retrieve useful records

• it saves space and prevents overcrowding

• it efficiently utilises filing equipment and computer storage space.

Having an effective file retention policy is therefore an essential aspect of maintaining a properly functioning filing system (Figure 8.4.1).

Retention periods for business documents are usually specified by law. In many countries business letters must be retained for at least three years and financial records must be kept for a minimum of seven years. Other records may be identified as **permanent records** that should never be destroyed. Some examples of permanent records are company registration documents, contracts and annual financial statements. In contrast, documents such as flyers are usually temporary and can be discarded almost immediately.

Several factors determine an organisation's retention policy:

• how often the record is requested or used

• what type of information it contains

• what laws govern the period of retention

• how useful the information will be in future decision making

• the organisation's capacity to effectively store files.

Table 8.4.1 provides a checklist for following retention policy.

Table 8.4.1 Retention policy checklist

The organisation should ensure that:
✓   Records are classified according to their purpose and retention period as Permanent, Temporary, Active and Inactive, for example. Each group of files should be kept in a separate storage location.
✓   Records are filed in an appropriate manual or electronic system. Most organisations use a combination of both systems.
✓   An inventory of records is maintained
✓   Files are examined periodically to determine whether they will be retained or disposed of.

Archiving

Archiving is the process of relocating records from the active filing area to storage. For example, scanned documents that are no longer in use can be stored in an archive. The archive can either be in a physical storage space or online.

Disposal of files

It is neither wise nor cost effective to retain records that are identified as worthless at the end of their retention period. They should be permanently removed from the archive and destroyed.

Treatment of sensitive documents

Sensitive documents contain information given in confidence, personal details about individuals, or commercial, legal or financial information. Hardcopies of sensitive documents must be shredded or incinerated. If old computers are discarded, their hard drives should be removed and destroyed to ensure the safety of sensitive information.

Traceability

Traceability is the ability to follow the sequence of changes that are made to a document. An easy way to maintain traceability is to name different versions of a saved file in numerical order. This allows you to keep track of work in progress. For example, for your SBA research project you may choose to name your versions as shown in Figure 8.4.2.

This technique makes it possible for an external verifier to confirm the authenticity of the documents you submit. It also ensures that the version you submit is the final version and that you do not omit any updates made.

Metadata

Metadata refers to data that is stored on documents, such as date created, date modified, date accessed, owner and access privileges (for example, whether it is read only or password protected). This metadata helps to ensure traceability of a document, because it shows information about when and on which computer a file was created. To view a document's metadata open the **Properties** dialogue box as shown in 8.3 and select the **Details** tab.

| Assignment 2.1 |
| Original document |

↓

| Assignment 2.2 |
| Document with improvements based on the teacher's comments |

↓

| Assignment 2.3 |
| Final version with formatting changes made after receiving approval |

Figure 8.4.2 | Suggested version names for updated documents

EXAM TIP

The documents created in the EDPM practical examinations must be saved on a CD and sent to CXC. Examiners could therefore view the metadata to verify whether the work is authentic.

DID YOU KNOW?

Microsoft Word can automatically track changes that are made in a document. This is very useful when several people are working collaboratively. Check how to use this feature in the Help section of the program.

9 Ethics

9.1

Intellectual property

LEARNING OUTCOMES

At the end of this topic you should be able to:

- explain the concept of intellectual property
- describe the rights that are protected by intellectual property laws
- discuss ethical standards with respect to intellectual property.

RESEARCH IT

Research and summarise the intellectual property laws of your country.

Intellectual property refers to the products of the minds of people, such as inventions, books, computer programs, architectural and technical drawings, works of art, films, songs and music. Intellectual property acknowledges that an individual can own the product of his or her creativity, innovation and self-expression. It grants the creator the legal right to determine how this product can be used, stored, reproduced and distributed.

Table 9.1.1 presents some terms associated with intellectual property and their meanings. Ensure that you can define each term.

Table 9.1.1 Intellectual property terms and their meanings

Term	Definition and examples
Patent	The right to produce and sell or rent a new invention, whether it is a product or a process, for a certain period of time (usually 20 years). The patent holder must register the product to obtain this right.
Industrial design right	The right to own and use the style or form of appearance of an industrial object such as the parts of an appliance, unique patterns on a piece of fabric or specially carved furniture.
Trade secret	The right to hold secret information concerning the commercial practices or knowledge of a business, for example KFC's 11 herbs and spices.
Trademark	The right to use a distinctive sign or words to differentiate the products or services produced by a particular business. Trademarks must be registered.

Rights protected by intellectual property laws

Intellectual property laws protect the *economic* and *moral* rights of the owner of the work.

Economic rights

Economic rights involve the right to receive payment for use of the product. For example, if you compose a short story that is later published in an anthology, you have the right to be paid for your work. Therefore photocopying a textbook instead of purchasing it violates the economic rights of the author.

Moral rights

Moral rights protect the integrity and reputation of the author from misrepresentation or misquoting of the work. This means that a person should not isolate sections from a work and then put them together in such a way that distorts the writer's original message. Falsely attributing work to an author is also a violation of moral rights.

DID YOU KNOW?

The Creative Commons licence gives authors the right to specify the conditions under which people can use, share or develop their work. For example, a developer of computer games might give websites permission to freely distribute but not sell their products.

For example Jehua Chalmers might write: 'I love Trinidad Carnival in all its glory. I am awed by the beauty and pageantry as thousands of masqueraders take the stage for what is called "The Greatest Show on Earth". However I am less thrilled by the vulgarity that is sometimes displayed.' It would violate that writer's moral rights to state: 'Jehua Chalmers loves the glory, beauty, pageantry, and vulgarity of Trinidad Carnival.'

Ethics and intellectual property

You have learned that intellectual property is protected by law. However, respect for intellectual property is also an ethical issue. It is sometimes challenging to decide whether a specific action is right or wrong. For example, have you ever downloaded and made copies of your favourite songs or movies to share with your friends? Have you ever used a photograph or drawing from the Internet in a research project without indicating the source? If so, it is quite possible that you have violated the intellectual property rights of a person, group or organisation.

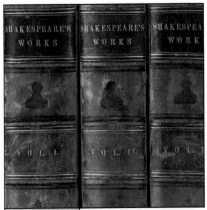

Figure 9.1.1 Many older books are now in the public domain, what does this mean for the authors' economic rights compared to their moral rights?

ACTIVITY

No permission was sought or obtained in each of the cases outlined below. State whether each was a violation of intellectual property. Give reasons for your answer.

1 Two journalists from rival newspapers investigate and write articles about the same car accident, so their information is almost exactly the same.

2 Terrell, an excellent tailor, decides to make a range of exercise wear for sale. He embellishes his clothes with the logos of the top NBA teams to make them more attractive.

3 Brittany cannot afford to buy a textbook, so she borrows her friend's textbook and writes notes about as much of it as she can.

4 Brittany decides to save time by photocopying several chapters of her friend's textbook.

5 Josiah invents an exciting new game for his technology education project. A couple of years later his teacher decides to make a few minor improvements and begins to produce the game for sale.

SUMMARY QUESTIONS

1 Define the following terms:
   a intellectual property
   b trademark
   c patent
   d trade secret.

2 Explain, with the use of appropriate examples, the concept of:
   a moral rights
   b economic rights.

9.2 Copyright and plagiarism

LEARNING OUTCOMES

At the end of this topic you should be able to:

- explain the concept of copyright
- explain the concept of plagiarism
- list guidelines to avoid plagiarism.

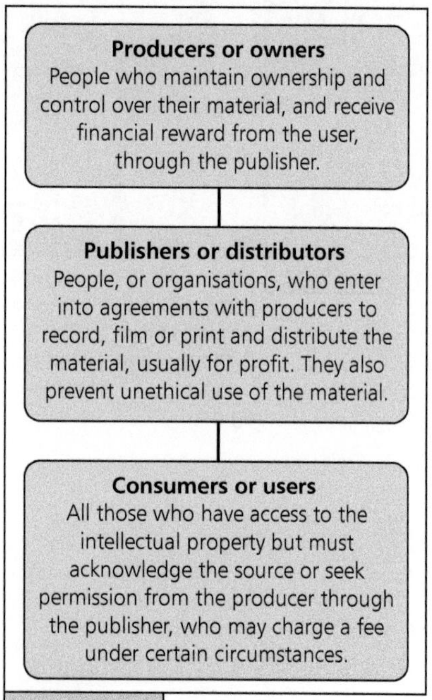
Producers or owners
People who maintain ownership and control over their material, and receive financial reward from the user, through the publisher.
Publishers or distributors
People, or organisations, who enter into agreements with producers to record, film or print and distribute the material, usually for profit. They also prevent unethical use of the material.
Consumers or users
All those who have access to the intellectual property but must acknowledge the source or seek permission from the producer through the publisher, who may charge a fee under certain circumstances.

Figure 9.2.1 People affected by copyright

Copyright

Copyright refers to the right to control the conditions under which others can print, publish, perform, record or adapt creative and artistic works. The works covered by copyright include music, books, software, films, paintings, architectural and engineering drawings and photographs. Copyright terms are normally valid for a certain period of time, unless they are renewed.

A copyright holder may allow or forbid people to:

- make copies by any means including typing, photocopying, scanning into a computer, taping live or recorded music and copying music and video disks
- issue copies of the work to the public (if a legal copy is already in circulation then the legal copy can be sold)
- rent their product, for example if a DVD is sold for home use only, then renting it out at a video club would be illegal
- publish the work on the Internet or make it available online for download to a computer
- broadcast or perform the work in public.

Figure 9.2.1 shows the people involved in the concept of copyright.

Plagiarism

Plagiarism is the act of using or closely imitating another people's words or ideas without acknowledging the source. The following guidelines will help you to avoid plagiarism when writing your own work:

- Use several different sources of information rather than relying on one or two texts.
- Read the source documents and make notes in your own words.
- Use the notes to develop your own ideas.
- Indicate when you are using another person's words.
- Acknowledge the source of any ideas, opinions or theories that are not your own.
- Obtain approval from the producer before using a substantial part of any work.
- State the source of any pieces of information that are not common knowledge including statistics, graphs, charts, drawings and photographs.

Citations

Citations are used to acknowledge the source of words or ideas used in your writing. Complete information, including the title, author's name, year of publication and the publisher, should be given so that the source can be located.

An in-text citation is a brief mention of the information source within the body of your document. It gives the surname of the author and the publication year of the cited information. The page number is included if a direct quotation or a paraphrase was used.

- If another person's exact words are used, they should be placed in quotation marks, for example:

Bailey (2008) stated that 'arguably no area of human endeavour has seen as much dramatic change over the past decade as in the field of information and communication technology' (p24).

- No quotation marks are used if the words are paraphrased. However, the source should still be acknowledged, for example:

Over the last 10 years information and communication has doubtlessly experienced more dramatic change than any other field of endeavour (Bailey, 2008, p24).

- If the quotation is longer than 40 words, an inset without quotation marks is used, as shown below:

Arguably no area of human endeavour has seen as much dramatic change over the past decade as in the field of information and communication technology. From cloud computing to 4G cellular networks, computing is becoming faster, more versatile and more mobile than ever before. (Bailey, 2008, p24)

Bibliography

A **bibliography** is a list of all the sources of information that you used in your document, including books, magazine articles and websites. You must include a bibliography whenever you prepare a document that uses information from other sources.

There are several internationally accepted styles for preparing bibliographies. CXC recommends that you use the style developed by the American Psychological Association, called the **APA style**. For example, a book reference following APA guidelines would look like this:

Bailey, F. R. (2013). *The information and communications technology revolution: A brief review*. New York: Academic Publishers International.

An Internet reference would be formatted as:

Bailey, F. R. (2013). Computing in the clouds: New and emerging technologies. *The Caribbean Information and Computer Technology Association Review*. Retrieved from http://www.cictar.edu/bailey_2003_1/

EXAM TIP

School-Based Assessments containing plagiarised material may be marked as ungraded by the Caribbean Examinations Council.

DID YOU KNOW?

Many educational institutions now use software that detects if a student's work contains plagiarised information.

ACTIVITY

Research other APA formats online. Prepare a bibliography using any four textbooks that are available to you and at least four articles from the Internet.

SUMMARY QUESTIONS

1 Define the terms:
  a plagiarism
  b copyright
  c bibliography.

2 Outline the guidelines that must be followed to:
  a avoid plagiarism
  b prepare an in-text citation
  c prepare a bibliography.

Standards of work

At the end of this topic you should be able to:

• plan and order priorities to ensure acceptable standards of work.

Figure 9.3.1 Workspace organisation affects productivity

The average adult spends one-third of his or her life, or half of all waking hours, at work. It is therefore essential to ensure that the workplace is organised for maximum health, safety and efficiency.

Organisation of work and work station

A well-organised workspace increases your comfort, confidence and productivity. Disorder can result in confusion and stress, which reduces efficiency (Figure 9.3.1). Table 9.3.1 lists tips for organising your work and work station.

Table 9.3.1 Tips for organising your work and work station

Arrange your work area so that you can function efficiently and effectively
✓ Ensure that items frequently used are always close at hand. ✓ Use a document holder to correctly position the copy of work to be typed. ✓ Follow the ergonomic and safety rules you have learned to ensure that you minimise the risk of work-related injury.
Eliminate clutter
✓ Proofread your work on-screen before printing the document. This will reduce your consumption of paper and ink and result in a cleaner work area. ✓ Sort through and discard unwanted documents. ✓ As far as possible, store a soft copy of your documents instead of a printout.
Organise your documents
✓ Save your documents with brief descriptive names so that they are easily recognised. Place these soft copies in appropriately named folders (see 8.2 and 8.4). ✓ Use a three-ring binder with clear document holders to organise hard-copy pages. This will enable you to quickly locate and select the documents that you need. For example, you can store prints of mailable samples of your work that will go into the reference manual that you are expected to submit for the SBA. It will also serve as a portfolio that you can show to potential employers.
Clean your work area before leaving after each work session, placing all objects where they belong.

Submission of assignments

You have been introduced to the wide range of documents that are used in the business environment. You are expected to produce samples of these documents for your School-Based Assessment. When submitting these, use the following guidelines:

• Make sure that the document is neat, well organised and free of errors.

• Make sure that business documents are prepared according to established rules and guidelines.

- Make sure that you present papers in a neatly labelled, attractive folder. Ensure that all pages are fastened together in the correct order.
- Make sure that you save electronically presented assignments, such as Microsoft PowerPoint presentations, on a well-labelled CD.

Effective time management

Time management is a challenge for many students. Students who lack time-management skills often wait until a deadline is at hand and then rush to complete assignments. As a result they may fail to produce the quality work of which they are capable.

The following guidelines will help you to manage your time more effectively:

- Always be punctual.
- Use an electronic or paper diary to record all assignments. Ensure that dates and times are correct and agreed upon. Aim to complete work assignments before the deadline date. Maintain a checklist and mark off assignments as you complete them.
- Develop a detailed plan or timetable of what needs to be done by a specified time so that the deadlines can be met comfortably. Ensure that assignments are allotted reasonable time for completion.
- If you are required to do group work, motivate your teammates to take early action and prepare a research timetable. Ensure that each team member understands what he or she is expected to do. Meet regularly for progress reports.
- Communicate any unresolved difficulties to your teacher in advance of the due date.

Follow-up procedures

Follow-up procedures are the set of steps that are taken to bring a task or project to a successful conclusion. Remember that there are specific objectives for each learning activity that you undertake. Your work is not over when you submit an assignment. Ultimately you are responsible for the level of success that you achieve. The following suggestions will help you to practise appropriate follow-up procedures.

- Prepare a checklist of the skills you are required to develop and assess yourself to determine the extent to which you have mastered each.
- When work is returned for improvement, make the required corrections promptly.
- Examine your performance and any feedback you receive to identify areas in which you need more practice.

EXAM TIP

You should consistently ensure that your assignments are of the highest possible quality.

EXAM TIP

Keep in mind that you will lose points for late submission of assignments.

SUMMARY QUESTION

Discuss at least three standards that relate to each of the following:

a organisation of work and work station

b submission of assignments

c effective time management

d follow-up procedures.

Desirable habits and attitudes

Table 9.4.1 How to demonstrate team spirit

✓	Work together with others to achieve common goals
✓	Suggest ideas, even if they are not eventually accepted by the group
✓	Respect the viewpoints of others, even if you do not agree with them
✓	Accept responsibility as a group member for the outcomes of the group's activities

As you prepare for adult responsibilities and the world of work, it is essential that you develop habits and attitudes that will make you an asset in any workplace.

Individual responsibility

Individual responsibility is the ability to be personally accountable for your thoughts, words and actions. It involves recognising that you are in charge of your actions and that your choices will determine the level of your success. It also involves being self-motivated and committed to working hard even when you are not closely monitored.

Willingness

Willingness means keenness or enthusiasm. It is the opposite of reluctance. A willing person is eager to accept responsibilities, fulfil duties, accept others and face new challenges.

Meeting deadlines

Meeting deadlines involves ensuring that all assignments are completed to required standards before they are due. Review effective time management in 9.3.

Team spirit

An increasing number of workplaces emphasise the importance of teamwork and collaboration among employees. Consequently it is important that you develop **team spirit**. Review Table 9.4.1.

Cooperation

Cooperation, the ability to work with others for a common purpose, is closely related to having team spirit. Although some environments are highly competitive, it is still essential that you are able to have a good working relationship with your colleagues. You should make a conscious effort to understand the thoughts, feelings, viewpoints and actions of others.

Recognition of diversity

Caribbean societies are generally multicultural and multi-ethnic. Moreover, an increasing number of organisations are operating internationally, with branches in many different countries. It is therefore essential that you develop tolerance and appreciate diversity. You should show equal respect and courtesy to all people, regardless of ethnicity, gender, gender identity, age, disabilities, political and religious affiliation, and socio-economic status.

Courtesy and respect for others

Courtesy involves showing politeness, consideration and kindness to others. Follow the guidelines in Table 9.4.2.

Table 9.4.2 How to be polite and considerate

✓	Be sure to use courteous expressions such as *please*, *thank you*, *I am sorry*, *how may I help?* and *you are welcome*
✓	Learn how to introduce yourself to strangers that you meet in the course of your work
✓	Ensure that you always treat others with dignity and honour
✓	Be considerate of the feelings of others and avoid causing offence by your words or actions

DID YOU KNOW?

While your qualifications might get you a job, it is your values and attitudes that will help to determine whether you will keep it.

Punctuality and regularity

Being punctual everyday will help you to become reliable and efficient. See Figure 9.4.1 for some helpful guidelines.

Good grooming

Your grooming and the style and condition of your clothes send a strong non-verbal message and significantly affect the way people see you. Even organisations that do not have strict dress codes expect the appearance of their workers to create a good impression. Follow the guidelines in Table 9.4.3.

Always arrive on time

Make allowances for unexpected delays such as traffic congestion or vehicle breakdowns

Avoid being absent, especially for trivial reasons

Figure 9.4.1 Punctuality and regularity

Table 9.4.3 How to demonstrate good grooming

✓	When dressing for business ensure that your back, chest, feet, abdomen, upper thighs and underwear are covered
✓	Frayed, torn, wrinkled or dirty clothing should never be worn
✓	Long hair should be tied back so that it does not fall into your face or cover your eyes
✓	Pay careful attention to your personal hygiene, including the length and condition of your fingernails
✓	Ensure that your cosmetics and perfume or cologne are subtle

Personal integrity

Integrity involves being completely trustworthy in all matters. You should be truthful and honest, not deceitful or corrupt. A person of integrity will do what is right, even when no one else is around.

Confidentiality

Confidentiality is the protection of information that should not be disclosed to others. Employees should not discuss information about their employers, colleagues or clients without permission. Confidentiality is essential. Clients can sue a business if their information is disclosed without authorisation and conflict can arise if employees gossip about each other.

SUMMARY QUESTION

The management of your company has asked you to prepare a handbook that clearly outlines desirable work habits and attitudes. This is to be used in its training programme for new employees. Prepare a well-presented document with appropriate graphics.

Practice exam questions

1 Type the following in 2.0 line spacing using Times New Roman size 12.

Visitors to the Regional Health Facility in most rural areas will be pleased with the variety and quality of services they offer. First-time patients may have been referred for attention by another health facility with a condition that requires urgent attention, or to keep a clinical appointment, attend a walk-in clinic on a specific day, or collect medication that is not available in their own area health facility. The emergency department offers a daily 24-hour service for which all patients must register upon arrival. The receptionist will record the information you give in the appointment register and in the patient's card.

People coming to the facility for the first time because of emergency must register in the Triage Department and undergo a preliminary examination designed to assess their condition. They will receive attention according to their status. Priority is given to infants, young children, emergencies such as people involved in serious motor vehicular accidents, and police emergency cases. Impatient people complain of discrimination but the wait for attention is not always very long. During the waiting period the blood sugar and pressure are measured and other conditions attended to. Some may require further examination that indicates whether they should be attended to and discharged, or taken to the general hospital for further attention, or referred directly to a hospital clinic.

From this year patients will be happy to be able to fill their prescriptions at a private pharmacy of their choice. This is the latest intervention under the National Health Plan. The intention is to help citizens cushion the extremely high cost of medical services and education, especially, treatment of the chronically ill and elderly patients. The Public Relations Division of the Ministry of Health is monitoring public response and is convinced that citizens are satisfied with the services they receive. From all accounts they appreciate the Health Plan and support the new health initiative while they hope for more improvements.

(10 marks)

2 Type the following letter on A4 with yesterday's date, using Times New Roman size 11. Use the following margins: 2.54 cm left and right. Correct all errors and do not use abbreviations. Address an envelope to the recipient. Print the letter.

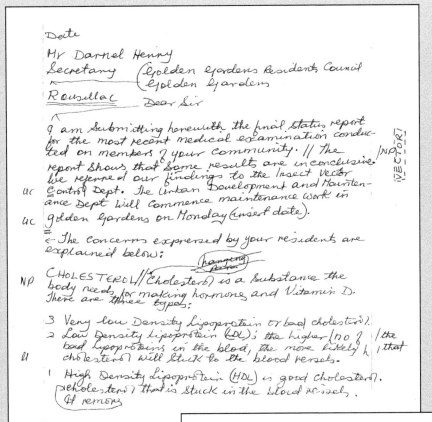

Date

Mr Darnel Henry
Secretary   (Golden Gardens Residents Council
             (Golden Gardens
Rousellac   Dear Sir

I am submitting herewith the final status report for the most recent medical examination conducted on members of your community. // The report shows that some results are inconclusive. We referred our findings to the Insect Vector [VECTOR] Control Dept. The Urban Development and Maintenance Dept will commence maintenance work in golden gardens on Monday (insert date).

← The concerns expressed by your residents are explained below:

CHOLESTEROL // Cholesterol is a substance the body needs for making hormone and Vitamin D. There are three types:

3 Very low Density Lipoprotein or bad cholesterol).
2 Low Density Lipoprotein (LDL); the higher (no of the bad lipoproteins in the blood, the more likely that cholesterol will stick to the blood vessels.
1 High Density Lipoprotein (HDL) is good cholesterol. cholesterol that is stuck in the blood vessels. (It removes

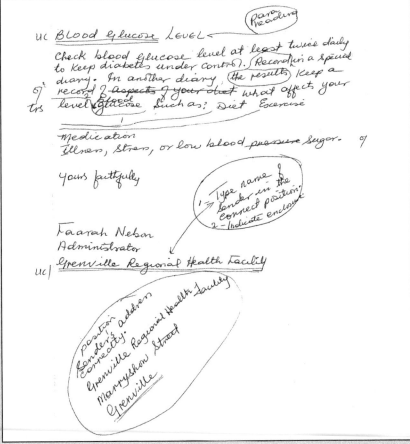

BLOOD GLUCOSE LEVEL ←
Check blood glucose level at least twice daily to keep diabetes under control. Record in a special diary. In another diary (the results) keep a record 2 aspects of your diet what affects your level glucose such as: Diet Exercise

Medication
Illness, stress, or low blood pressure sugar.

Yours faithfully

1→ Type name of sender in the correct position
2 - Indicate enclosure

Faarah Nelson
Administrator
Grenville Regional Health Facility

position address
sender's entity:
correctly.
Grenville Regional Health Facility
Marryshow Street
Grenville

(24 marks)

3 Type the following manuscript using 2.0 line spacing. Correct all errors and follow all instructions.

No abbreviations

NATIONAL REGIONAL HEALTH FACILITIES

The country is divided into health regions. Each [lc] Regional Health facility is in charge of a number of health centres. They all have their own catchment area. District health centres are, open to the public daily from ~~Friday to Monday~~ at 0800 hrs. [trs] Regional health facilities are open 24 hrs daily and will attend to anyone seeking their services.

[stet] Patients are treated and referred to one of the facility's clinics, to their area health centre, or to the General Hospital for further treatment.

Awareness and control of diseases caused by mosquitos, water borne diseases and chronic diseases, is is of paramount importance. Each health centre must submit quarterly statistics to the Regional Health [lc] facility. It will be sent to the Ministry of Health where it will be collated with reports from ~~other~~ regions and sent to the Central Statistical Office to become [stet] Part of the ~~Annual~~ national statistical report. ~~yearly~~

Para 5 // NO HEARTBEAT, NO LIFE! (Shoulder hdg) The heart // is our physical life support. We all risk developing at least one type of coronary ~~heart~~ of disease, and should ~~A risk factor~~ know what the risk factors are. increases the likelihood of coronary [trs] disease heart such as a heart ~~attack~~ angina pectoris (chest pain), or heart attack. We should therefore be interested in risk factors which may be one or more of the following:

numbered

Typist prepare a list of the following
Heart enlargement
Advanced age   Male gender   High or low blood
Pressure   Smoking   Diabetes   Family history
of heart ~~disease~~ attacks among youths   High or
low ~~blood pressures~~ density lipoprotein cholesterol
(not enough cholesterol)   a sedentary lifestyle
(not enough exercise)   The established presence
of coronary heart diseases.

Para 3   MAINTAIN YOUR HEALTH (Shoulder) heading
Our health is our most valuable ~~health~~ asset. Therefore we should be careful. avoid health problems.
The early detection of diseases may add years to our lives. The key to living to a ripe old age is a healthy lifestyle. A healthy diet and recommended, regular exercise physical will help.

Para 4 → Patients of all health facilities get free medical services, medication and advice. They learn about correct use of medication and the importance of refilling prescriptions on time to prevent medication ~~errors~~. They learn to follow instructions carefully and that should be only taken with other medication and foods as prescribed medication.

(28 marks)

4 a Display the below in a spreadsheet. Use the following column widths: column 1 – 25.71 points; columns 2–5 – 22.57 points. Correct all errors.

(24 marks)

4 b Create a database for arriving emergency patients at Grenville Regional Health Facility's emergency department. Print one copy on A4 paper. Correct all errors.

(14 marks)

Further practice questions and examples can be found on the accompanying CD.

Glossary

Actor's script The rehearsal script for an individual performer in a play.

Address bar The section of a web browser in which the website's URL is displayed. In a spreadsheet the address bar shows the column name and row number of the active cell.

Agenda A list of the issues that will be discussed at a meeting.

Animations Motion effects that are applied to individual items such as a text or graphics on a presentation slide.

Antivirus A program that is designed to protect a computer against malicious software such as viruses.

Appendix A section that contains additional supporting material that is placed at the end of a document such as a report or proposal.

Applicable standards The quality of work and materials that is required, according to the law of the country and the standards of the industry.

Application software A computer program that is designed to be used to perform specific tasks (e.g. word-processing software).

Archiving The process of moving data and files that are no longer actively being used to another location for long-term storage.

Attestation clause The section of a legal document (e.g. a will or contract) that is signed by the witnesses, who thereby swear that the document is authentic.

Audio conference A call by telephone or Internet in which there are three or more participants who are in different locations.

Audio message A spoken message that is recorded, typically by an answering machine.

Autosum Used in spreadsheets to add up the contents of many cells.

Background Colours, patterns or pictures that cover the page in a document behind the main text.

Backing storage Memory external to the central processing unit used for storage of large quantities of data or large programs.

Balance sheet A summary of the assets, liabilities and owner's equity of a business. It provides a 'snapshot' of the financial condition of the business.

Bank statement A printed record of the deposits to and withdrawals from a bank account over a specified period.

Bar code A series of lines of varying widths that are used to identify products. Bar codes are read by a scanner.

Bibliography A list of the books, websites and other reference material that were cited in a document.

Bill of quantity A document that lists the quantities, descriptions and prices of the items of labour, materials and parts that are required to complete a project.

Blocked paragraph A paragraph with no indentations.

Border A plain or decorative line that surrounds items such as text or pictures.

Bullet A symbol that is used at the start of each item in a list.

Business card A small rectangle that displays the contact information of an individual or an organisation.

Cell A rectangular box in a spreadsheet or table that is created by the intersection of a column and a row.

Cell address The unique designation of a cell in a spreadsheet. The cell address consists of the column letter followed by the row number.

Central-processing unit (CPU) Considered the brain of the computer. It is the piece of hardware that carries out all the instructions from the software.

Chairman's agenda A specially-prepared list of the matters to be discussed in a meeting, with a wide right column in which the chairman can write notes.

Character A letter, digit, punctuation mark or other symbol that is represented in a computer.

Character keys A key on the keyboard that instructs the computer to display a printable character (e.g. a letter or punctuation mark).

Chart A function of spreadsheet software that allows you to present the data entered into a worksheet as a graph.

Citations Material that is quoted or referred to in a document. Citations are used to illustrate, explain or support a point.

Cloud computing The use of servers on the Internet to store and manage data and processes.

Column heading The heading on the top row of a table or spreadsheet that describes the category of data contained in the column.

Command keys (system keys) Keys that are used alone or in combination with other keys to give instructions to the computer.

Committee documents Documents used in connection with meetings, specifically the notice, agenda, chairman's agenda and minutes.

Compact disk (CD) An optical disk that is used to store data.

Computer An electronic machine or device that accepts and processes data to produce information.

Confidentiality The protection of information that should not be disclosed to others.

Connector A circle on a flow chart that depicts a jump from one point in the process flow to another. Also a line that is used to link two symbols on a flow chart.

Contacts The names and email addresses of people.

Continuation sheet The specially formatted pages that are used for the second and subsequent pages of a letter or memorandum.

Continuous page printer A printer such as a line printer and dot-matrix printer that uses continuous paper that is folded like a fan.

Contractor A person or organisation that enters into a legal agreement to provide materials or labour for a project at a specified price.

Conveyance document A legal document that transfers the ownership of property from one party to another (also known as a deed of conveyance).

Copy The written or printed document that is to be typed.

Copy notation A notation that sometimes appears at the end of a document indicating that copies were sent to other people. It can also be used when sending an email.

Copy paper Good quality of paper that is suitable for use in a photocopier or laser printer.

Copyright The right to control reproduction or adaptation of creative and artistic works for a certain period of time.

Counterpart A duplicate copy of a legal document for signature.

Cut-off slip A response form attached to a letter that the recipient is expected to complete and return to the sender.

Data processing A series of operations that are performed to organise, classify and store data.

Data source The document containing personalised information such as names and addresses that is used in a mail merge.

Database A collection of data organised in tables.

Database management system (DBMS) A set of programs that control the storage of and access to data.

Designation The office or job title of the sender of a letter.

Digital video disk (DVD) An optical disk that is capable of storing large volumes of data.

Document cover Relatively thick, durable paper, which is used for making covers for publications such as pamphlets and brochures.

Document scanner A device that converts existing images or documents to a digital image on the computer.

Domain name A series of characters that serve as the address of a computer network.

Dot-matrix printer An impact printer that uses a series of dots to create an image.

Draft A copy of a legal document that is sent to each party for approval or amendments.

Drafts folder An email storage location for documents that have been written but not yet sent.

Driver The program that is used to control a peripheral device.

Drop caps The first letter in a block of text that is printed larger than the rest of text.

Drop-down menu A list of options that appear under a clicked item.

E-commerce Business that is conducted electronically, particularly on the Internet.

Economic rights Rights to receive payment for use of a product that one has created. This is one form of intellectual property rights.

Editing The process of making changes, especially corrections, to a printed document.

Electronic communication The transmission of messages that have been created in digital format.

Electronic filing system A system for organising and storing files on a computer.

Electronic mail (email) A method of sending and receiving written communication via the computer.

Ellipsis A series of three dots used to indicate that words have been left out from a quotation.

Email address The unique set of characters that is used to identify an email account.

Embedded object An object such as a chart or graph that is placed in a document.

Enclosure line A notation that indicates that additional documents were sent with a letter.

Encryption The process of scrambling the code that makes up a file so that it appears in a different pattern, making the file impossible to read.

Endnote A section at the end of a document used to cite sources of information that were used.

Endorsement A brief statement of the nature of a business document, printed on the outside of the envelope into which the document is placed.

Engrossment The final copy of a legal document for signature.

Enumeration The numbering that is used to show the sequence of items in a list.

Ergonomics The science of designing the job, equipment and workplace to fit the worker, reducing fatigue, discomfort and injury.

Executor (male) or **executrix** (female) The person responsible for ensuring that the terms of the will are carried out.

F

Facsimile (fax) An exact copy of a document that is converted to a code and transmitted via telephone lines or the Internet.

Fax modem A device that enables a computer to send and receive documents as faxes.

Fax transmission form A form sent with a fax that contains information such as the sender's name, subject of the document, number of pages and recipient's name.

Field The smallest unit of data that is stored in a database.

File extension A set of characters at the end of a file name that indicates the type of file and the program to which it is related.

File integrity The maintenance of a file in the exact condition that it was originally stored.

File security The protection of files from damage, destruction and unauthorised access, whether accidental or deliberate.

Filing system A method of classifying files for efficient storage and retrieval.

Firewall A set of programs that protects a computer or a network from unauthorised access.

Flash drive A small, portable storage device that connects to the computer via a USB port.

Floppy disk (diskette) A flexible magnetic disk that is enclosed in a plastic casing.

Flow chart A pictorial representation of the steps, sequence and relationship of operations in a process.

Glossary

Flyer An announcement printed on a single sheet of paper that is designed to be widely distributed, usually in a public place or by mail.

Follow-up procedure The set of steps that are taken to bring a task or project to a successful conclusion.

Font The shape and design of the characters.

Footer An area of the bottom margin of a document into which text or graphics can be inserted.

Footnote A notation at the bottom of a page that is used to explain, comment on, or provide references.

Form A preprinted document with blank spaces into which information is entered.

Form letter A standardised letter that can be personalised by merging it with a data source.

Formulae Code that is used to perform calculations in a spreadsheet by using the cell addresses and signs (operands) such as +, -, * and /.

Forums Online discussion sites that are designed for readers to post brief messages related to a topic.

Function A preset code that is used to perform calculations in a spreadsheet.

Function keys The keys on the keyboard that are labelled F1 to F12.

G

Goods Those products that are identified in the agreement (e.g. a car or appliance).

Grievance arrangement The step-by-step procedure that an employee must follow if he/she has a complaint against an employer.

Guide keys The A key and semicolon key (;) on which the little fingers are placed, making it easy for the other fingers to find their respective home keys naturally.

H

Hanging indent A form of indentation in which all except the first line of a paragraph begin a specified distance from the margin.

Hard-disk drive A metallic case that contains a set of inflexible disks that are stacked one above the other on a spindle.

Hardware The physical components of a computer system, including the computer itself, as well as input, output and storage devices.

Header An area of the top margin of a document into which text or graphics can be inserted.

Heading Text that indicates the topic of a document or section within a document.

Hierarchical file structure The organisation of files into folders and sub-folders, making it easier to locate them.

Hire purchase agreement The agreement between the hirer and the owner in relation to the goods.

Hirer In a hire purchase agreement, the customer who enters into the agreement with the owner.

Home keys In touch keyboarding, the eight keys over which the fingers are positioned when starting to type.

Hyperlinks Specially formatted text or graphic that leads to another webpage when it is clicked.

I

Immediate access storage The memory within the central processor.

Impact printer A printer that creates a printout by using metal pins to press an inked ribbon onto a sheet of paper.

Inbox The section of an email account in which received letters are stored.

Income and expenditure statement (income statement; profit and loss statement) A summary of the sales and expenses of a business over a specific period of time.

Indented paragraph A paragraph in which the first line only begins a distance from the left margin.

Index card A card typically used in a manual filing system (e.g. to type the names and related information of clients, employees, patients and stock).

Industrial design right The right to own and use the style or form of appearance of an industrial object (e.g. the parts of an appliance or unique patterns on a piece of fabric).

Information management system A system for storing, organising and retrieving information.

Initial capitals (title case) The use of capitals (upper-case letters) for the first letter of each word.

Inkjet printer A non-impact printer that creates a printout by shooting fine jets of ink onto paper.

Input device Any piece of hardware that is used to give data or to control signals to the computer.

Inset A section of text that begins and ends further from the left and right margins than the rest of the document.

Integrity Being completely trustworthy in all matters.

Intellectual property The products of the minds of people (e.g. inventions, books, music).

Internet A network that links individual computers and networks throughout the world via telephone lines, cables and satellites.

Invoice A bill that a business sends to a customer.

K

Keyboard An input device used to enter information and instructions into a computer by pressing various keys.

L

Label A small piece of material such as paper or plastic that gives information about the object to which it is attached.

Landscape The horizontal orientation of a document, so that its width is greater than its height.

Laser printer A printer that uses a beam of light to attach powdered ink called toner to paper.

Leader A series of dots or dashes used to guide the eyes of the reader from items in one column to related items in the next column (e.g. in a table of contents).

Leaflet A sheet of paper, usually printed on both sides, that is folded to create pages.

Lease An agreement by which one person conveys to another party the rights to possess and use an asset for a specified period of time.

Legal document A document that contains a legally enforceable agreement (e.g. a lease or will).

Legal-sized paper Paper measuring 216mm × 356mm (8.5 inches × 14 inches) used for printing legal documents.

Lessee In a lease, the person or organisation receiving permission to use the asset.

Lessor In a lease, the owner of an asset. In the case of land or buildings, the lessor is also called the landlord.

Letter-sized paper Paper that measures 216 mm × 279 mm (8.5 inches × 11 inches).

Letterhead Predesigned business stationery that displays the organisation's name, logo and contact information.

Light pen A light-sensitive input device which when it touches the screen detects the presence or absence of light.

Line printer A high-speed impact printer that uses pins to strike the paper.

Line spacing The distance between two lines of text.

Linked object An object in a document, such as a chart, that is connected to a data file, so that the object is automatically updated whenever the data is changed.

Literary work Any piece of composition or creative writing.

Logo A distinctive picture that represents the organisation.

M

Machine-readable document A document that can be scanned directly into the computer and does not need to be manually typed in by a person.

Magnetic disk A circular plate on which electronic data can be stored magnetically.

Mailing list A list of the names and addresses of people and organisations to which correspondence is sent.

Main heading The title of a document, usually displayed in the largest font.

Mainframe A large-scale computer with a variety of peripheral devices, large storage capacity and a fast central processing unit.

Manual filing system A system used for the organisation and storage of hard copy by hand.

Manuscript The original handwritten or typewritten work of an author that is used to prepare an error-free document.

Margin The edge or border of a document.

Marginal heading (side heading) A heading set to the left in a document that is used when typing displayed work such as minutes of meetings, programmes, plays and specifications.

Memorandum (memo) A specially formatted document that is used for communicating within a business.

Memory card A small plastic-coated rectangle that can be used to store data on computers, digital cameras, music players, cellphones and game consoles.

Menu An organised listing of the meals that are served at a restaurant or event.

Metadata Data that is stored on documents (e.g. date created, date modified, date accessed).

Microcomputer Also called a personal computer (PC) – a computer based on a single microprocessor, designed to be used by one person.

Microphone A device used to input audio to a computer.

Minicomputer A computer whose size, speed and capabilities lie between those of a mainframe and a microcomputer.

Minutes A written record of all official proceedings, from the start of the meeting to its conclusion.

Modifier keys The Caps Lock and Shift keys, which modify (change) the function of the character keys.

Monitor A television-like device used to display data (also known as a visual display unit or VDU).

Moral rights Rights that protect the integrity and reputation of the author from misrepresentation or misquoting of the work.

Mouse A handheld input device that controls the movement of the cursor, or the pointer, that is seen on a computer screen.

Multifunctional device A device that combines a scanner, printer, photocopier and fax machine in a single unit.

Multimedia projector A device that takes the image from a computer and projects it onto a screen or wall so that it can be seen by a large audience.

N

Network A system of communication that is created when two or more computers are linked, either by cables or wirelessly, so that they are able to share information and resources.

Newsletter A short, regularly published bulletin that is distributed to interested people (e.g. members of an organisation).

Non-impact printer A printer that does not strike the paper to create a printout.

Notice A document that clearly and concisely presents urgent or important information to its readers.

Notice of meeting A formal, written announcement indicating the date, time and purpose of a meeting.

O

Oblique heading Headings that are set at an angle to the page, used in tables.

Operands The mathematical symbols =, -, * and /.

Operating system software A set of programs that coordinate the activities among computer devices.

Optical character recognition (OCR) The scanning and conversion of paper documents into text that can be edited or changed.

Glossary

Optical disk A disk that stores data as microscopic light-and-dark spots on the disk surface.

Optical mark reader (OMR) A device that is used to recognise dark pencil marks that are made in specific positions on forms.

Organisation chart A diagram that represents the structure of an organisation in terms of levels of authority, lines of responsibility and reporting relationships.

Orientation The direction in which a rectangular page is displayed or printed.

Outbox folder The section of an email account in which sent letters are stored.

Output devices Used to send messages out of the computer in the form of text, images, sounds or coded signals, either directly to the user or to another computer.

P

Page break A marker in a word-processing program that shows where one page ends and another begins.

Page printer A printer such as an inkjet or laser, which prints and ejects one sheet of paper before beginning to print another sheet.

Paragraph heading A heading placed at the start of the first line of a paragraph that is used to indicate the specific idea of the paragraph.

Patent The right to produce and sell or rent a new invention, whether it is a product or a process, for a certain period of time (usually 20 years).

Payment receipt A document prepared as proof of payment.

Peripheral Any hardware device connected to and controlled by the central processing unit.

Permanent record A document that is always retained by a business, because of its administrative, financial, legal or historical importance.

Phishing The fraudulent sending of emails that are designed to get individuals to reveal confidential information such as bank account numbers.

Placeholder A pre-designed section of a document into which you may put text, graphics or other objects.

Plagiarism The act of using or closely imitating other people's words or ideas without acknowledging the source.

Podcast A digital audio recording that is distributed via the Internet, and can be downloaded to computers or portable media players.

Pointing device Device used to move an arrow on a computer screen (e.g. a mouse, trackpoint or trackpad).

Portrait The vertical orientation of a document, so that its height is greater than its width.

Postscript A brief note at the bottom of a letter that is used to send a personal message or to give information that is not directly related to the subject of the letter.

Presentation program Used to create slides containing a variety of elements such as text, pictures, sounds, graphs and video clips.

Press release A concisely-written document that contains information sent to a media house in the hope that it will be published (also called a news release, media release or press statement).

Process symbol A shape used on a flow chart.

Programme A sequential list of activities that are scheduled to take place at an event.

Proofreading The process of carefully reading through a document to identify and correct errors.

Protocol The set of rules on which the website is based.

Public domain Any item that is not subject to copyright and so can be freely used, copied and distributed.

Query A database tool that is used to automatically find and select information from tables for specific purposes.

R

Range A set of adjacent cells.

Receipt A document that is created to provide proof that a payment was received.

Record A set of data about a specific subject, such as a person or product.

References The sources of information that were cited in a document.

Repetitive strain injuries Injuries that occur when the muscles, tendons, nerves or other tissue experience stress or strain because a task is performed repeatedly.

Response form *See* Cut-off slip.

Retention period The period of time for which a specific document must be kept by a business.

Retention system A systematic method for identifying and dealing with outdated files.

Root directory The drive on which the files and folders are stored.

Row heading Used to describe the category of data that the row contains.

S

Sales receipt A document prepared as proof of payment when goods are purchased.

Scan to file A feature of a scanner program that enables a document to be scanned and saved to a storage medium.

Scan to mail A feature of a scanner program that enables a document to be scanned and sent by email.

Scope of works A document that sets out the requirements for performance of work so that the objectives of a project will be achieved.

Search bar A section of a webpage into which keywords for an Internet search can be typed.

Search engine A program that is designed to search for information on the World Wide Web.

Shoulder heading A heading placed between two paragraphs that is used to indicate the specific ideas of the section of a document.

Slide A 'page' in a presentation program.

Slide master A feature that stores information about the slide template that is being used in a presentation.

Slide transitions A motion effects feature of presentation programs.

Smart phones Mobile devices that combine cellular phone service with a wide range of computer applications, including high-speed internet access and on-screen drawing.

Social media A range of easily accessible, user-friendly, interactive applications that are available on the Internet (e.g. blogs and wikis).

Social networking The use of a website to create profiles, link with other users, exchange messages and share a wide range of content, including photographs and videos.

Software A collection of programs, procedures and routines that direct the operations of a computer.

Source documents The records that are created whenever business is conducted (e.g. cheques, credit and debit notes, and contracts of work).

Spam Unsolicited email, usually advertisements.

Specification A precise statement of the exact material, method, process, service, and/or work for every aspect of a proposed project.

Spreadsheet A program in which data is displayed in table format.

Static forces Pressures exerted on parts of the body that are caused by maintaining the same position for a prolonged period of time.

Stationery Paper and envelopes used in the production of documents.

Storage The process by which data is retained on a computer for future use.

Storage device The equipment that is used for recording data.

Storage medium The material on which the data is recorded.

Stylus A pointed device, similar to a pen, designed to be detected by a touch screen.

Subheading The heading for a subsection of a document.

Tab stop A preset point in a document to which the cursor moves when the Tab key is pressed.

Table In a database, where related records are stored.

Task pane A section of a window that typically opens on the right side of the screen, which allows the user to select from a set of options when performing a complex task.

Team spirit The willingness to support a group and work together with other members to achieve common goals.

Telecommuting Working at home or from another location by using a computer that is electronically linked to a central place of employment.

Teleconference A meeting using telephone or Internet in which there are three or more participants in different locations. (*Also see* Audio conference and Video conference.)

Template A preset design for a document.

Testator (male) or **testatrix** (female) In a will, the owner of the assets, whose will is being prepared.

Text wrapping The feature that controls how text behaves in relation to a graphic in a document.

Thumbnail In a presentation program, a small representation of the slide that is displayed to the left of the window.

Time management The process of planning and controlling how time is spent on activities to ensure that work is performed efficiently and effectively.

Touch keyboarding The process of typing data into a computer without looking at the keyboard.

Touch screen The screen for a computer or other device that is sensitive to human touch, so users can select and move objects with their fingers or a stylus.

Traceability The ability to follow the sequence of changes that are made to a document.

Trade secret The right to hold secret information concerning the commercial practices or knowledge of a business.

Trademark The right to use a distinctive sign to differentiate the products or services produced by a particular business. Trademarks must be registered.

Trash folder The storage location on a computer in which deleted files are placed.

Trial balance A worksheet that lists the totals of all accounts from the ledger in debit and credit columns, in an effort to detect whether errors were made when recording transactions.

Turnaround document A paper or electronic document that is sent to an external party to gather data, which is then returned to the company's computer system as input.

Uniform resource locator (URL) The address of a webpage, which typically begins with http://

Vertical heading A table heading that is displayed perpendicular to the page.

Vidcast A digital video recording that is distributed via the Internet, and can be downloaded to computers or portable media players.

Video conference A teleconference in which the participants can hear and see each other.

Virus A harmful program that destroys files or damages the operation of a computer.

Watermark Text or a picture that is placed behind the text in a document.

Weblogs (blogs) Online journals that allow users to regularly share information, opinions, photographs and other content.

Webpage A document that can contain any combination of text, graphics, videos, sounds and content placeholders called frames.

Wikis Websites that allow users to collaboratively write information.

Will A legal declaration that clearly states the way in which a person's assets should be distributed after his or her death.

Wizard A tool that helps the user to perform a task by using dialogue boxes to present a series of clearly defined steps.

Worksheet A 'page' in a spreadsheet.

World Wide Web All the public websites that are available on the Internet.

Write-protect To set the properties of a file so that users cannot change its contents.

Index

A

abbreviations 24
actors' scripts, literary works 136–8
agendas 92–5
    Annual General Meetings (AGMs)
        93–5
agreements 126–7
    hire purchase agreements 126–7
alignments, paragraphs 39
animations, presentations 54
Annual General Meetings (AGMs),
    agendas 93–5
antivirus software 12, 161
application software 12, 13
archiving 167
attitudes and habits, desirable 174–5
audio messages 88–9
AutoCorrect, word processing 45
AutoShapes, Microsoft Word 98–9
Autosum, spreadsheets 48

B

backgrounds, page 42
balance sheets 140–1
bank statements 144–5
bar codes 7
bibliographies 171
bills of quantity 132–3
blocked letter format 64–5
blocked paragraphs 22
borders
    paragraphs 41
    spreadsheets 46–7
bullets, paragraphs 40
business cards, creative displays 102–3
business communication
    audio messages 88–9
    composition 86–9
    skeleton notes 86–8
business letters 58–61
    blocked letter format 64–5
    circular letters 72–3
    continuation sheets 70–1
    effective communication 58–9
    enumeration 78–9
    envelopes 82–5
    formats 64–9
    indented letter format 68–9
    insets 76–7
    labels 84
    letterheads 62–3
    mail merge 74–5, 84–5
    semi-blocked letter format 66–7
    short and long letters 70–1
    skeleton letters 86
    skeleton notes 86–8
    structure 59–61
    tables 80–1

C

central processing units (CPUs) 4
character keys, keyboarding 17
character readers 7
charts 110–11
    embedded objects 110–11
    flow charts 106–7
    linked objects 110–11
    Microsoft Word 98–9
    organisation charts 108–9
    spreadsheets 49
circular letters 72–3
citations 170–1
cloud computing 158
columnar work 100–1
command keys, keyboarding 17
committee documents 92–7
communication
    business communication 86–9
    communication media 158–9
    effective communication 55, 58–9
    electronic communication 150–9
compact disks (CDs) 11
computers 4–5
    cloud computing 158
    computer care 14–15
    usage, advantages/disadvantages 5
confidentiality 175
continuation sheets, business letters
    70–1
contracts 128–9
conveyance documents 124–5
copyright 170–1
correction signs, manuscript 20–1
counterparts, legal documents 118
courtesy 175
Creative Commons licences 168
creative displays 102–5
    business cards 102–3
    flyers 104
    invitations 103
    leaflets 104–5
    menus 103
    notices 102
    programmes 104–5
credit notes, spreadsheets 51
currency symbols, typing 25
cut-off slips, circular letters 72–3

D

data processing 162
database management systems
    (DBMS) 13, 30–3

features 30–1
fields 30–1
purposes 30, 35
queries 32–3
records 31
tables 31
dates, typing 25
debit notes, spreadsheets 50–1
digital cameras 7
digital video disks (DVDs) 11
diversity, respecting 174
document scanners 7
drop caps 112–13

E

economic rights, intellectual property
    168
editing 44–5
effective communication
    business letters 58–9
    presentations 55
electronic communication
    Internet 152–3
    scan to mail/scan to file 151
    social media 151
    telecommuting 150
    teleconferencing 151
    types 150–1
electronic filing systems 160–3
ellipsis, typing 25
email 156–7
embedded objects, charts/graphs
    110–11
employment contracts 128–9
encryption, file security 164–5
endnotes 43
endorsements, legal documents 118
engrossments, legal documents 118
enumeration, business letters 78–9
envelopes, business letters 82–5
ergonomics 14–15
Escape (Esc) key, keyboarding 16
ethics, intellectual property 169

F

facsimile (fax) 154–5
fields, database management systems
    (DBMS) 30–1
figures, typing 25
file extensions 162
file integrity 164–5
file retention 166–7
file security 164–5
filing systems 160–3
flash drives 11

flow charts 106–7
flyers, creative displays 104
follow-up procedures 173
font
    formatting 36–7
    presentations 53
    styles 36–7
footers
    letterheads 63
    page 42–3
footnotes 43
formats
    business letters 64–9
formatting
    characters 36–7
    font 36–7
    headings 22, 23, 46
    pages 42–3
    paragraphs 38–41
    spreadsheets 46–7
forms 146–7
formulae, spreadsheets 48
fractions, typing 25
function keys, keyboarding 16
functions, spreadsheets 48

G
graphics 98–9
    AutoShapes 98–9
    charts/graphs 49, 98–9, 106–7,
        108–9, 110–11
    presentations 53
    WordArt 98–9
graphs 110–11
    embedded objects 110–11
    linked objects 110–11
    Microsoft Word 98–9
    spreadsheets 49
grooming, good 175
guide keys, keyboarding 16

H
habits and attitudes, desirable 174–5
hanging indents 22
hard-disk drives 10–11
hardware 4
headers 42–3
headings
    formatting 22, 23, 46
    spreadsheets 46–7
hire purchase agreements 126–7
home keys, keyboarding 16

I
income and expenditure statements
        142–3
indented letter format 68–9

indented paragraphs 22
indents, hanging indents 22
inkjet printers 9
input devices 6–7
Insert mode, word processing 45
insets
    business letters 76–7
    paragraphs 23
integrity 175
intellectual property 168–9
Internet
    advantages/disadvantages 153
    electronic communication 152–3
    uniform resource locators (URLs)
        152
    web browsers 152
    vs World Wide Web 152
invitations, creative displays 103
invoices, spreadsheets 50–1

K
keyboarding 16–17
keyboards 6, 16–17

L
labels, business letters 84
laser printers 9
leaflets, creative displays 104–5
leases 122–3
legal documents 118
letterheads 62–3
    see also business letters
    footers 63
    logos 62–3
    text wrapping 63
letters, business see business letters
light pens 6
line spacing, paragraphs 38–9
linked objects, charts/graphs 110–11
literary works 136–9
    actors' scripts 136–8
    plays 136–8
    poetry 136
logos, letterheads 62–3
long and short letters 70–1

M
magnetic disks 10
mail merge 74–5, 84–5
main headings 22, 23
mainframes 4
manual filing systems 160–1
manuscript correction signs 20–1
marginal headings (side headings)
        22, 23
memoranda 90–1

memory cards 11
menus, creative displays 103
metadata 167
microcomputers 4–5
microphones 6
Microsoft Excel see spreadsheets
Microsoft Word see word processing
minicomputers 4
minutes of meetings 96–7
modifier keys, keyboarding 17
monitors 8
moral rights 168–9
mouse, computer 6
multifunctional devices 154–5
multimedia projectors 9

N
newsletters 112–13
notices
    creative displays 102
    meetings 92–3
numbering
    in letters 78–9
    paragraphs 41
numbers, typing 25

O
operating system software 12
optical character recognition (OCR) 7
optical disks 10
optical mark readers (OMRs) 7
organisation charts 108–9
organisation of work 172–3
output devices 8–9
Overwrite mode, word processing 45
overwrite protection, file integrity 165

P
pages
    backgrounds 42
    endnotes 43
    footers 42–3
    footnotes 43
    formatting 42–3
    headers 42–3
    watermarks 42
paper layout 57
paper sizes 56
paragraph headings 22, 23
paragraphs 22–3, 38–41
    alignments 39
    blocked paragraphs 22
    borders 41
    bullets 40
    formatting 38–41

Index

hanging indents 22
indented paragraphs 22
insets 23
line spacing 38–9
numbering 41
shading 41
tabs 39–40
password protection, file integrity 164
peripherals, computer 4
plagiarism 170–1
plays, literary works 136–8
poetry, literary works 136
pointing devices, computer 6
presentation software 13, 34–5
features 34
purposes 34, 35
presentations
animations 54
creating 52–5
effective communication 55
fonts 53
graphics 53
layouts 52–3
slides 52, 53, 54
timing 54–5
transitions 54
press releases 116–17
printers 8–9
profit and loss statements 142–3
programmes, creative displays 104–5
proofreading 44
proposals 114–15
public domain 169
punctuation 18–19

Q

queries, database management
systems (DBMS) 32–3

R

receipts 145
records, database management
systems (DBMS) 31
repetitive strain injuries 14
reports 114–15
retention systems, file 166–7

S

safety 14–15
scan to mail/scan to file, electronic
communication 151
scopes of works 134–5
semi-blocked letter format 66–7

shading, paragraphs 41
short and long letters 70–1
shortcut buttons
spreadsheets 29
word processors 27, 36, 38
shoulder headings 22, 23
signs, manuscript correction 20–1
skeleton letters 86
skeleton notes 86–8
slides
presentation software 34
presentations 52, 53, 54
transitions 54
smart phones 158
social media, electronic
communication 151
software 4, 12–13
speakers 9
specifications 130–1
spelling/grammar checker 44–5
spreadsheets 28–9
Autosum 48
borders 46–7
charts/graphs 49
credit notes 51
debit notes 50–1
features 28–9
formatting 46–7
formulae 48
functions 48
headings 46
invoices 50–1
purposes 28, 35
shortcut buttons 29
software 13
tabulation 46–51
standards of work 172–3
static forces 14
stationery 56–7
paper sizes 56
types 57
storage media 10–11
styluses, touch screen 6
subheadings 22, 23
symbols 37
typing 25
system backup, file security 165

T

tables
business letters 80–1
database management systems
(DBMS) 31

tabs, paragraphs 39–40
tabulation, spreadsheets 46–51
team spirit 174
telecommuting, electronic
communication 150
teleconferencing, electronic
communication 151
templates
database management systems
(DBMS) 32
Microsoft Word 148–9
word processing 26, 148–9
text wrapping, letterheads 63
time management 173
times, typing 25
touch keyboarding 16
touch screens 6
traceability, document 167
transitions, presentations 54
trial balances 140–1
Type Over mode, word processing 45

U

uniform resource locators (URLs),
Internet 152

V

video conference 151
viruses, computer 12, 161

W

watermarks 42
web browsers, Internet 152
wills 120–1
wizards 148–9
word processing 26–7
AutoShapes 98–9
charts 98–9
features 26–7
formatting 36–43
graphs 98–9
purposes 26, 35
templates 26, 148–9
WordArt 98–9
word-processing software 13
WordArt, Microsoft Word 98–9
World Wide Web, vs Internet 152